THE MIGHTY CRUSADERS

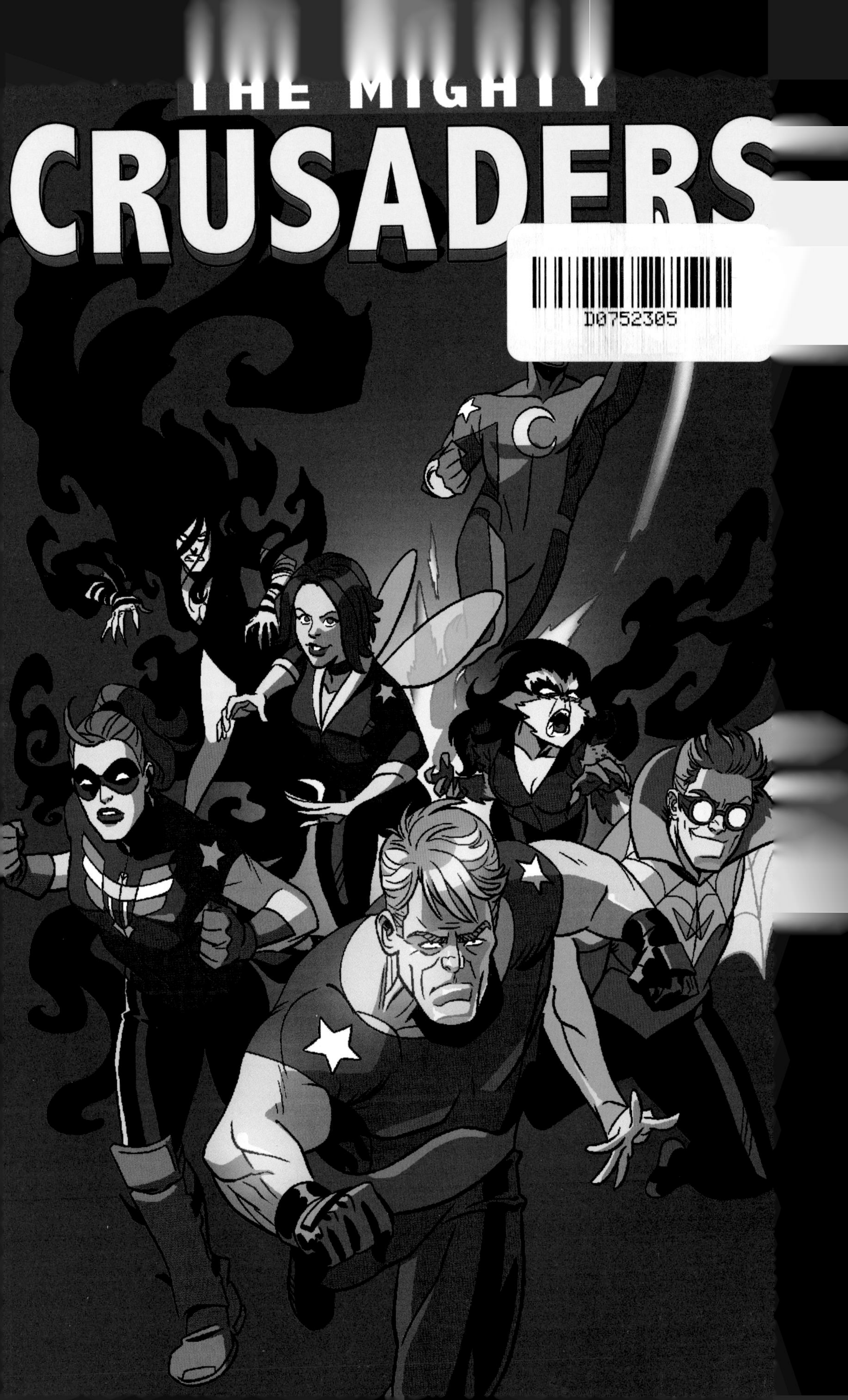

MLJ

STORY BY
IAN FLYNN

PENCILS & INKS BY
KELSEY SHANNON
Inks Chap. 1-2, Chap. 4 (p. 6, 11 & 20)

LETTERING BY
JACK MORELLI

INKS BY
RYAN JAMPOLE
Chap. 3, Chap. 4 (p. 1-5, 7-10, 12-19)

EDITOR-IN-CHIEF
VICTOR GORELICK

COLORS BY
MATT HERMS

PUBLISHER
JON GOLDWATER

EDITORS
ALEX SEGURA AND
VINCENT LOVALLO

ASSOCIATE EDITOR
STEPHEN OSWALD

ASSISTANT EDITOR
JAMIE LEE ROTANTE

INTRODUCTION BY IAN FLYNN

You can't keep a good hero down. No matter what obstacles they face–aliens, super villains, limited print runs–they always persevere. Therefore the Mighty Crusaders are truly mighty as they continue to return to protect us. They've taken on many forms over the decades, but their mission has remained the same: keep us safe.

One of the most interesting things about the Mighty Crusaders, at least for me, is that they're never very glamorous. In just about every incarnation they start at the bottom, things get even worse, and then they win the day. They don't so much function as a team as they endure as a group. They have a unique, dysfunctional underdog family vibe to them that I don't think you really see too much in other superhero comics.

Mighty Crusaders is something of a spiritual successor to New Crusaders rather than a direct sequel. If you missed out on that team's premier adventure, or Victoria Adams's solo book, we didn't want you to feel completely out of the loop. At the same time a great deal of love and effort went into those incarnations of the heroes, so we wanted to use their legacy as an inspiration for where we went this time.

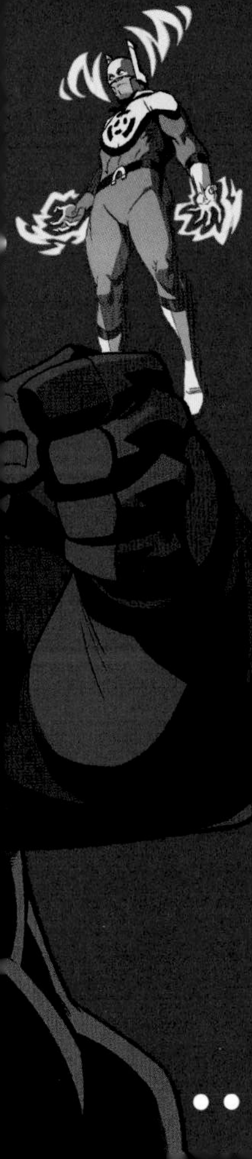

So when you see the connections between the "New" and the "Mighty" with *Dark Tomorrow*, you're free to take it as canon as you want. A great deal happened to the team between their battle in Impact City and the events in Washington D.C., and they all saw some drastic changes. Or this is a new look at the group, and you totally get all the references now. They're flexible like that.

However you choose to read them, I thank you for joining them on their adventures. I've had a blast writing them in every form they've taken. And who knows? Next time we might get to see the kids tackle Brain Emperor. Maybe we'll see what diabolical plan Eternos has cooking. Or maybe we'll slip down a different strand of the Blue Ribbon and see something altogether new and fantastic.

It's a mighty fine idea, if you ask me.

Ian Flynn
Writer, *The Mighty Crusaders*

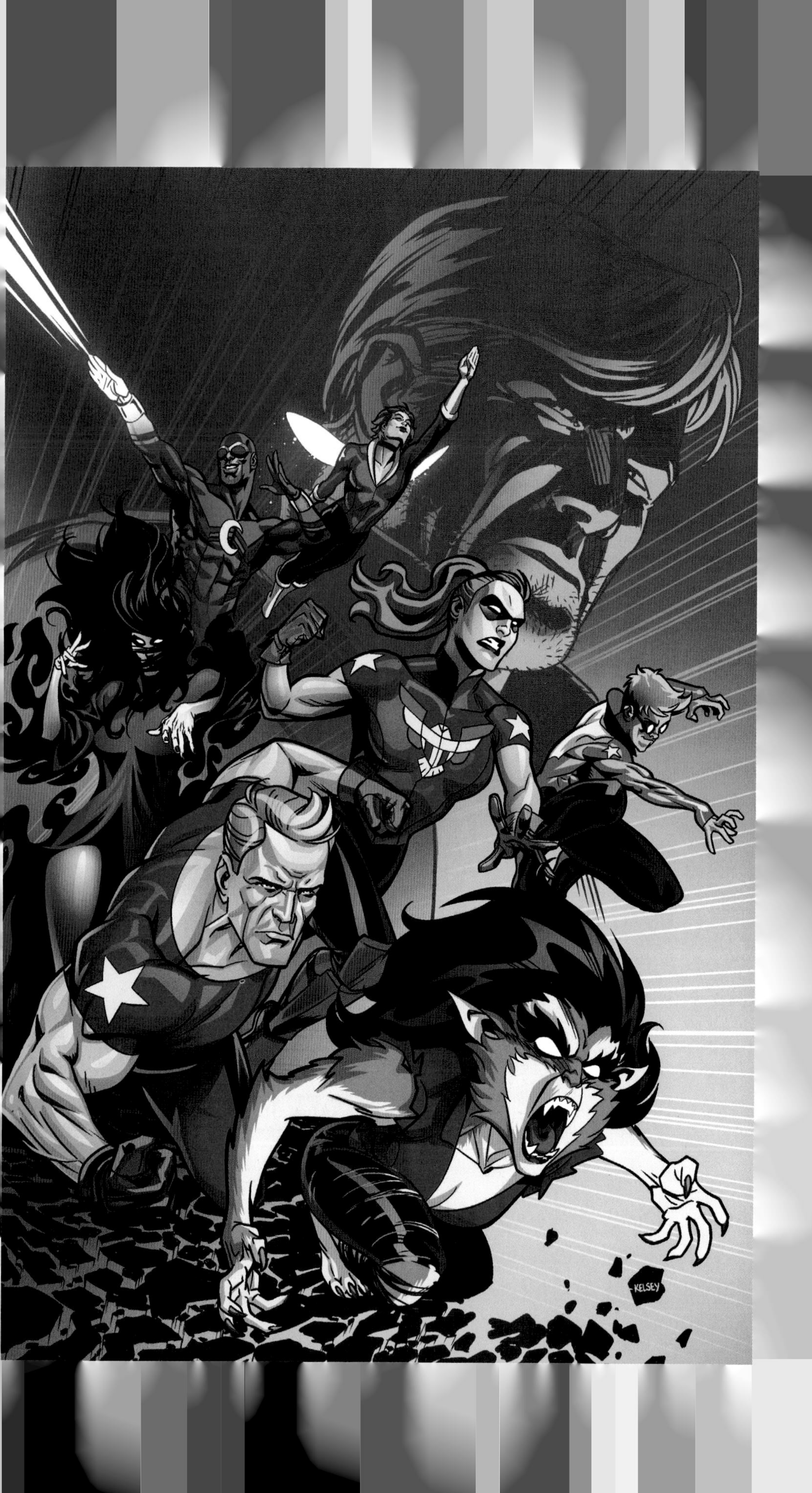
KELSEY

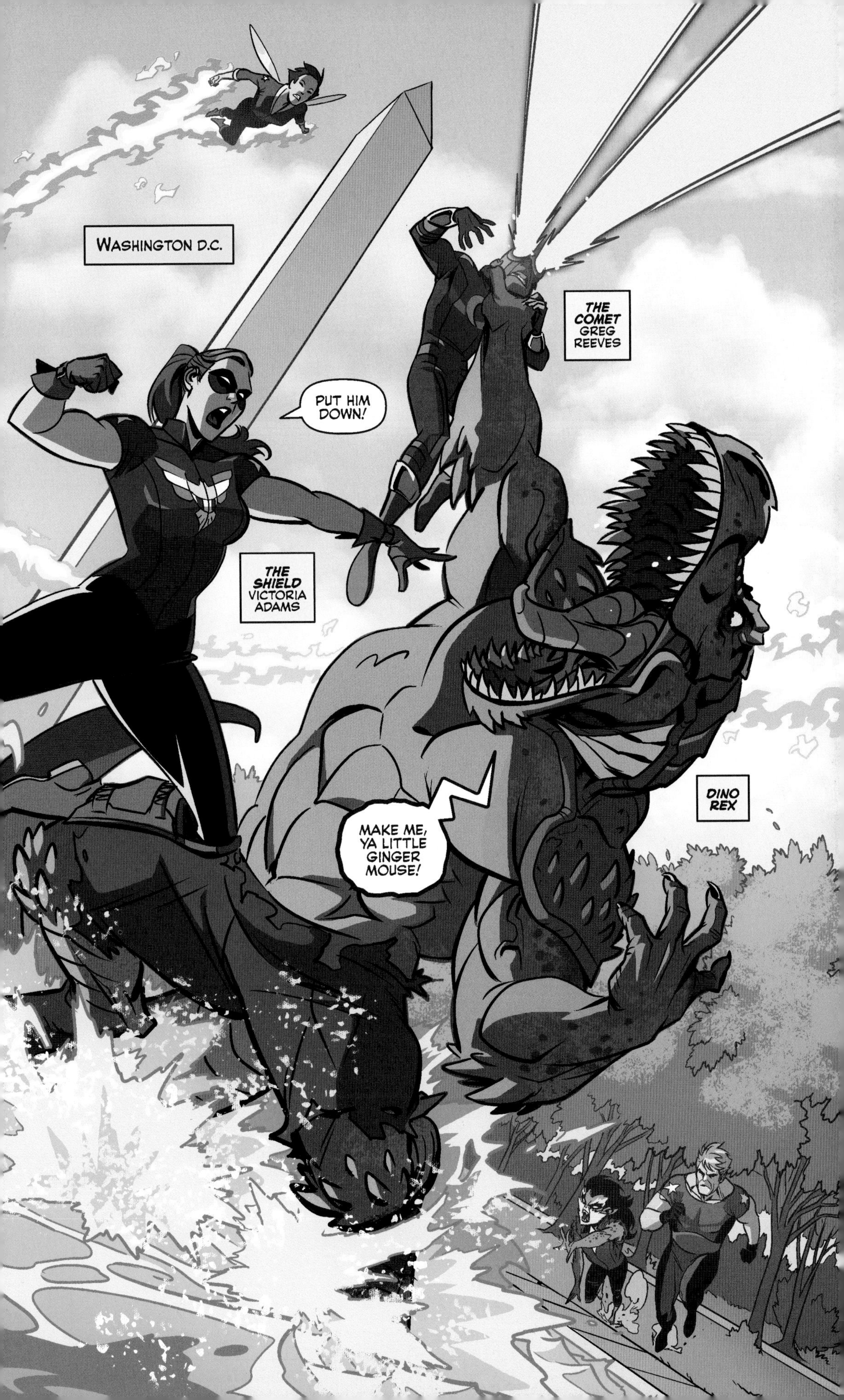
WASHINGTON D.C.
THE COMET GREG REEVES
PUT HIM DOWN!
THE SHIELD VICTORIA ADAMS
DINO REX
MAKE ME, YA LITTLE GINGER MOUSE!

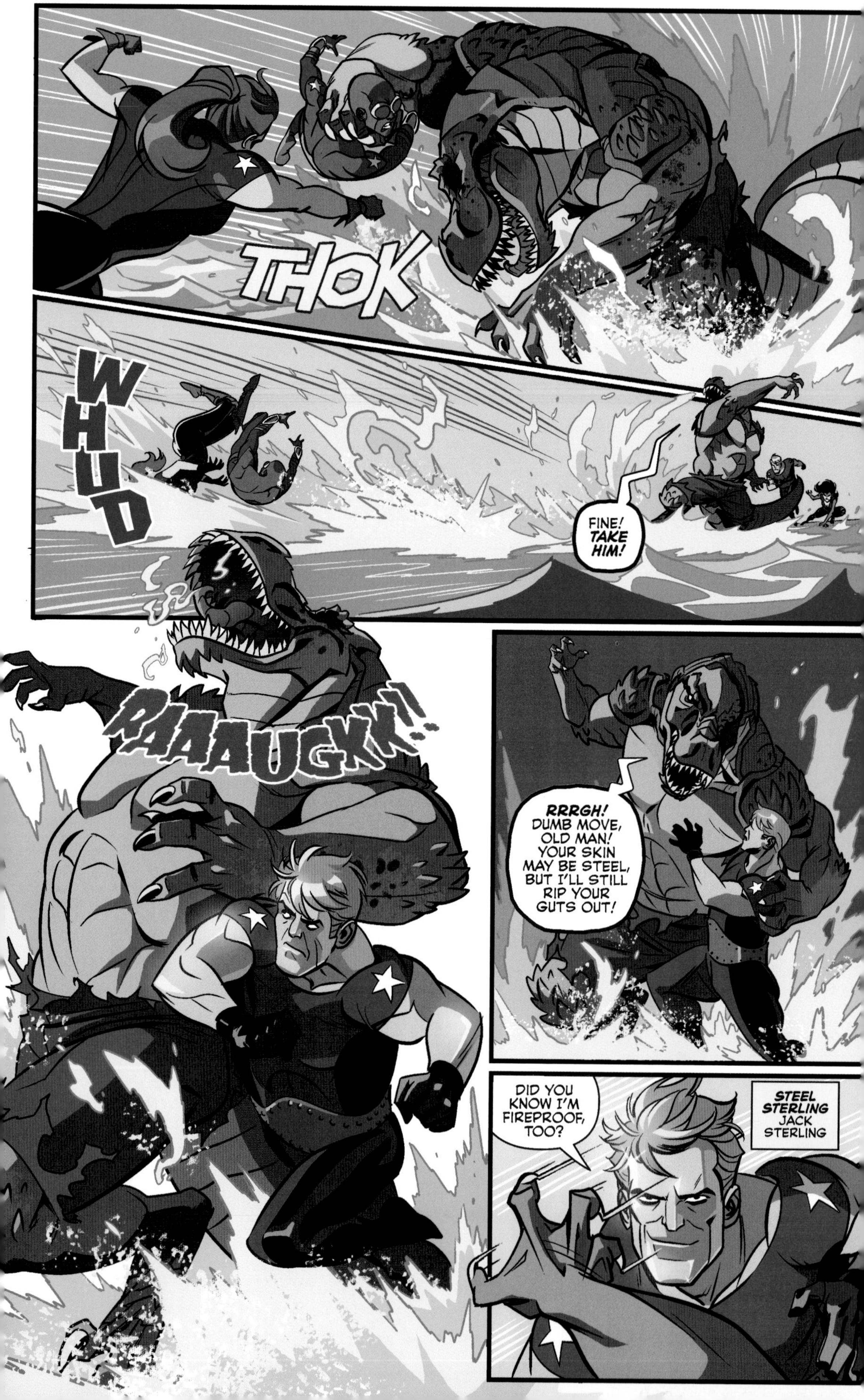
THOK
WHUD
FINE! TAKE HIM!
RAAAUGKK!!
RRRGH! DUMB MOVE, OLD MAN! YOUR SKIN MAY BE STEEL, BUT I'LL STILL RIP YOUR GUTS OUT!
DID YOU KNOW I'M FIREPROOF, TOO?
STEEL STERLING JACK STERLING

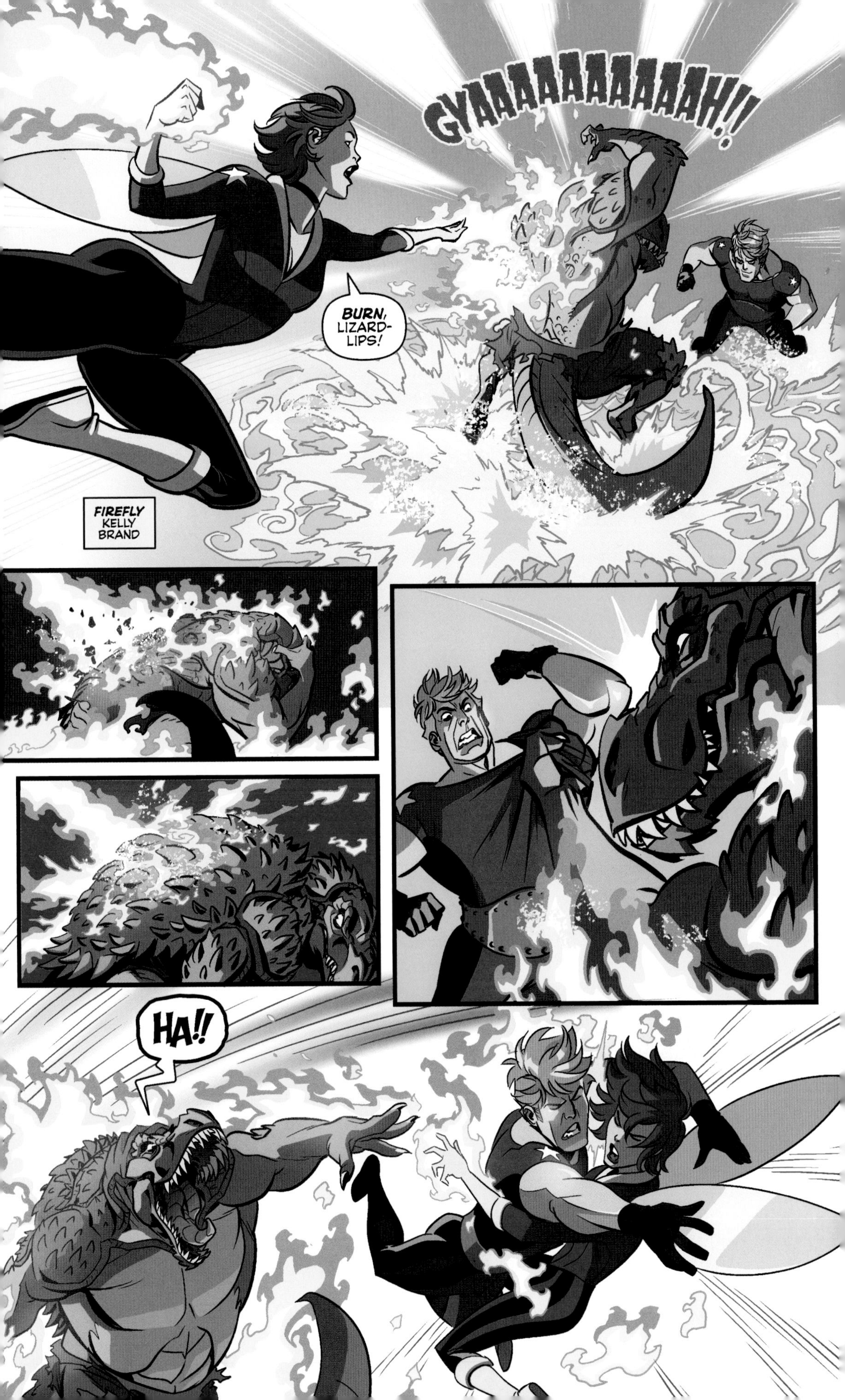

GYAAAAAAAAAAH!!
BURN, LIZARD-LIPS!
FIREFLY
KELLY BRAND
HA!!

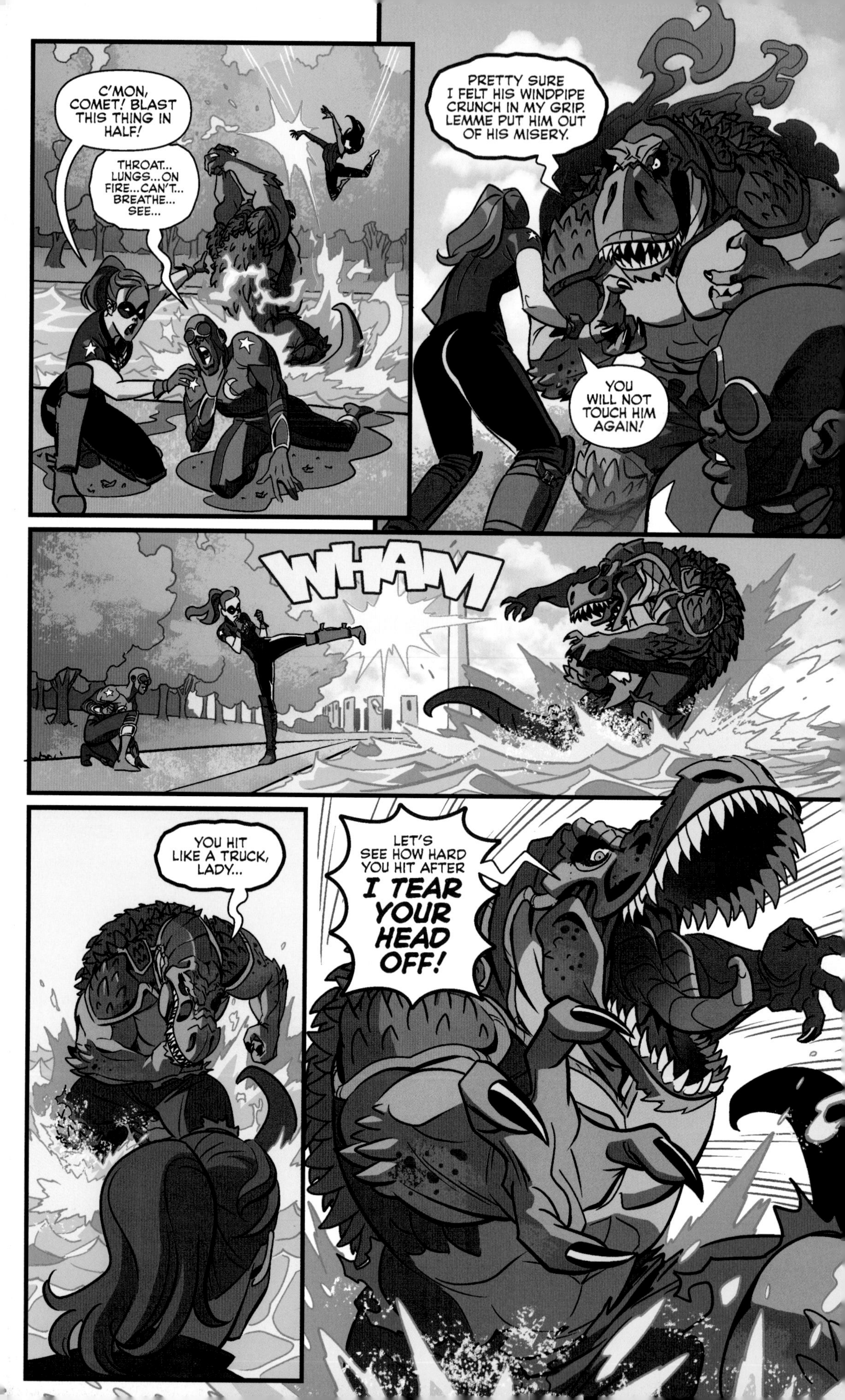

C'MON, COMET! BLAST THIS THING IN HALF!
THROAT... LUNGS...ON FIRE...CAN'T... BREATHE... SEE...
PRETTY SURE I FELT HIS WINDPIPE CRUNCH IN MY GRIP. LEMME PUT HIM OUT OF HIS MISERY.
YOU WILL NOT TOUCH HIM AGAIN!
WHAM
YOU HIT LIKE A TRUCK, LADY...
LET'S SEE HOW HARD YOU HIT AFTER I TEAR YOUR HEAD OFF!

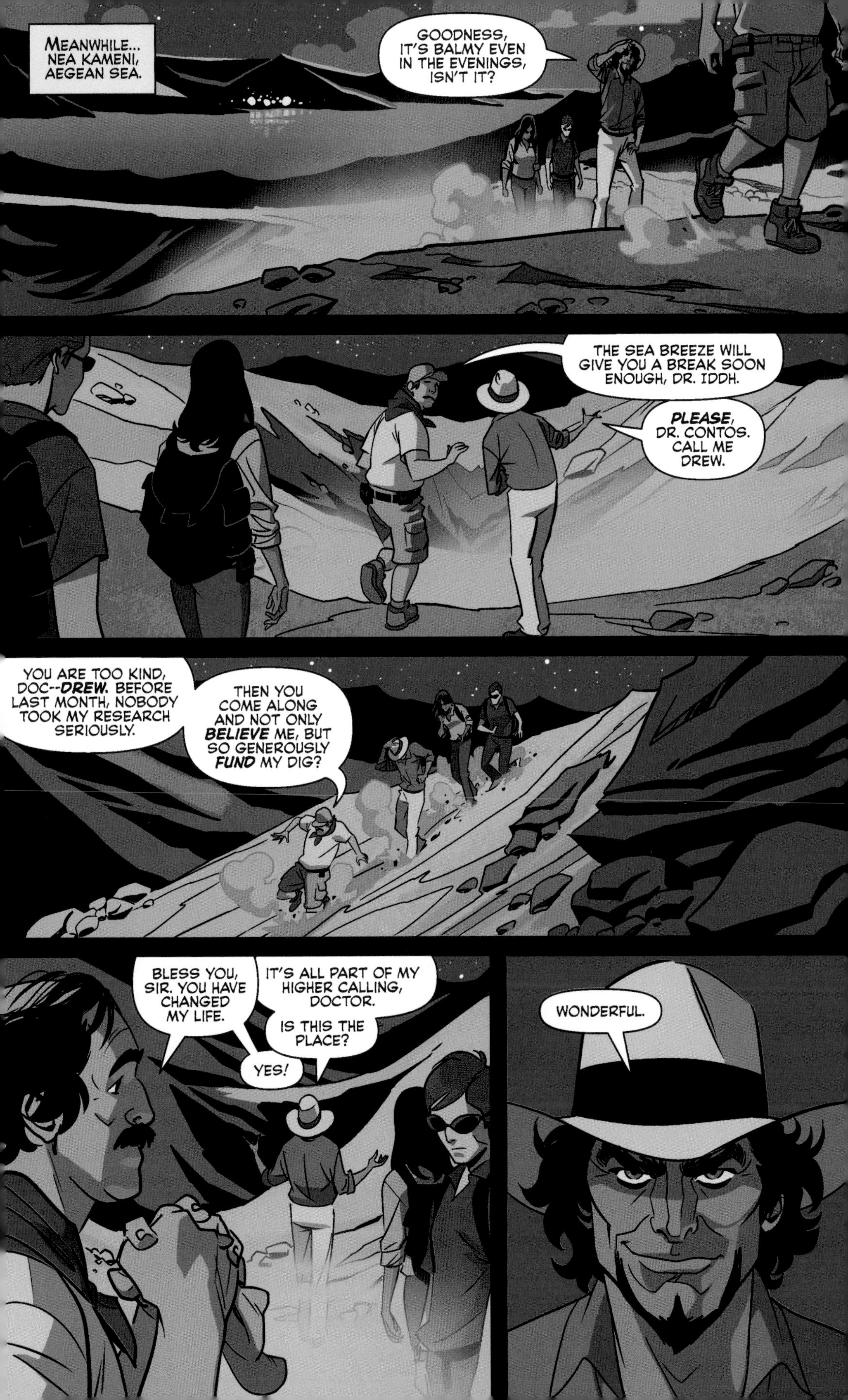
MEANWHILE... NEA KAMENI, AEGEAN SEA.
GOODNESS, IT'S BALMY EVEN IN THE EVENINGS, ISN'T IT?
THE SEA BREEZE WILL GIVE YOU A BREAK SOON ENOUGH, DR. IDDH.
PLEASE, DR. CONTOS. CALL ME DREW.
YOU ARE TOO KIND, DOC--**DREW.** BEFORE LAST MONTH, NOBODY TOOK MY RESEARCH SERIOUSLY.
THEN YOU COME ALONG AND NOT ONLY ***BELIEVE*** ME, BUT SO GENEROUSLY ***FUND*** MY DIG?
BLESS YOU, SIR. YOU HAVE CHANGED MY LIFE.
IT'S ALL PART OF MY HIGHER CALLING, DOCTOR.
IS THIS THE PLACE?
YES!
WONDERFUL.

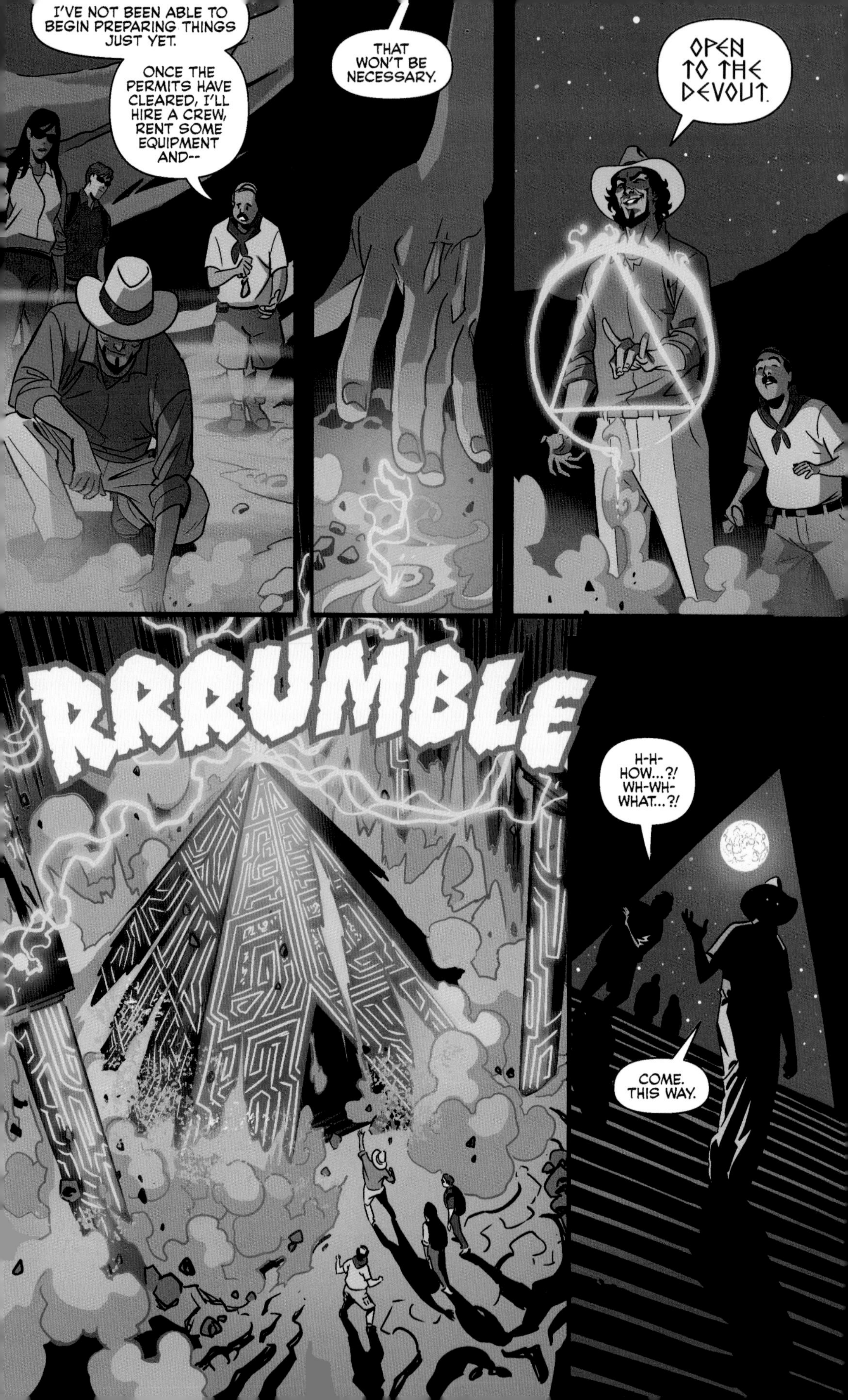
I'VE NOT BEEN ABLE TO BEGIN PREPARING THINGS JUST YET.
ONCE THE PERMITS HAVE CLEARED, I'LL HIRE A CREW, RENT SOME EQUIPMENT AND--
THAT WON'T BE NECESSARY.
OPEN TO THE DEVOUT.
RRRUMBLE
H-H-HOW...?! WH-WH-WHAT...?!
COME. THIS WAY.

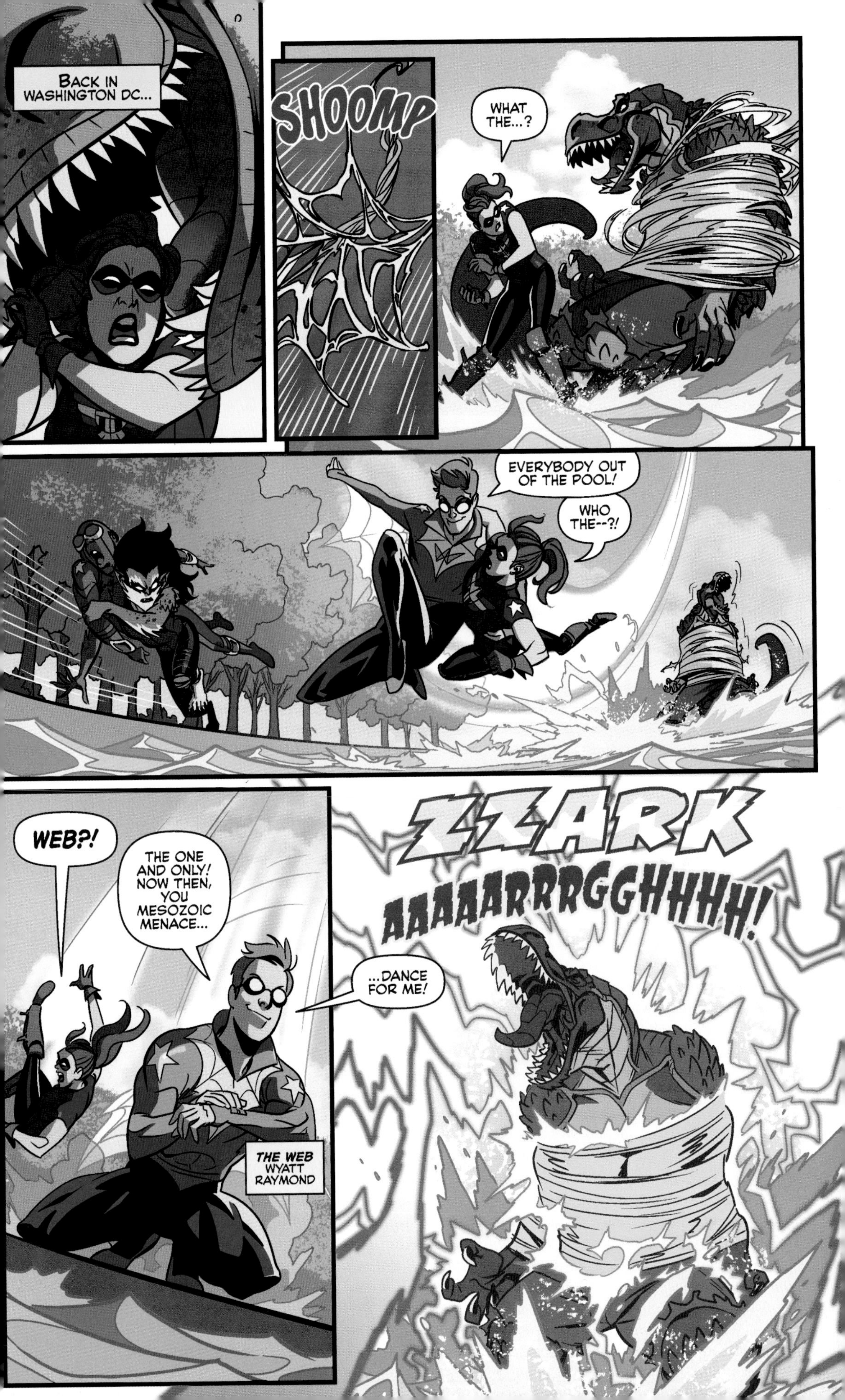

BACK IN WASHINGTON DC...
SHOOMP
WHAT THE...?
EVERYBODY OUT OF THE POOL!
WHO THE--?!
WEB?!
THE ONE AND ONLY! NOW THEN, YOU MESOZOIC MENACE...
...DANCE FOR ME!
THE WEB WYATT RAYMOND
ZZARK
AAAAARRRGGHHHH!

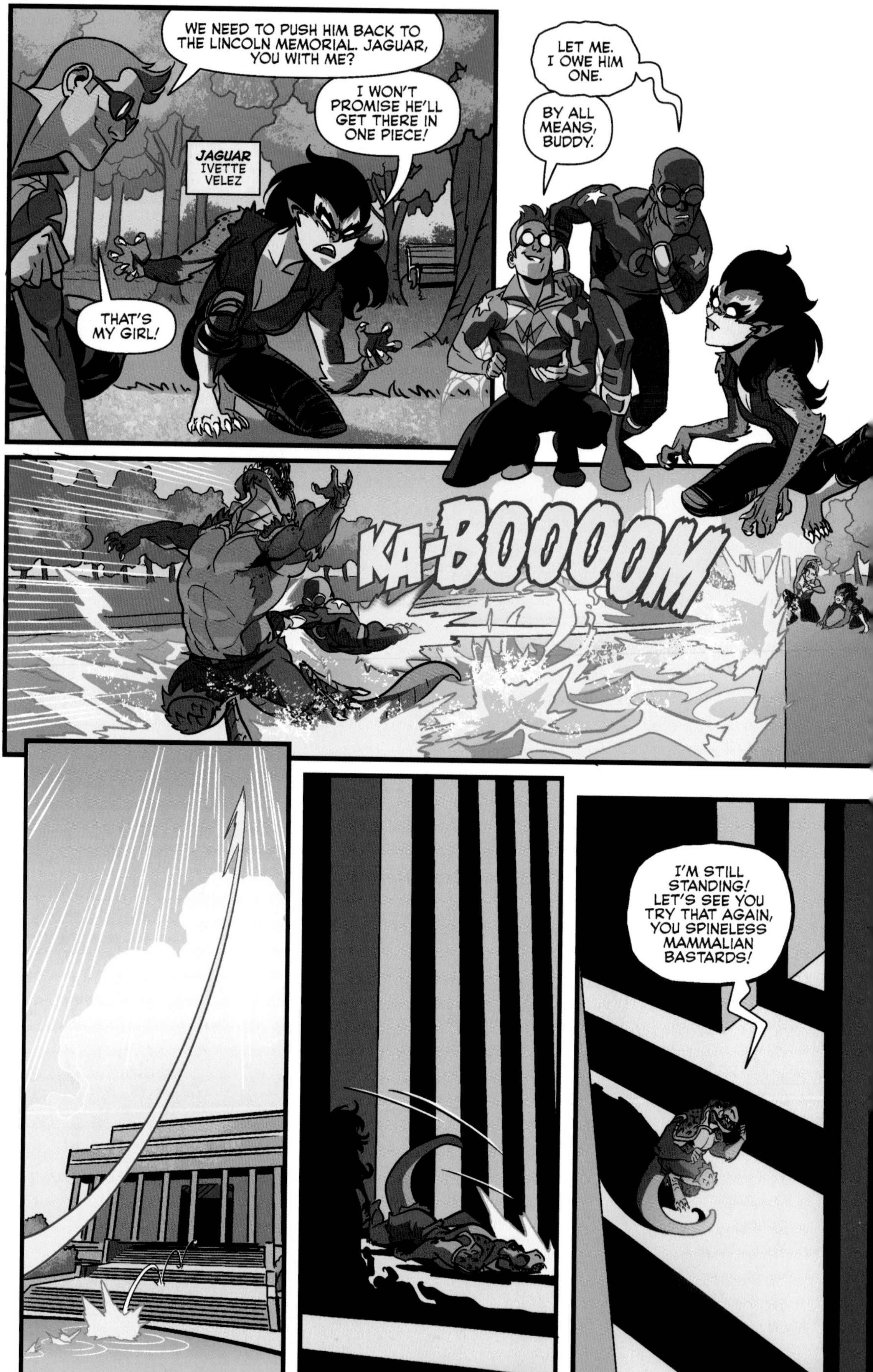
WE NEED TO PUSH HIM BACK TO THE LINCOLN MEMORIAL. JAGUAR, YOU WITH ME?
JAGUAR IVETTE VELEZ
I WON'T PROMISE HE'LL GET THERE IN ONE PIECE!
THAT'S MY GIRL!
LET ME. I OWE HIM ONE.
BY ALL MEANS, BUDDY.
KA-BOOOOM
I'M STILL STANDING! LET'S SEE YOU TRY THAT AGAIN, YOU SPINELESS MAMMALIAN BASTARDS!

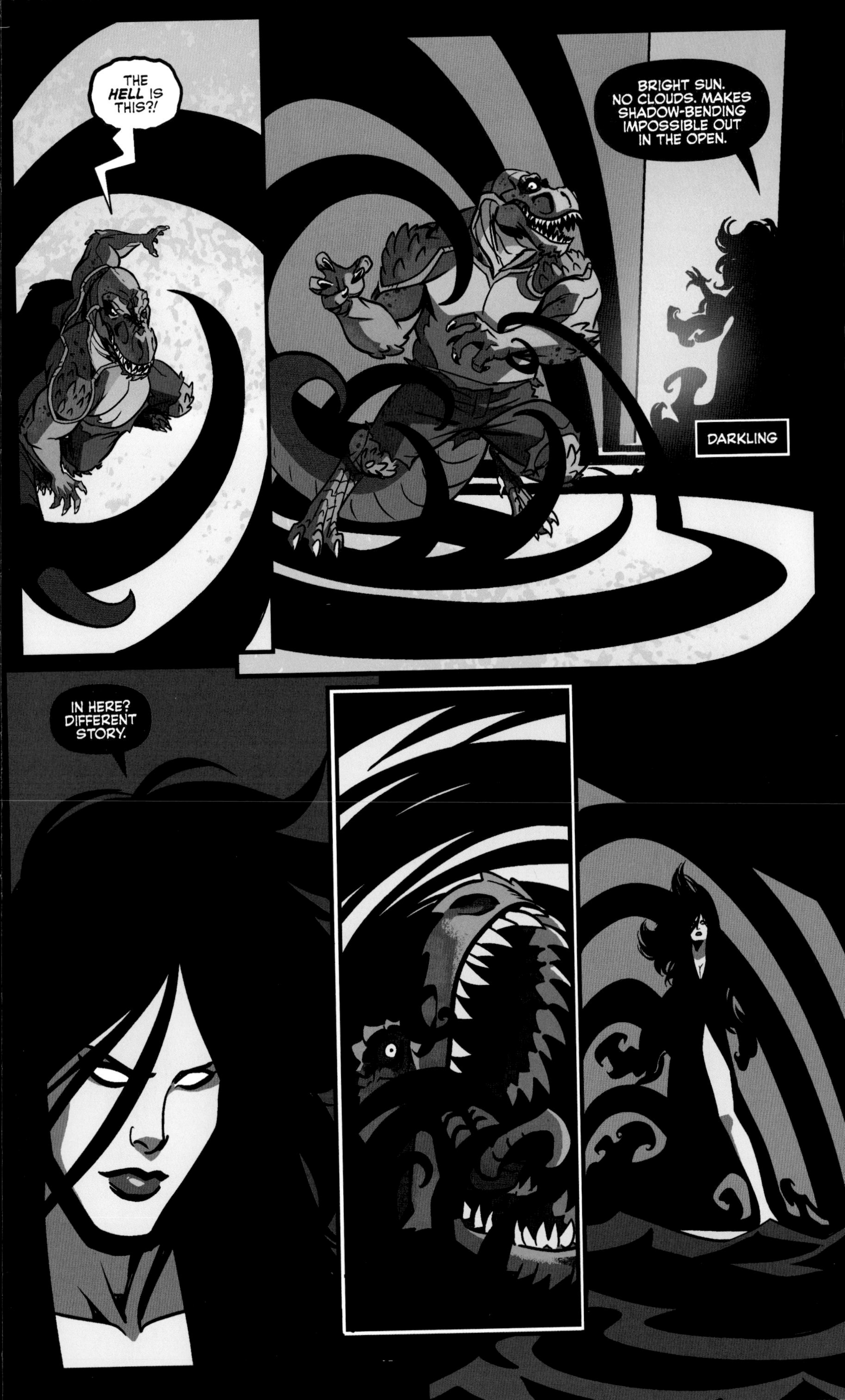
THE *HELL* IS THIS?!
BRIGHT SUN. NO CLOUDS. MAKES SHADOW-BENDING IMPOSSIBLE OUT IN THE OPEN.
DARKLING
IN HERE? DIFFERENT STORY.

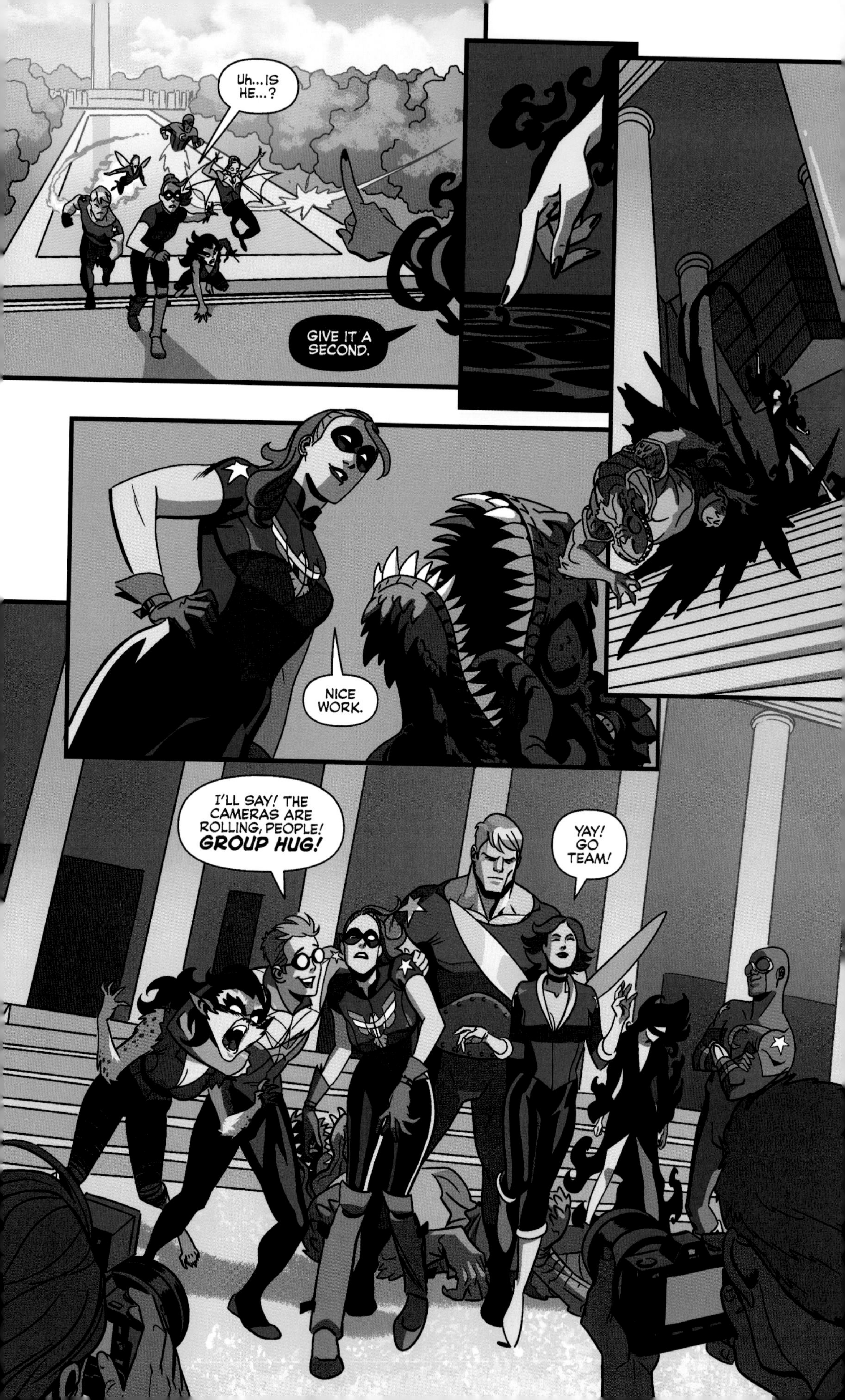
Uh...IS HE...?
GIVE IT A SECOND.
NICE WORK.
I'LL SAY! THE CAMERAS ARE ROLLING, PEOPLE! GROUP HUG!
YAY! GO TEAM!

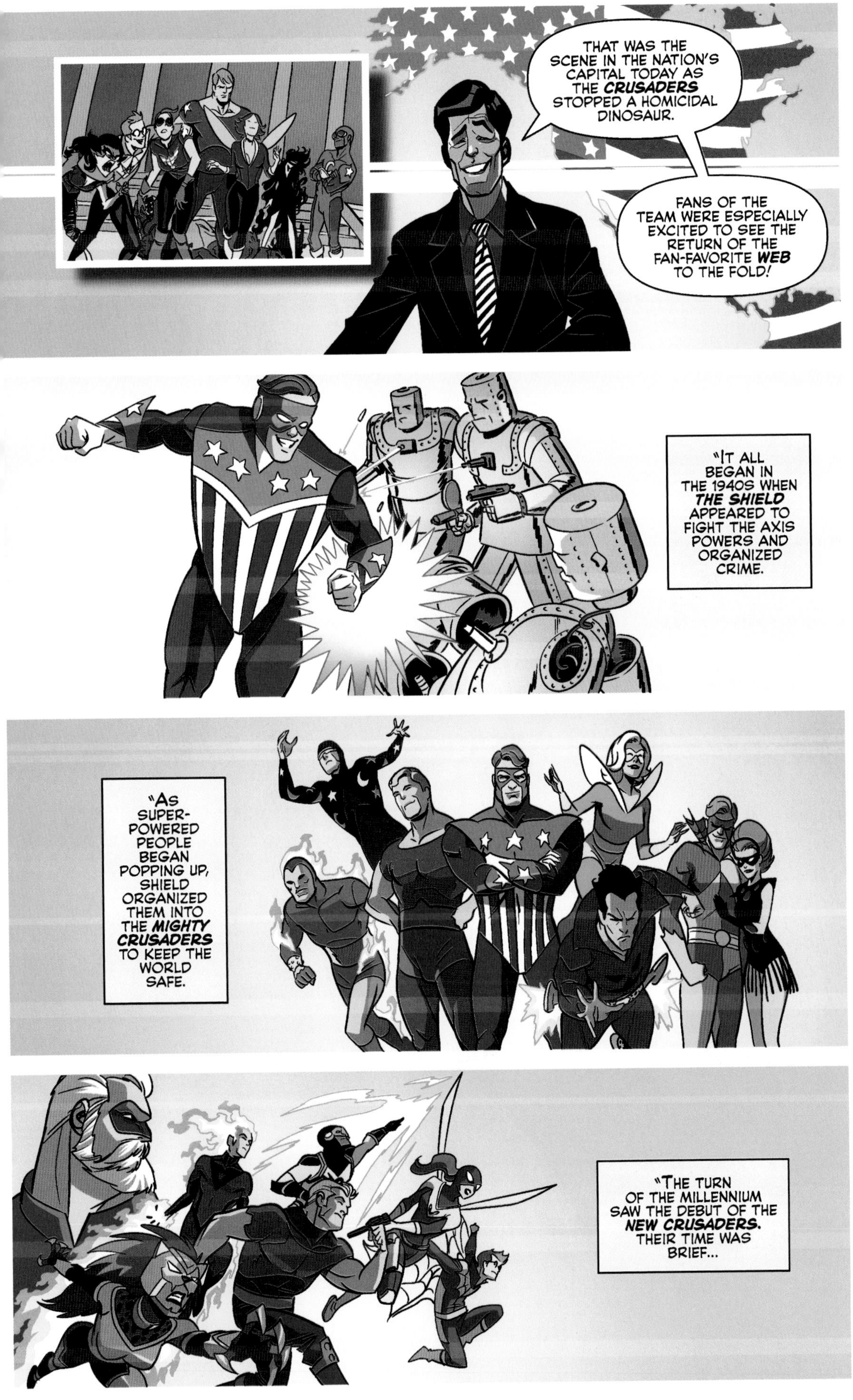
THAT WAS THE SCENE IN THE NATION'S CAPITAL TODAY AS THE **CRUSADERS** STOPPED A HOMICIDAL DINOSAUR.
FANS OF THE TEAM WERE ESPECIALLY EXCITED TO SEE THE RETURN OF THE FAN-FAVORITE **WEB** TO THE FOLD!
"IT ALL BEGAN IN THE 1940S WHEN **THE SHIELD** APPEARED TO FIGHT THE AXIS POWERS AND ORGANIZED CRIME.
"AS SUPER-POWERED PEOPLE BEGAN POPPING UP, SHIELD ORGANIZED THEM INTO THE **MIGHTY CRUSADERS** TO KEEP THE WORLD SAFE.
"THE TURN OF THE MILLENNIUM SAW THE DEBUT OF THE **NEW CRUSADERS.** THEIR TIME WAS BRIEF...

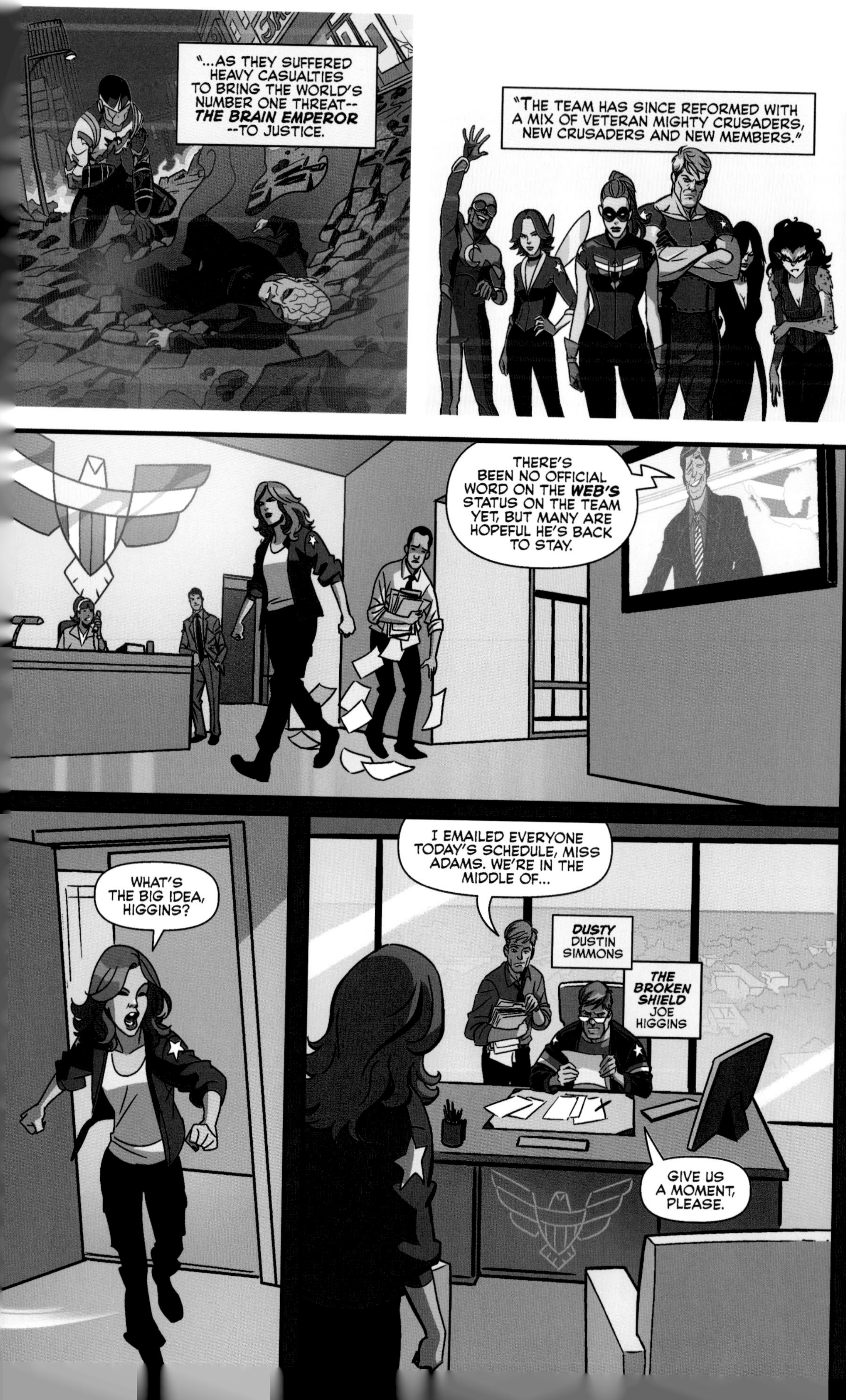
"...AS THEY SUFFERED HEAVY CASUALTIES TO BRING THE WORLD'S NUMBER ONE THREAT-- THE BRAIN EMPEROR --TO JUSTICE.
"THE TEAM HAS SINCE REFORMED WITH A MIX OF VETERAN MIGHTY CRUSADERS, NEW CRUSADERS AND NEW MEMBERS."
THERE'S BEEN NO OFFICIAL WORD ON THE WEB'S STATUS ON THE TEAM YET, BUT MANY ARE HOPEFUL HE'S BACK TO STAY.
WHAT'S THE BIG IDEA, HIGGINS?
I EMAILED EVERYONE TODAY'S SCHEDULE, MISS ADAMS. WE'RE IN THE MIDDLE OF...
DUSTY DUSTIN SIMMONS
THE BROKEN SHIELD JOE HIGGINS
GIVE US A MOMENT, PLEASE.

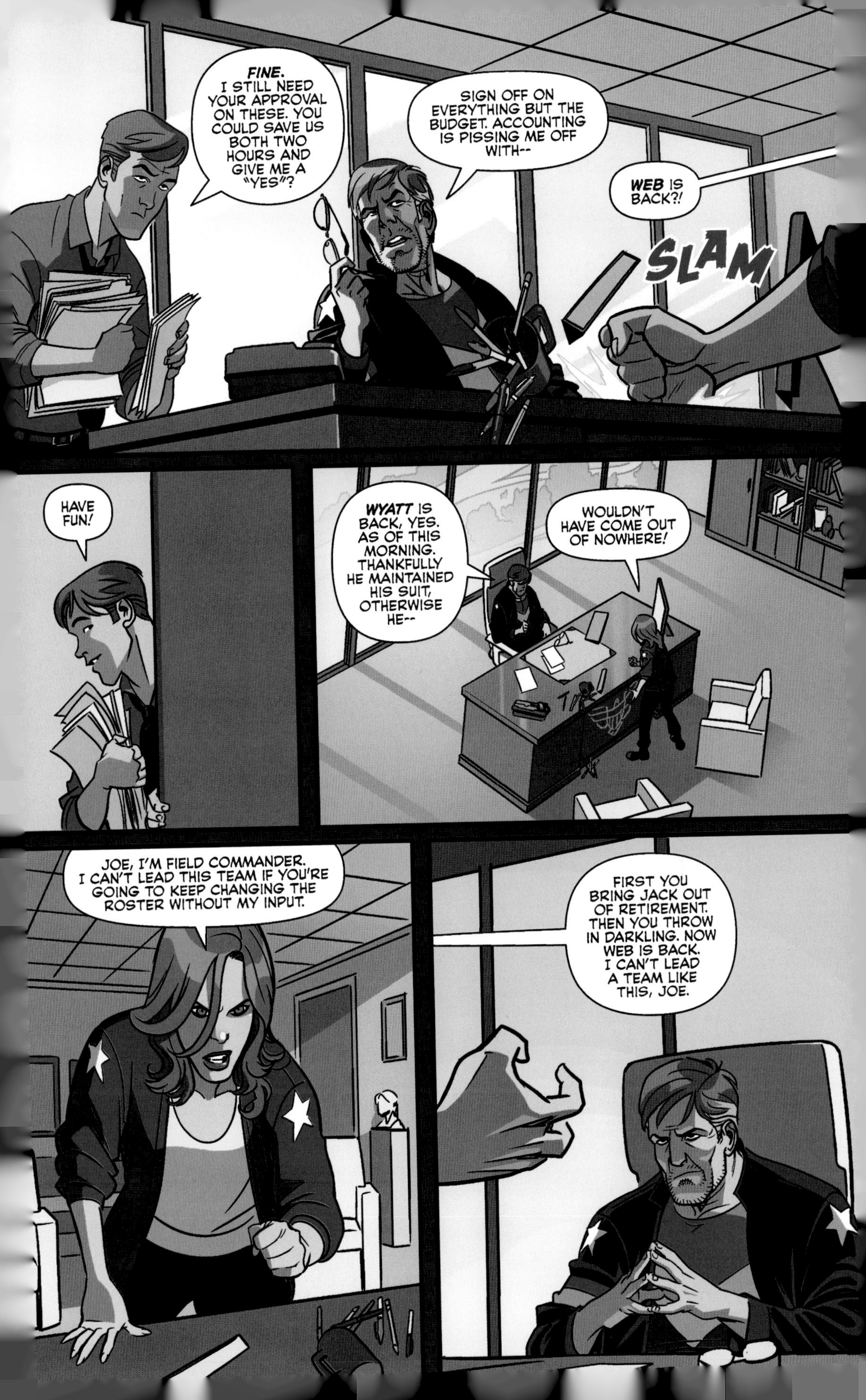
FINE. I STILL NEED YOUR APPROVAL ON THESE. YOU COULD SAVE US BOTH TWO HOURS AND GIVE ME A "YES"?
SIGN OFF ON EVERYTHING BUT THE BUDGET. ACCOUNTING IS PISSING ME OFF WITH--
WEB IS BACK?!
SLAM
HAVE FUN!
WYATT IS BACK, YES. AS OF THIS MORNING. THANKFULLY HE MAINTAINED HIS SUIT, OTHERWISE HE--
WOULDN'T HAVE COME OUT OF NOWHERE!
JOE, I'M FIELD COMMANDER. I CAN'T LEAD THIS TEAM IF YOU'RE GOING TO KEEP CHANGING THE ROSTER WITHOUT MY INPUT.
FIRST YOU BRING JACK OUT OF RETIREMENT. THEN YOU THROW IN DARKLING. NOW WEB IS BACK. I CAN'T LEAD A TEAM LIKE THIS, JOE.

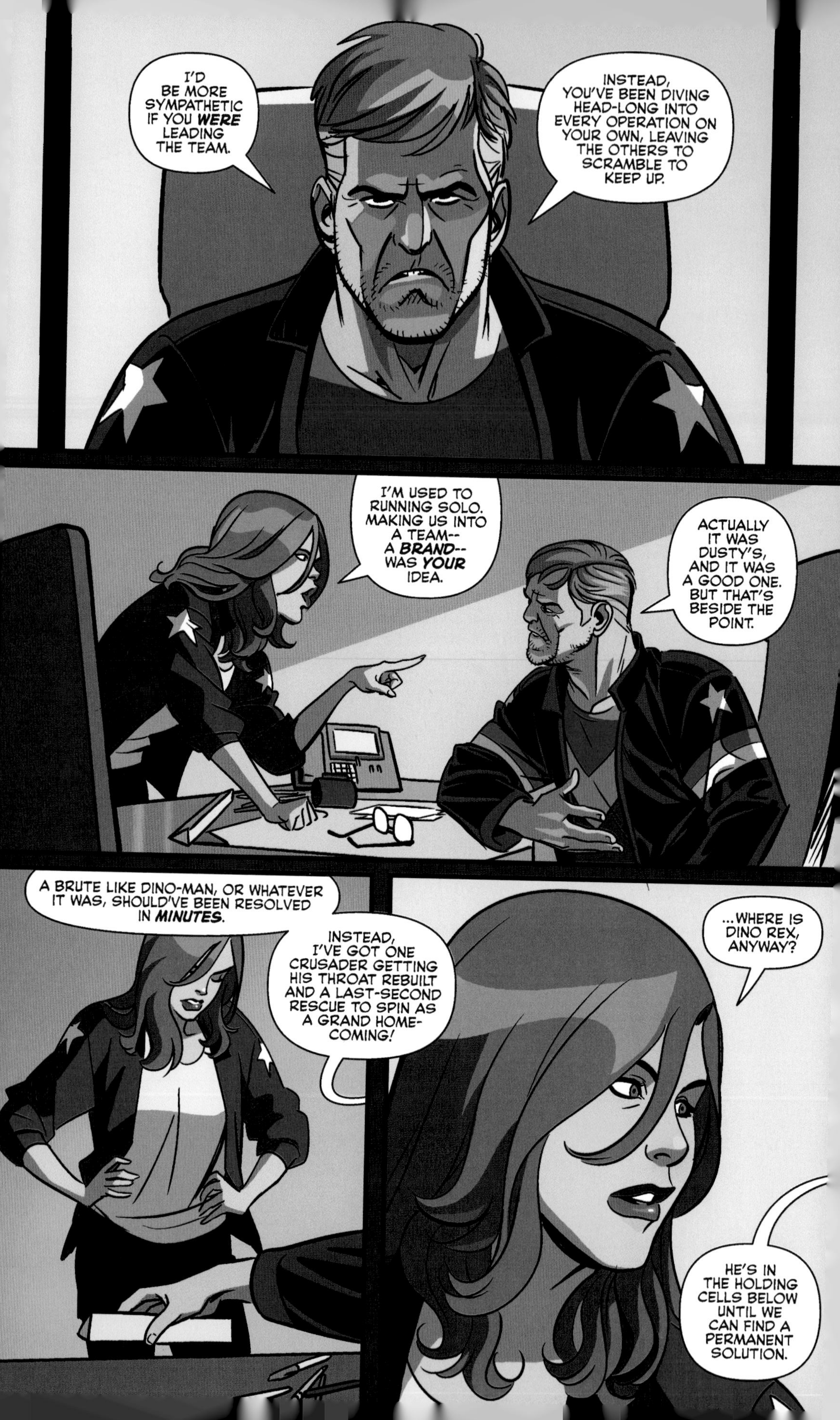
I'D BE MORE SYMPATHETIC IF YOU *WERE* LEADING THE TEAM.
INSTEAD, YOU'VE BEEN DIVING HEAD-LONG INTO EVERY OPERATION ON YOUR OWN, LEAVING THE OTHERS TO SCRAMBLE TO KEEP UP.
I'M USED TO RUNNING SOLO. MAKING US INTO A TEAM-- A *BRAND*-- WAS *YOUR* IDEA.
ACTUALLY IT WAS DUSTY'S, AND IT WAS A GOOD ONE. BUT THAT'S BESIDE THE POINT.
A BRUTE LIKE DINO-MAN, OR WHATEVER IT WAS, SHOULD'VE BEEN RESOLVED IN *MINUTES*.
INSTEAD, I'VE GOT ONE CRUSADER GETTING HIS THROAT REBUILT AND A LAST-SECOND RESCUE TO SPIN AS A GRAND HOME-COMING!
...WHERE IS DINO REX, ANYWAY?
HE'S IN THE HOLDING CELLS BELOW UNTIL WE CAN FIND A PERMANENT SOLUTION.

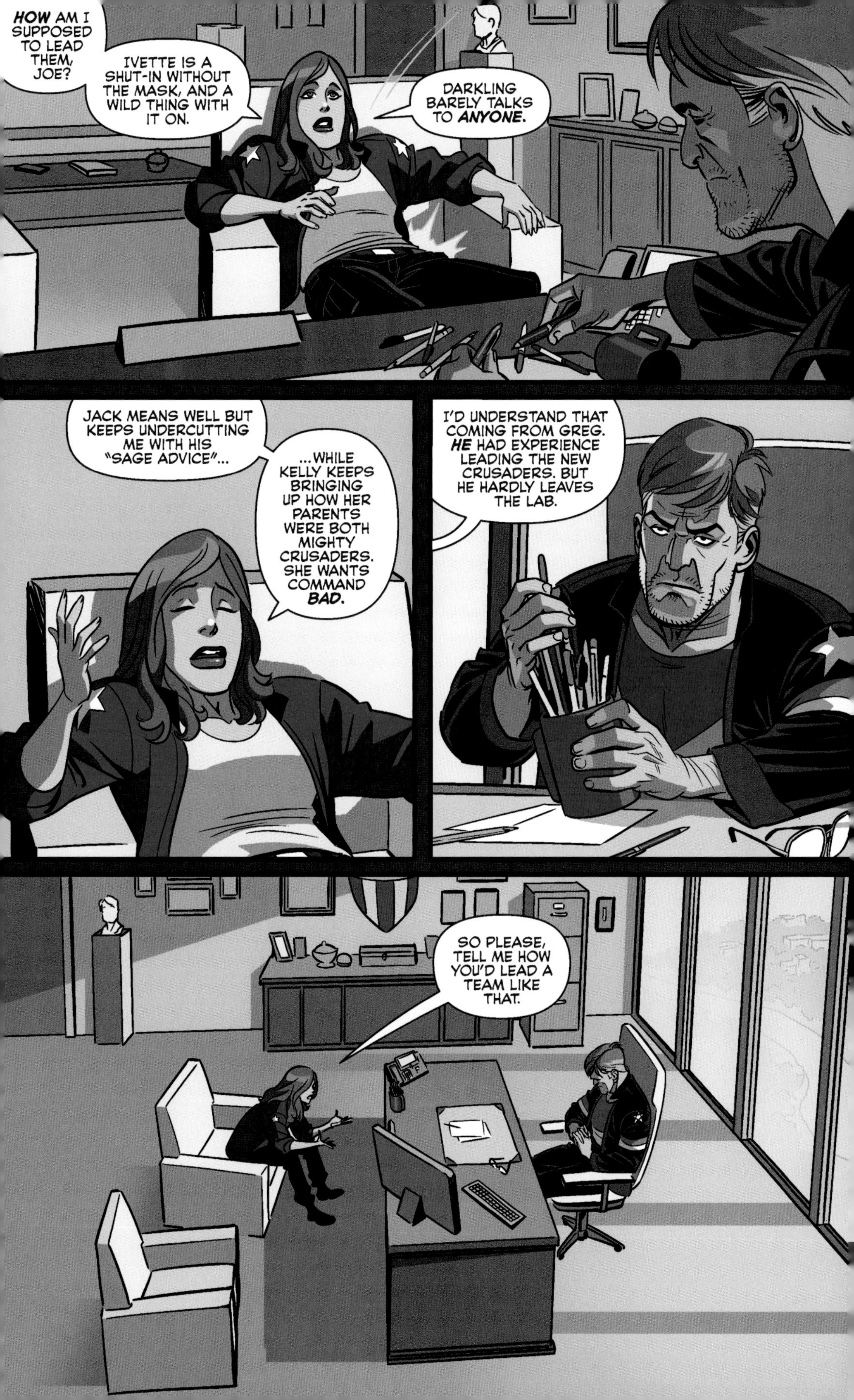
HOW AM I SUPPOSED TO LEAD THEM, JOE?
IVETTE IS A SHUT-IN WITHOUT THE MASK, AND A WILD THING WITH IT ON.
DARKLING BARELY TALKS TO ANYONE.
JACK MEANS WELL BUT KEEPS UNDERCUTTING ME WITH HIS "SAGE ADVICE"...
...WHILE KELLY KEEPS BRINGING UP HOW HER PARENTS WERE BOTH MIGHTY CRUSADERS. SHE WANTS COMMAND BAD.
I'D UNDERSTAND THAT COMING FROM GREG. HE HAD EXPERIENCE LEADING THE NEW CRUSADERS. BUT HE HARDLY LEAVES THE LAB.
SO PLEASE, TELL ME HOW YOU'D LEAD A TEAM LIKE THAT.

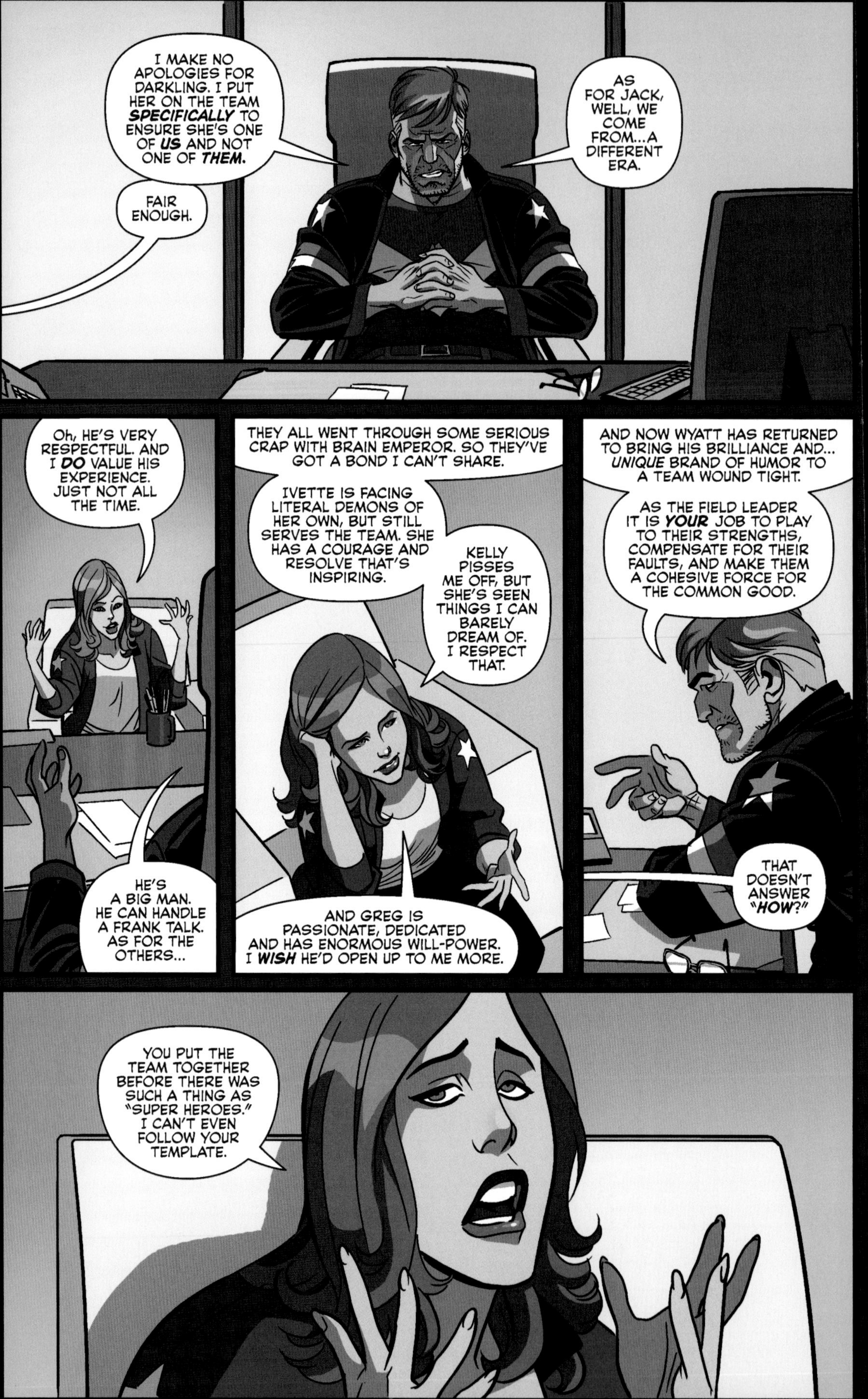

I MAKE NO APOLOGIES FOR DARKLING. I PUT HER ON THE TEAM **SPECIFICALLY** TO ENSURE SHE'S ONE OF **US** AND NOT ONE OF **THEM.**
AS FOR JACK, WELL, WE COME FROM...A DIFFERENT ERA.
FAIR ENOUGH.
Oh, HE'S VERY RESPECTFUL. AND I **DO** VALUE HIS EXPERIENCE. JUST NOT ALL THE TIME.
HE'S A BIG MAN. HE CAN HANDLE A FRANK TALK. AS FOR THE OTHERS...
THEY ALL WENT THROUGH SOME SERIOUS CRAP WITH BRAIN EMPEROR. SO THEY'VE GOT A BOND I CAN'T SHARE.
IVETTE IS FACING LITERAL DEMONS OF HER OWN, BUT STILL SERVES THE TEAM. SHE HAS A COURAGE AND RESOLVE THAT'S INSPIRING.
KELLY PISSES ME OFF, BUT SHE'S SEEN THINGS I CAN BARELY DREAM OF. I RESPECT THAT.
AND GREG IS PASSIONATE, DEDICATED AND HAS ENORMOUS WILL-POWER. I **WISH** HE'D OPEN UP TO ME MORE.
AND NOW WYATT HAS RETURNED TO BRING HIS BRILLIANCE AND... *UNIQUE* BRAND OF HUMOR TO A TEAM WOUND TIGHT.
AS THE FIELD LEADER IT IS **YOUR** JOB TO PLAY TO THEIR STRENGTHS, COMPENSATE FOR THEIR FAULTS, AND MAKE THEM A COHESIVE FORCE FOR THE COMMON GOOD.
THAT DOESN'T ANSWER "**HOW**?"
YOU PUT THE TEAM TOGETHER BEFORE THERE WAS SUCH A THING AS "SUPER HEROES." I CAN'T EVEN FOLLOW YOUR TEMPLATE.

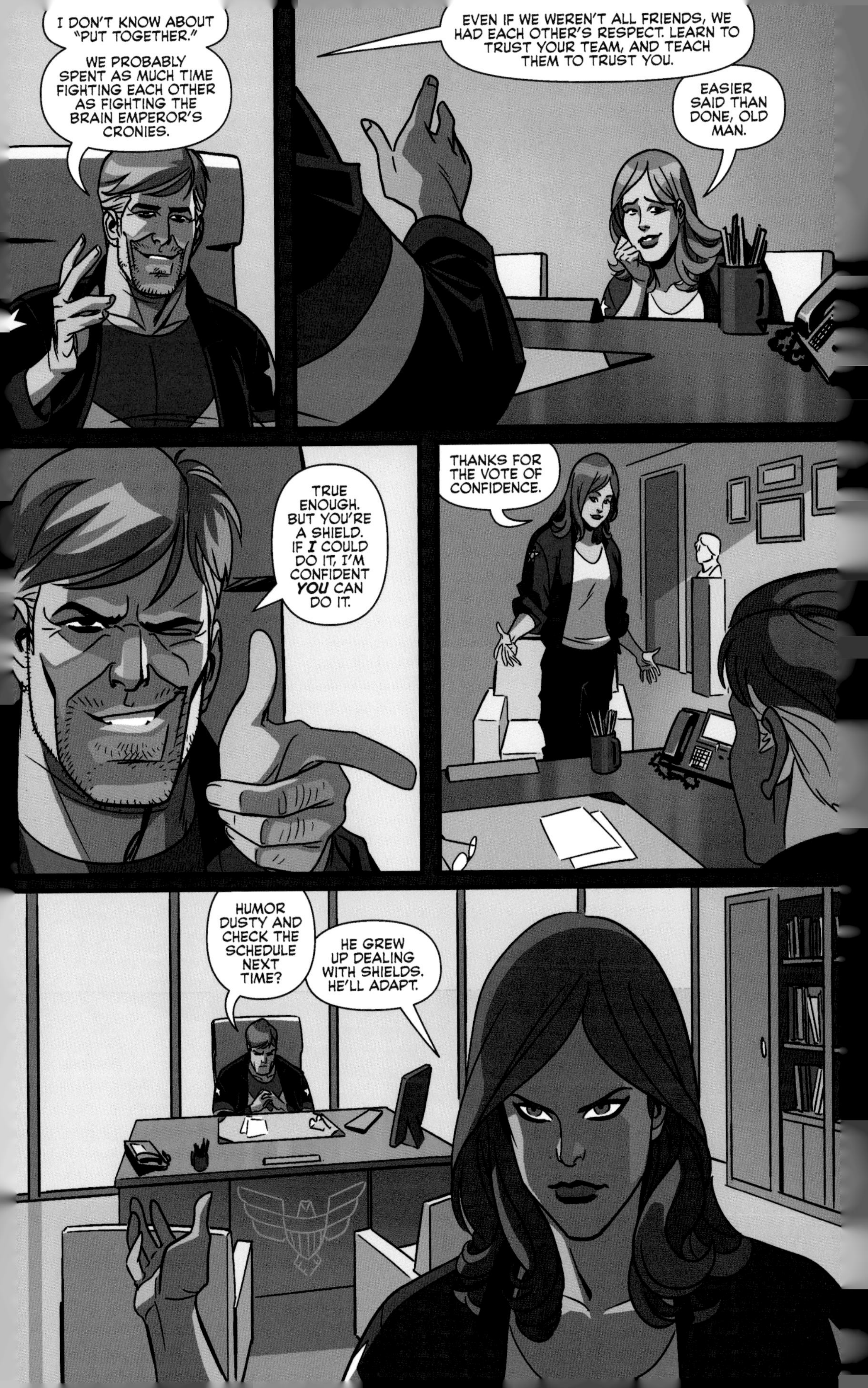
I DON'T KNOW ABOUT "PUT TOGETHER."
WE PROBABLY SPENT AS MUCH TIME FIGHTING EACH OTHER AS FIGHTING THE BRAIN EMPEROR'S CRONIES.
EVEN IF WE WEREN'T ALL FRIENDS, WE HAD EACH OTHER'S RESPECT. LEARN TO TRUST YOUR TEAM, AND TEACH THEM TO TRUST YOU.
EASIER SAID THAN DONE, OLD MAN.
TRUE ENOUGH. BUT YOU'RE A SHIELD. IF *I* COULD DO IT, I'M CONFIDENT *YOU* CAN DO IT.
THANKS FOR THE VOTE OF CONFIDENCE.
HUMOR DUSTY AND CHECK THE SCHEDULE NEXT TIME?
HE GREW UP DEALING WITH SHIELDS. HE'LL ADAPT.

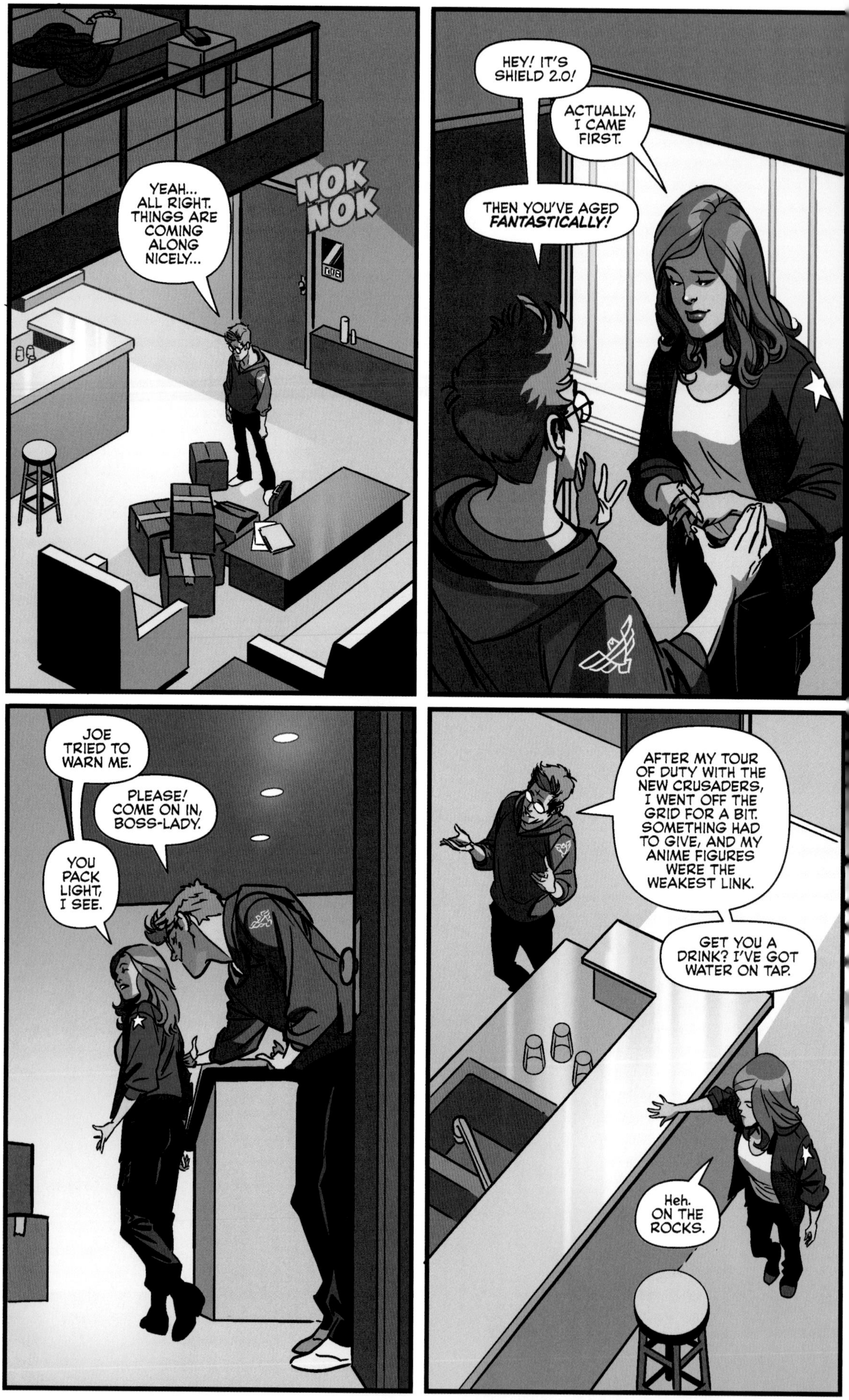
YEAH... ALL RIGHT. THINGS ARE COMING ALONG NICELY...
NOK NOK
HEY! IT'S SHIELD 2.0!
ACTUALLY, I CAME FIRST.
THEN YOU'VE AGED *FANTASTICALLY!*
JOE TRIED TO WARN ME.
PLEASE! COME ON IN, BOSS-LADY.
YOU PACK LIGHT, I SEE.
AFTER MY TOUR OF DUTY WITH THE NEW CRUSADERS, I WENT OFF THE GRID FOR A BIT. SOMETHING HAD TO GIVE, AND MY ANIME FIGURES WERE THE WEAKEST LINK.
GET YOU A DRINK? I'VE GOT WATER ON TAP.
Heh. ON THE ROCKS.

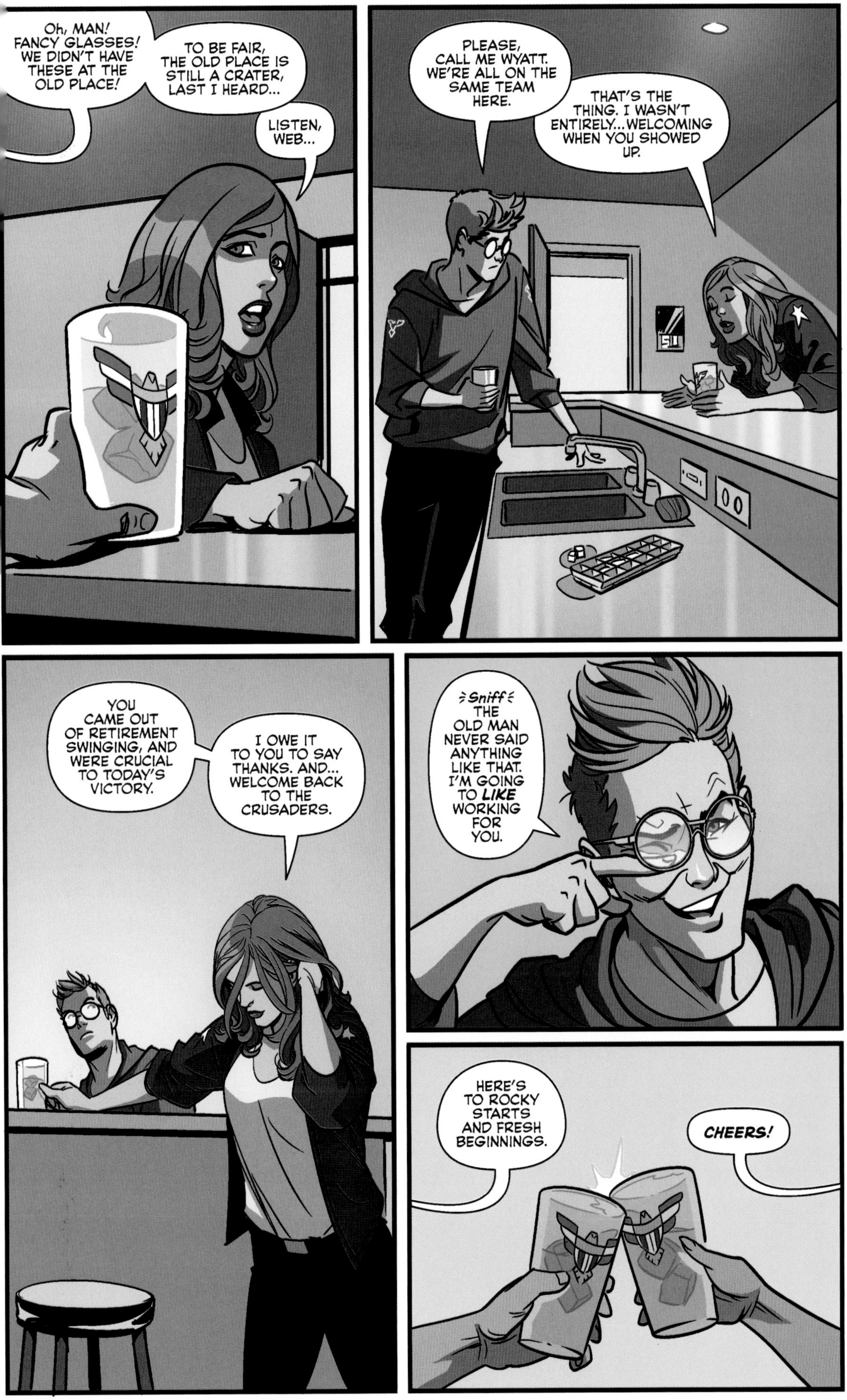
Oh, MAN! FANCY GLASSES! WE DIDN'T HAVE THESE AT THE OLD PLACE!
TO BE FAIR, THE OLD PLACE IS STILL A CRATER, LAST I HEARD...
LISTEN, WEB...
PLEASE, CALL ME WYATT. WE'RE ALL ON THE SAME TEAM HERE.
THAT'S THE THING. I WASN'T ENTIRELY...WELCOMING WHEN YOU SHOWED UP.
YOU CAME OUT OF RETIREMENT SWINGING, AND WERE CRUCIAL TO TODAY'S VICTORY.
I OWE IT TO YOU TO SAY THANKS. AND... WELCOME BACK TO THE CRUSADERS.
Sniff THE OLD MAN NEVER SAID ANYTHING LIKE THAT. I'M GOING TO *LIKE* WORKING FOR YOU.
HERE'S TO ROCKY STARTS AND FRESH BEGINNINGS.
CHEERS!

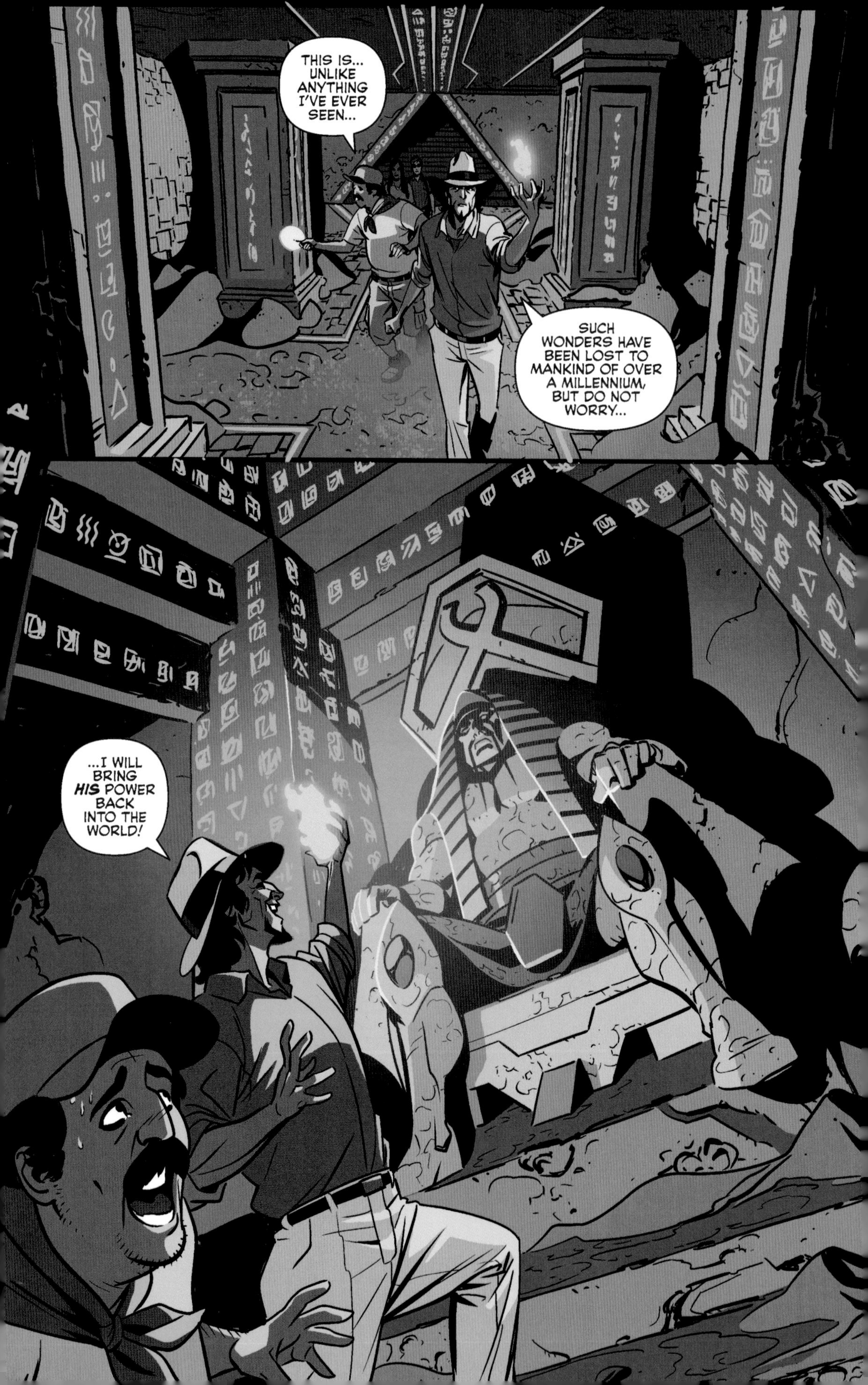
THIS IS... UNLIKE ANYTHING I'VE EVER SEEN...
SUCH WONDERS HAVE BEEN LOST TO MANKIND OF OVER A MILLENNIUM, BUT DO NOT WORRY...
...I WILL BRING *HIS* POWER BACK INTO THE WORLD!

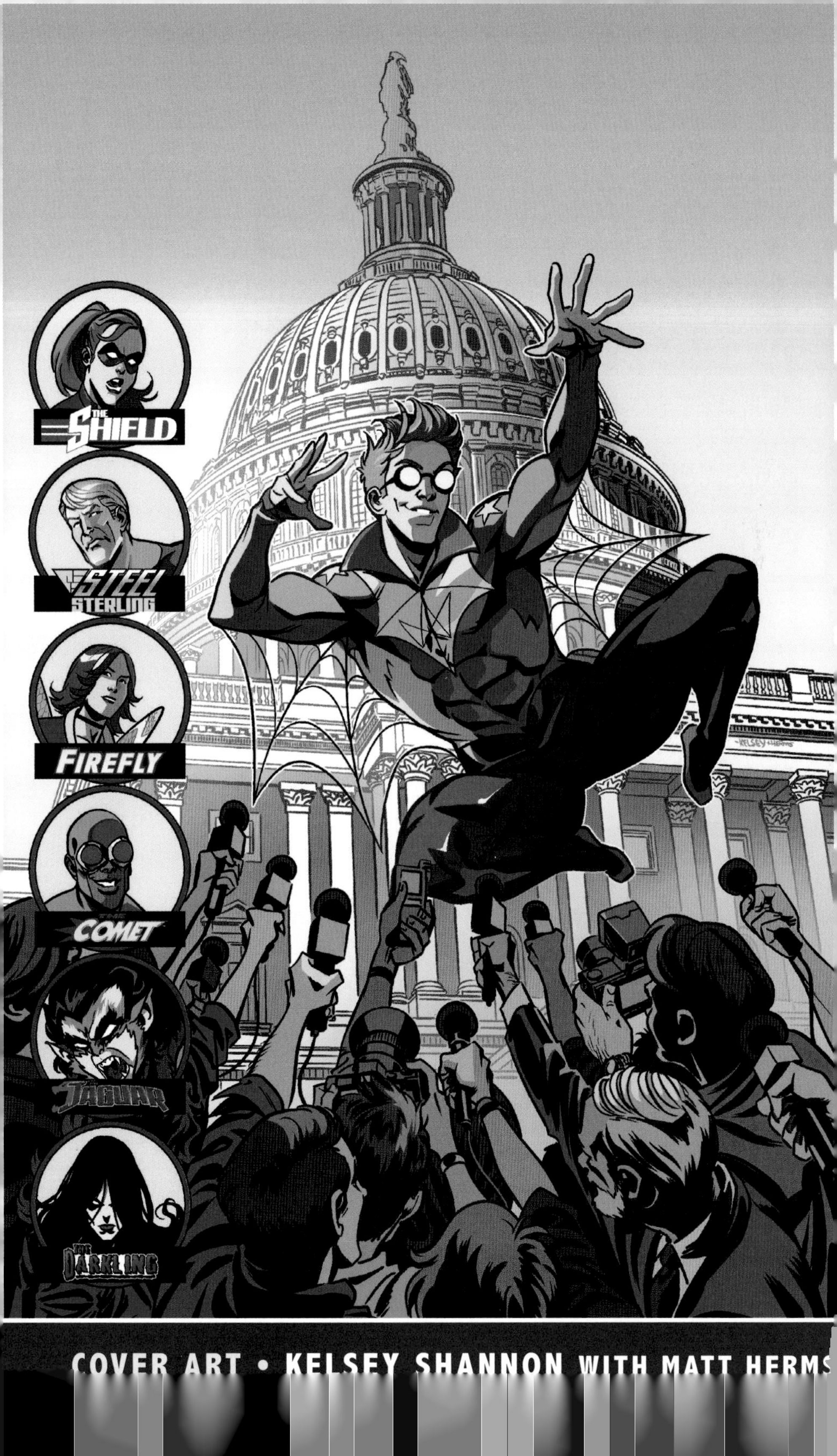
THE SHIELD
STEEL STERLING
FIREFLY
COMET
JAGUAR
THE DARKLING
COVER ART • KELSEY SHANNON WITH MATT HERMS

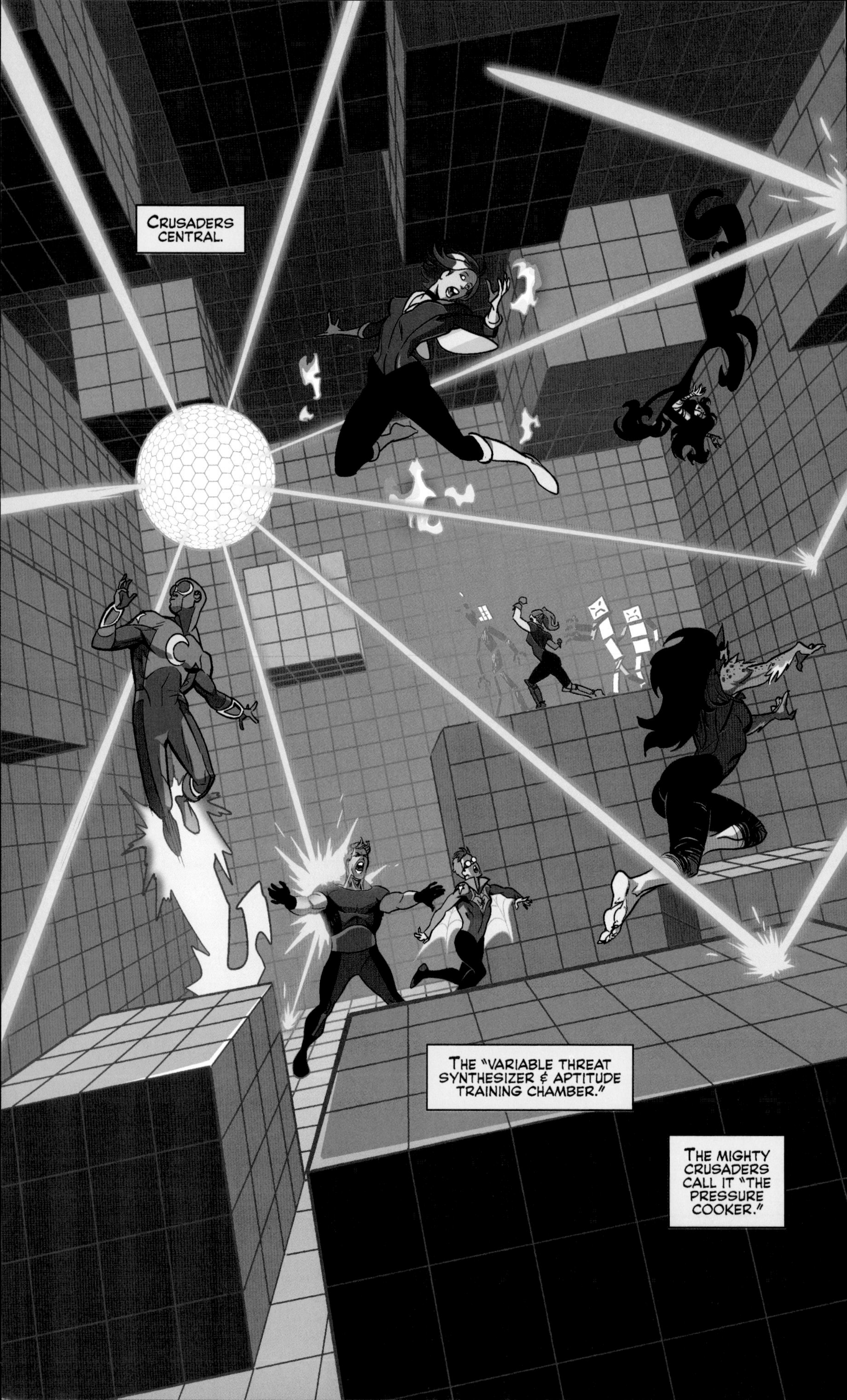
CRUSADERS CENTRAL.
THE "VARIABLE THREAT SYNTHESIZER & APTITUDE TRAINING CHAMBER."
THE MIGHTY CRUSADERS CALL IT "THE PRESSURE COOKER."

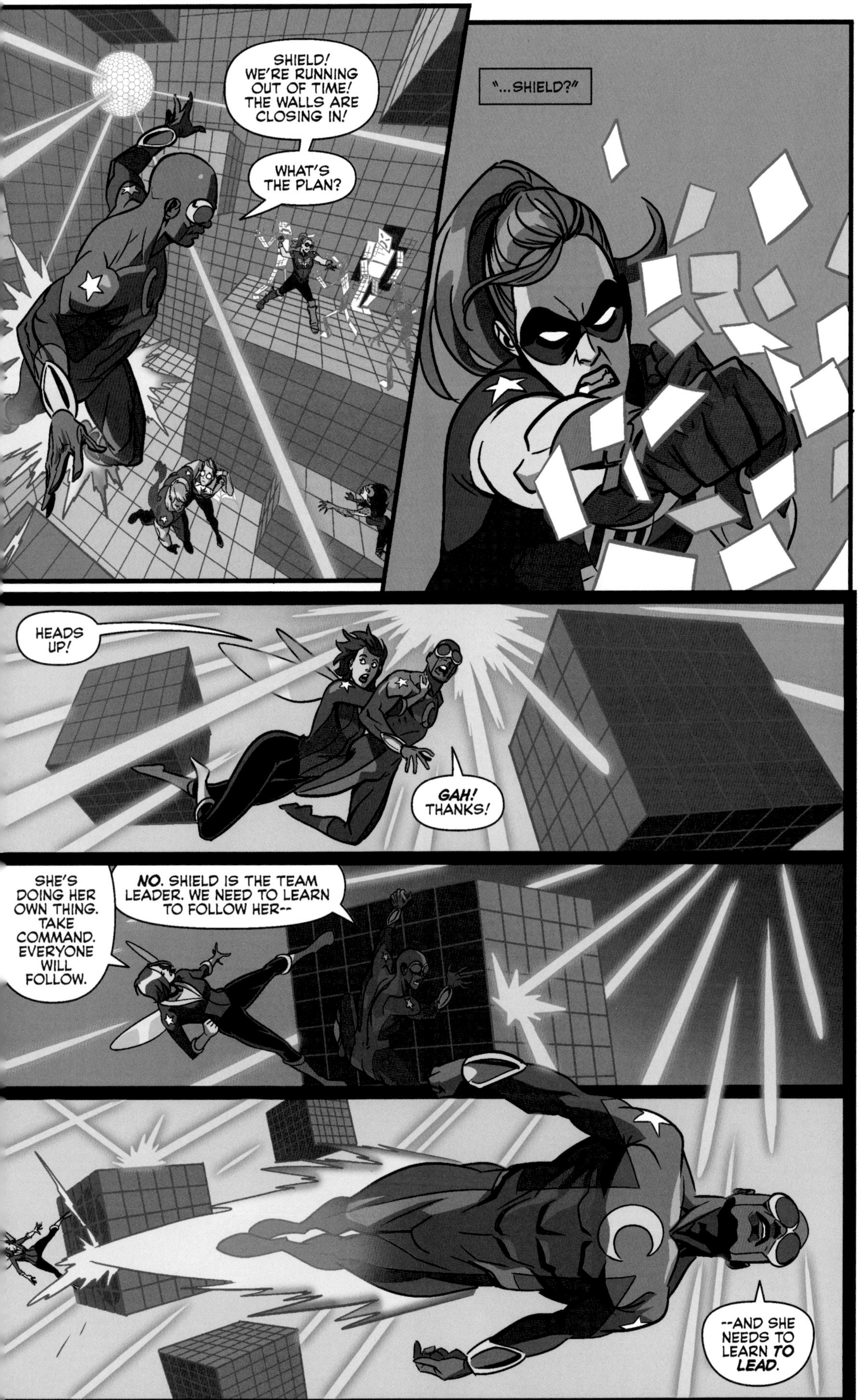

SHIELD! WE'RE RUNNING OUT OF TIME! THE WALLS ARE CLOSING IN!
WHAT'S THE PLAN?
"...SHIELD?"
HEADS UP!
GAH! THANKS!
SHE'S DOING HER OWN THING. TAKE COMMAND. EVERYONE WILL FOLLOW.
NO. SHIELD IS THE TEAM LEADER. WE NEED TO LEARN TO FOLLOW HER--
--AND SHE NEEDS TO LEARN TO LEAD.

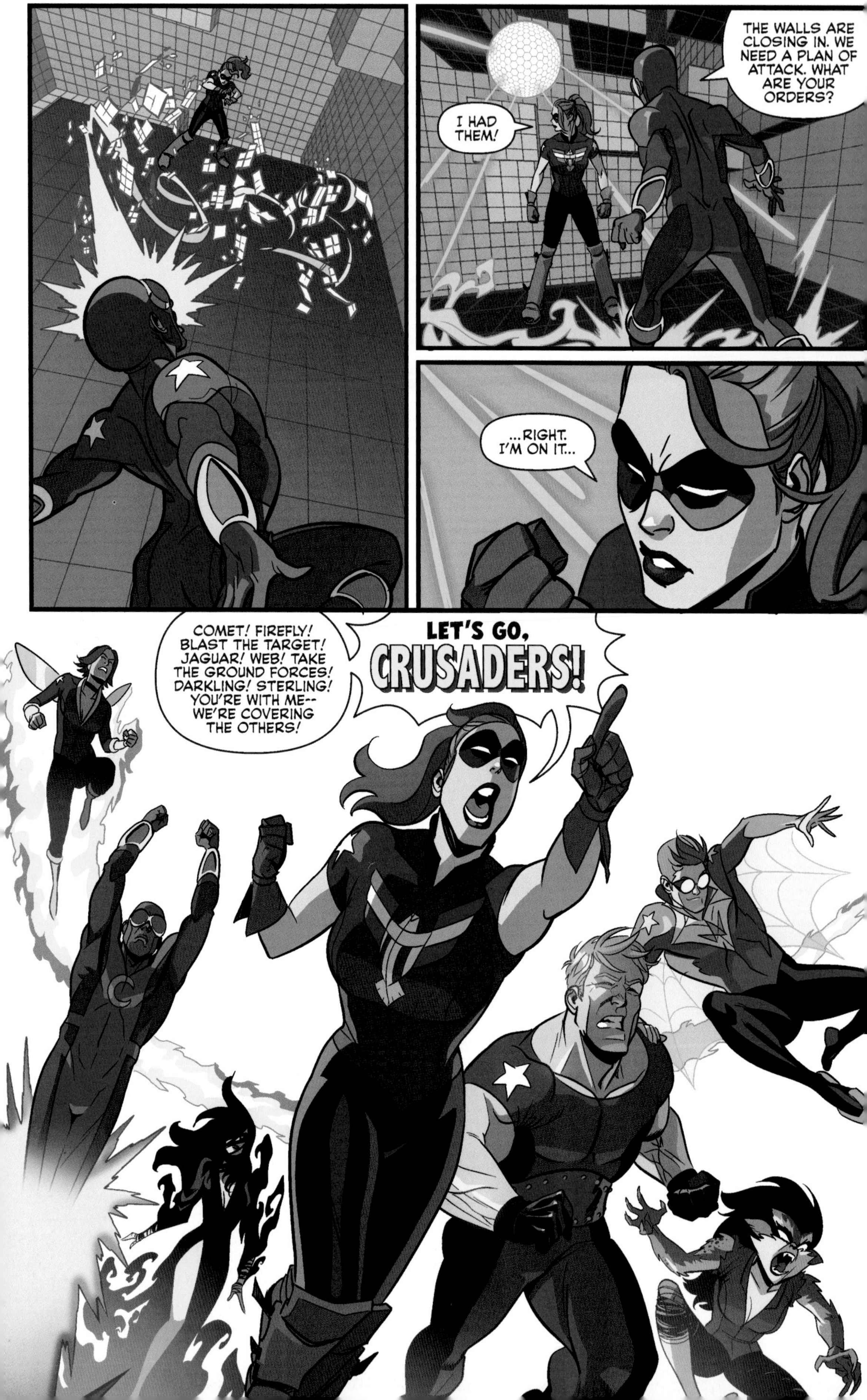
THE WALLS ARE CLOSING IN. WE NEED A PLAN OF ATTACK. WHAT ARE YOUR ORDERS?
I HAD THEM!
...RIGHT. I'M ON IT...
COMET! FIREFLY! BLAST THE TARGET! JAGUAR! WEB! TAKE THE GROUND FORCES! DARKLING! STERLING! YOU'RE WITH ME-- WE'RE COVERING THE OTHERS!
LET'S GO, CRUSADERS!

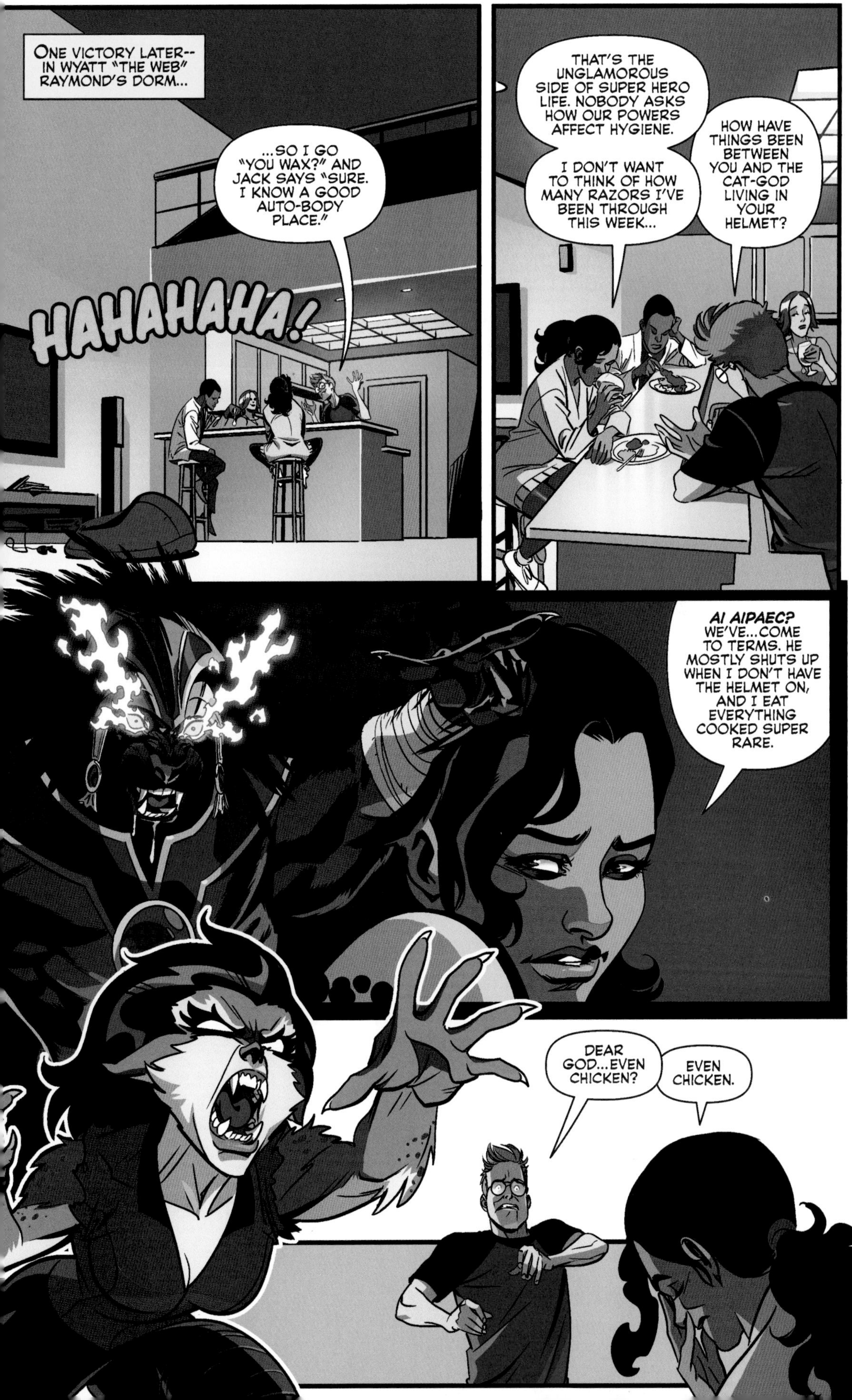
ONE VICTORY LATER--
IN WYATT "THE WEB" RAYMOND'S DORM...
...SO I GO "YOU WAX?" AND JACK SAYS "SURE. I KNOW A GOOD AUTO-BODY PLACE."
HAHAHAHA!
THAT'S THE UNGLAMOROUS SIDE OF SUPER HERO LIFE. NOBODY ASKS HOW OUR POWERS AFFECT HYGIENE.
I DON'T WANT TO THINK OF HOW MANY RAZORS I'VE BEEN THROUGH THIS WEEK...
HOW HAVE THINGS BEEN BETWEEN YOU AND THE CAT-GOD LIVING IN YOUR HELMET?
AI AIPAEC? WE'VE...COME TO TERMS. HE MOSTLY SHUTS UP WHEN I DON'T HAVE THE HELMET ON, AND I EAT EVERYTHING COOKED SUPER RARE.
DEAR GOD...EVEN CHICKEN?
EVEN CHICKEN.

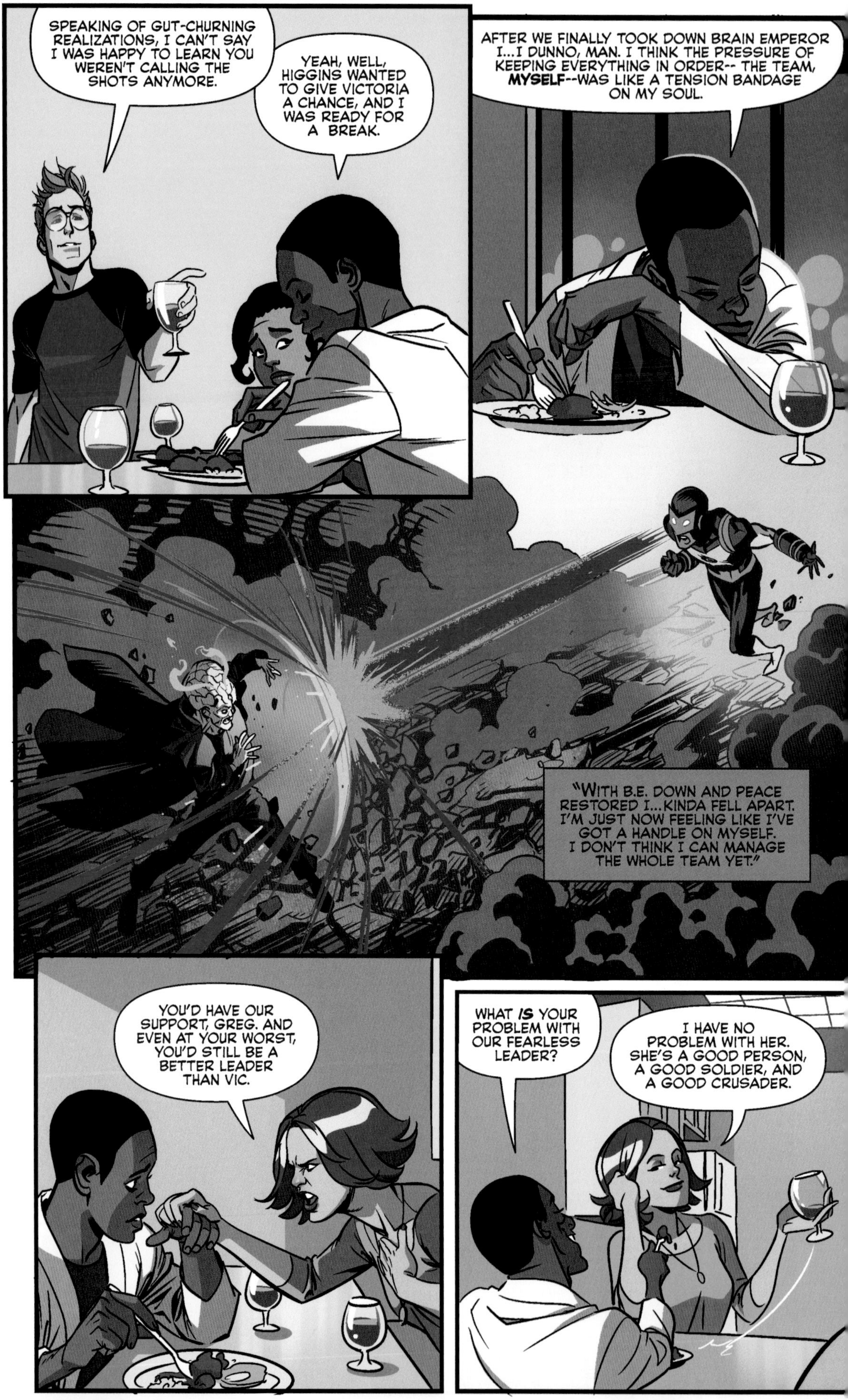
SPEAKING OF GUT-CHURNING REALIZATIONS, I CAN'T SAY I WAS HAPPY TO LEARN YOU WEREN'T CALLING THE SHOTS ANYMORE.
YEAH, WELL, HIGGINS WANTED TO GIVE VICTORIA A CHANCE, AND I WAS READY FOR A BREAK.
AFTER WE FINALLY TOOK DOWN BRAIN EMPEROR I...I DUNNO, MAN. I THINK THE PRESSURE OF KEEPING EVERYTHING IN ORDER-- THE TEAM, **MYSELF**--WAS LIKE A TENSION BANDAGE ON MY SOUL.
"WITH B.E. DOWN AND PEACE RESTORED I...KINDA FELL APART. I'M JUST NOW FEELING LIKE I'VE GOT A HANDLE ON MYSELF. I DON'T THINK I CAN MANAGE THE WHOLE TEAM YET."
YOU'D HAVE OUR SUPPORT, GREG. AND EVEN AT YOUR WORST, YOU'D STILL BE A BETTER LEADER THAN VIC.
WHAT *IS* YOUR PROBLEM WITH OUR FEARLESS LEADER?
I HAVE NO PROBLEM WITH HER. SHE'S A GOOD PERSON, A GOOD SOLDIER, AND A GOOD CRUSADER.

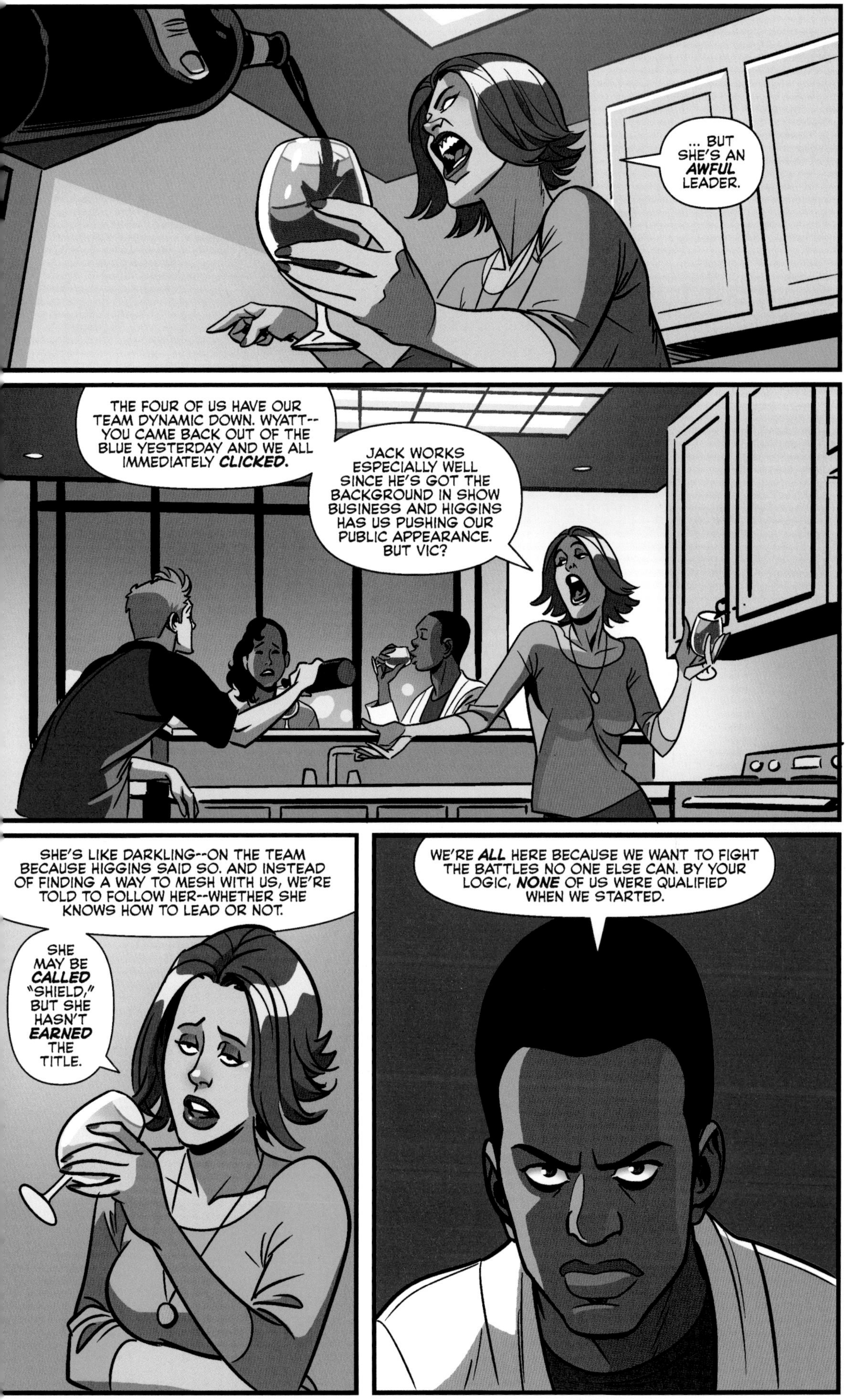
... BUT SHE'S AN AWFUL LEADER.
THE FOUR OF US HAVE OUR TEAM DYNAMIC DOWN. WYATT-- YOU CAME BACK OUT OF THE BLUE YESTERDAY AND WE ALL IMMEDIATELY CLICKED.
JACK WORKS ESPECIALLY WELL SINCE HE'S GOT THE BACKGROUND IN SHOW BUSINESS AND HIGGINS HAS US PUSHING OUR PUBLIC APPEARANCE. BUT VIC?
SHE'S LIKE DARKLING--ON THE TEAM BECAUSE HIGGINS SAID SO. AND INSTEAD OF FINDING A WAY TO MESH WITH US, WE'RE TOLD TO FOLLOW HER--WHETHER SHE KNOWS HOW TO LEAD OR NOT.
SHE MAY BE CALLED "SHIELD," BUT SHE HASN'T EARNED THE TITLE.
WE'RE ALL HERE BECAUSE WE WANT TO FIGHT THE BATTLES NO ONE ELSE CAN. BY YOUR LOGIC, NONE OF US WERE QUALIFIED WHEN WE STARTED.

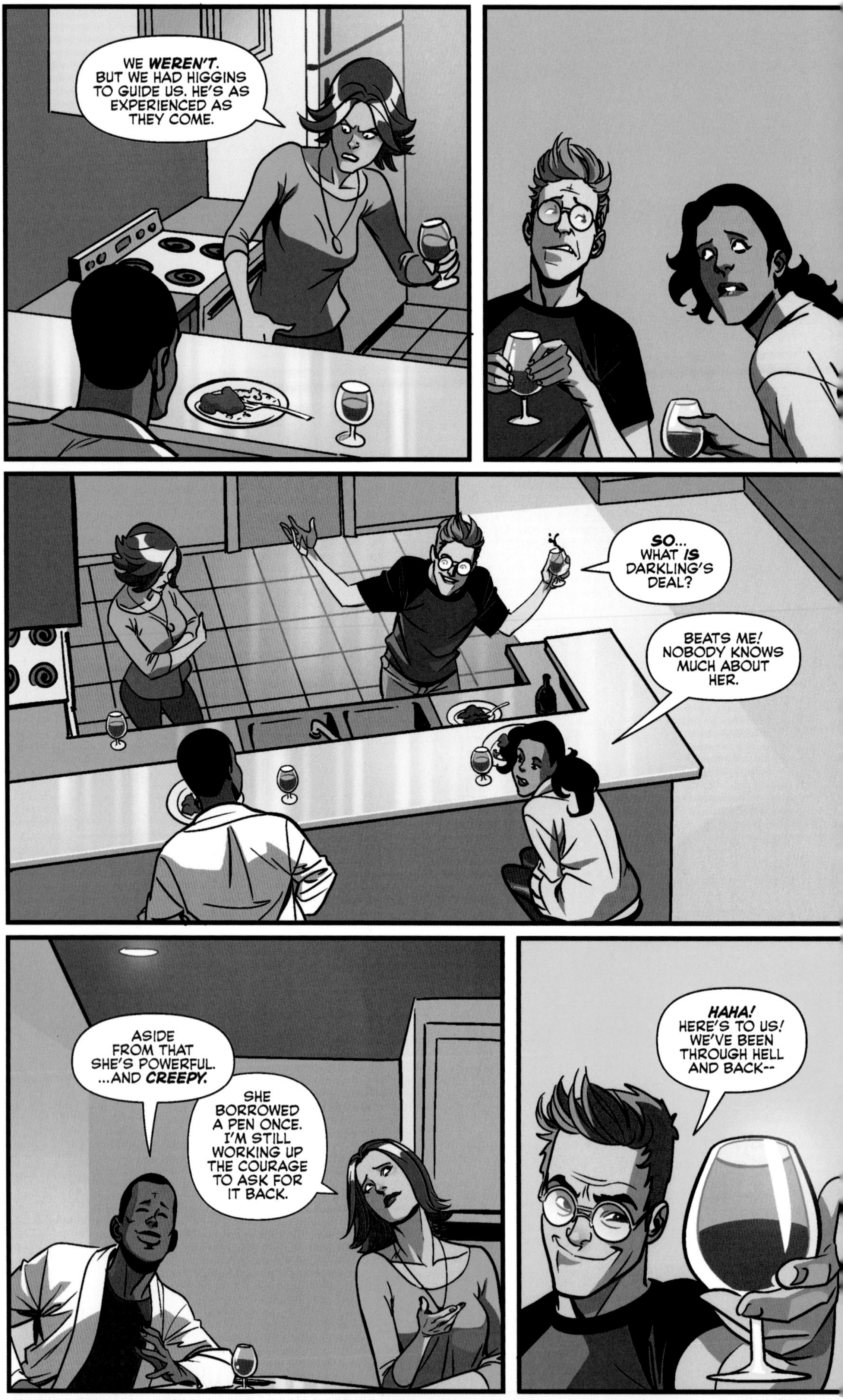
WE *WEREN'T*. BUT WE HAD HIGGINS TO GUIDE US. HE'S AS EXPERIENCED AS THEY COME.
SO... WHAT *IS* DARKLING'S DEAL?
BEATS ME! NOBODY KNOWS MUCH ABOUT HER.
ASIDE FROM THAT SHE'S POWERFUL. ...AND *CREEPY.*
SHE BORROWED A PEN ONCE. I'M STILL WORKING UP THE COURAGE TO ASK FOR IT BACK.
HAHA! HERE'S TO US! WE'VE BEEN THROUGH HELL AND BACK--

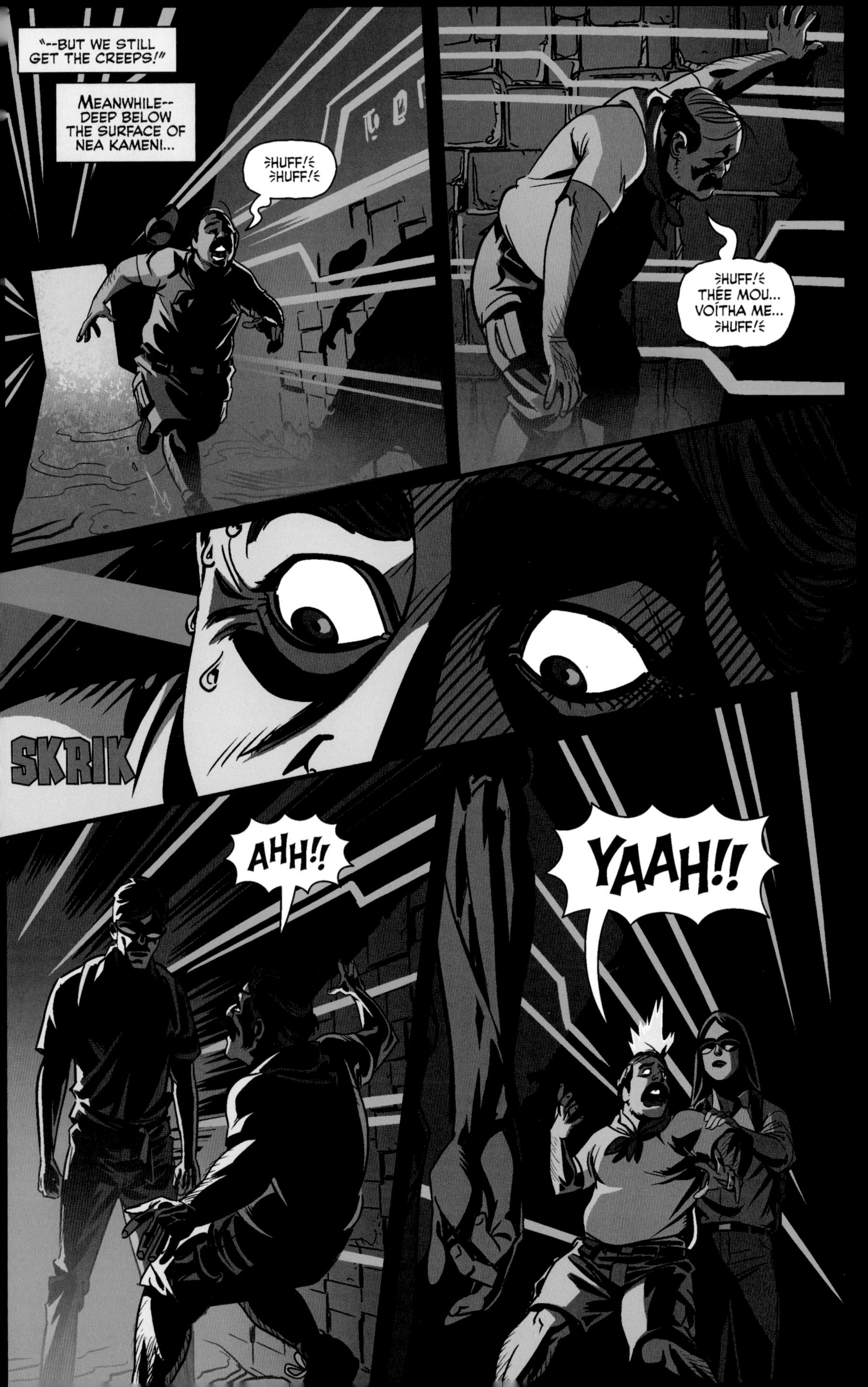
"--BUT WE STILL GET THE CREEPS!"
MEANWHILE-- DEEP BELOW THE SURFACE OF NEA KAMENI...
HUFF! HUFF!
HUFF! THÉE MOU... VOÍTHA ME... HUFF!
SKRIK
AHH!!
YAAH!!

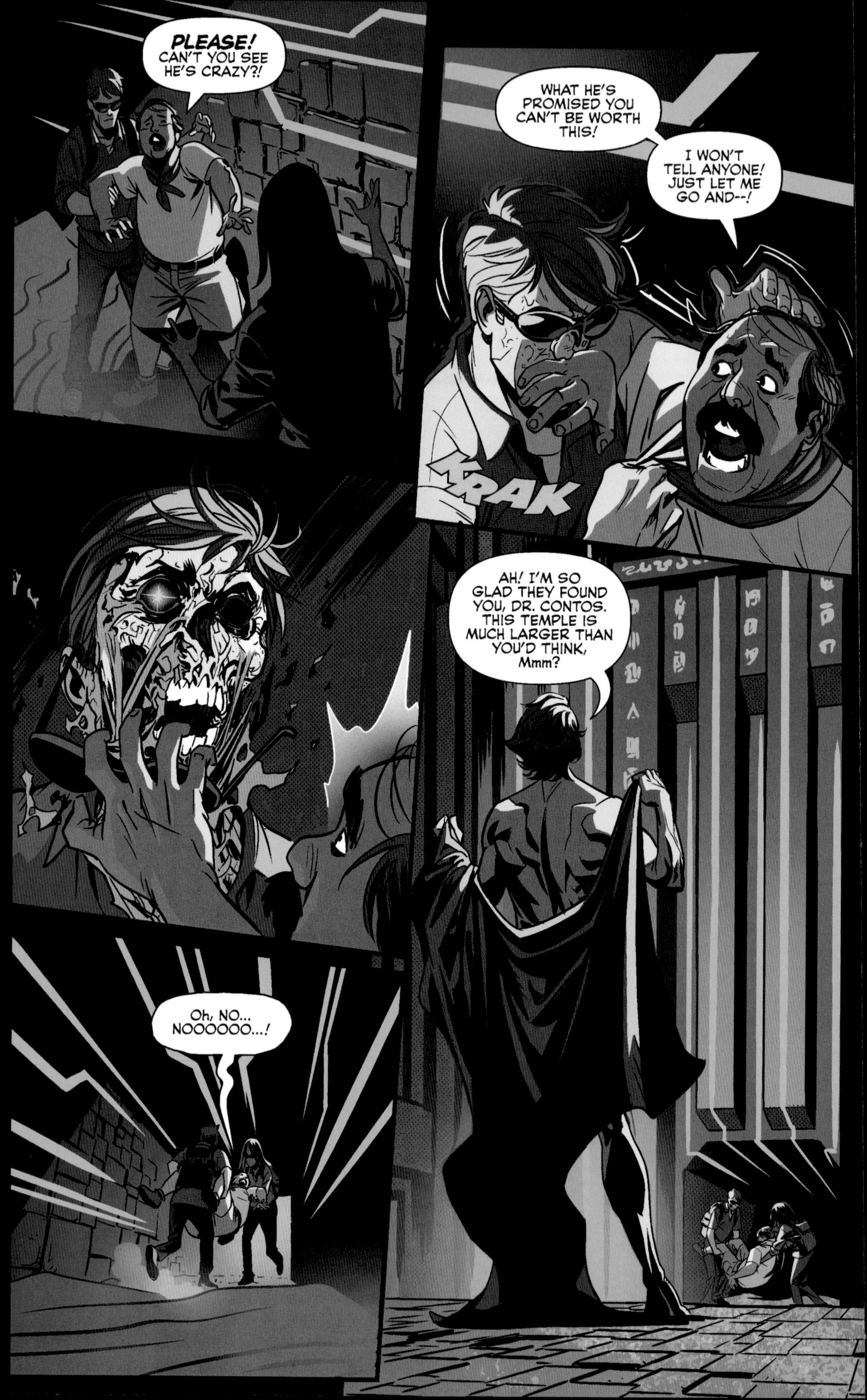
PLEASE! CAN'T YOU SEE HE'S CRAZY?!
WHAT HE'S PROMISED YOU CAN'T BE WORTH THIS!
I WON'T TELL ANYONE! JUST LET ME GO AND--!
KRAK
AH! I'M SO GLAD THEY FOUND YOU, DR. CONTOS. THIS TEMPLE IS MUCH LARGER THAN YOU'D THINK, Mmm?
Oh, NO... NOOOOOO...!

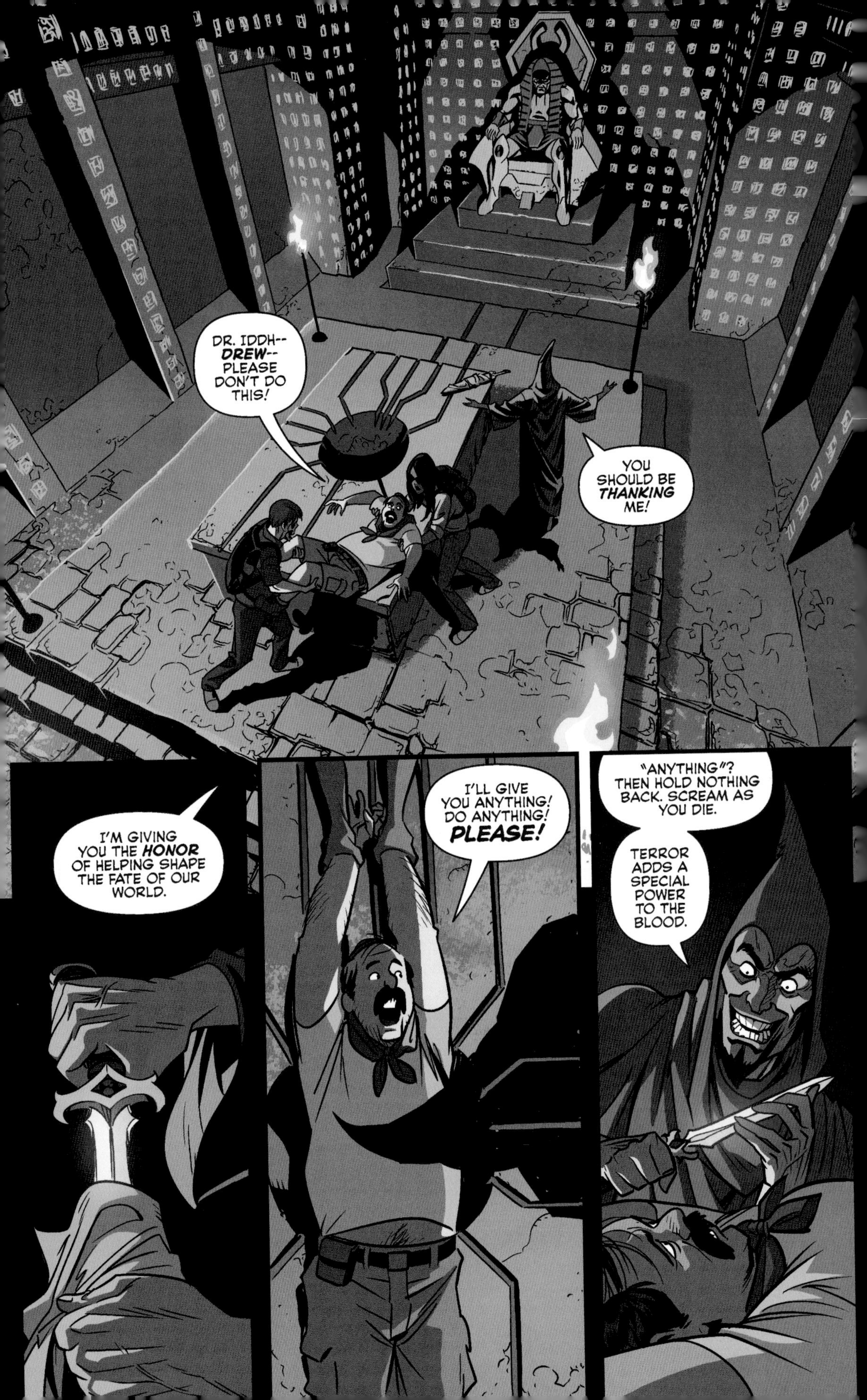

DR. IDDH-- DREW-- PLEASE DON'T DO THIS!
YOU SHOULD BE THANKING ME!
I'M GIVING YOU THE HONOR OF HELPING SHAPE THE FATE OF OUR WORLD.
I'LL GIVE YOU ANYTHING! DO ANYTHING! PLEASE!
"ANYTHING"? THEN HOLD NOTHING BACK. SCREAM AS YOU DIE.
TERROR ADDS A SPECIAL POWER TO THE BLOOD.

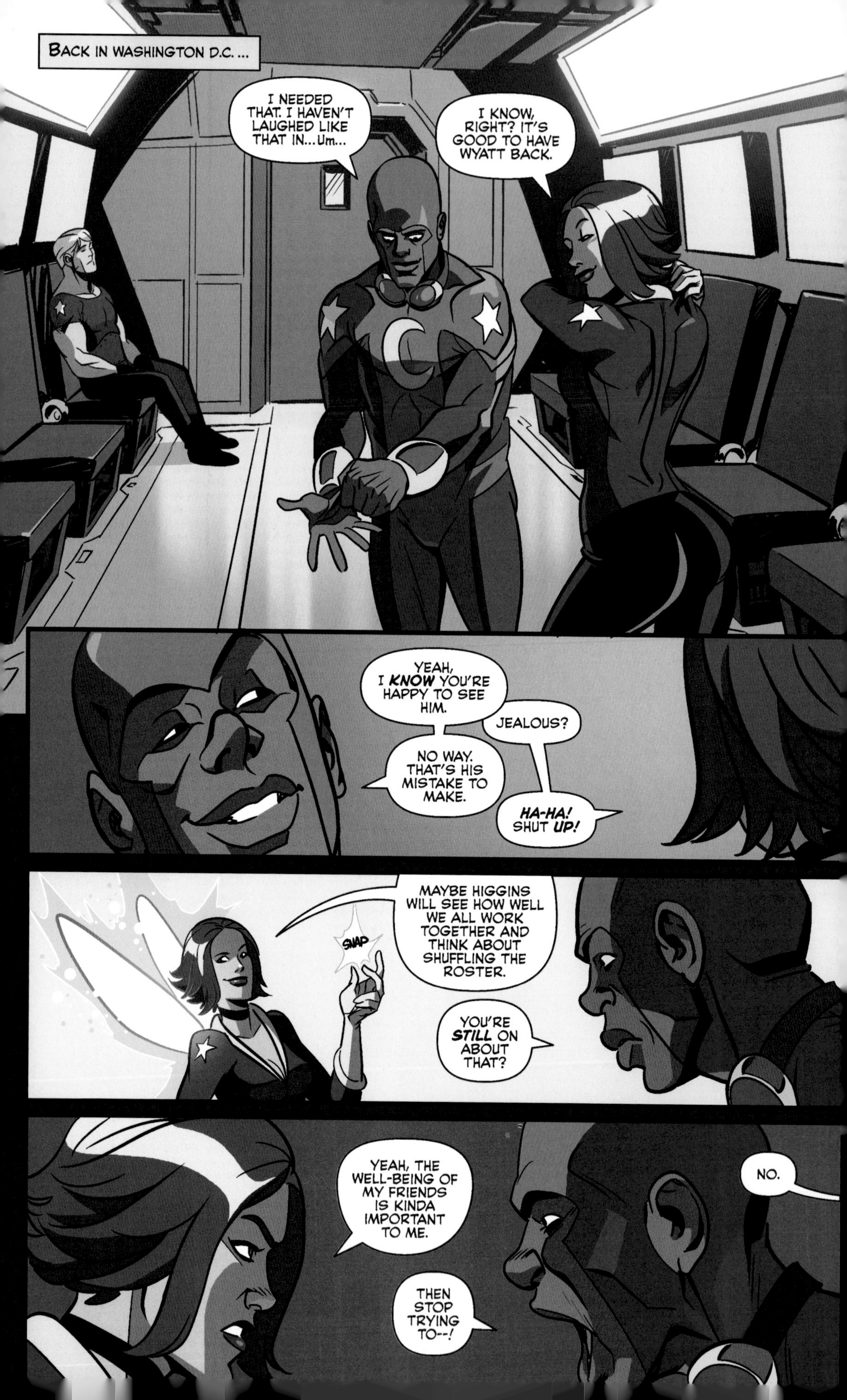
BACK IN WASHINGTON D.C. ...
I NEEDED THAT. I HAVEN'T LAUGHED LIKE THAT IN...Um...
I KNOW, RIGHT? IT'S GOOD TO HAVE WYATT BACK.
YEAH, I KNOW YOU'RE HAPPY TO SEE HIM.
JEALOUS?
NO WAY. THAT'S HIS MISTAKE TO MAKE.
HA-HA! SHUT UP!
MAYBE HIGGINS WILL SEE HOW WELL WE ALL WORK TOGETHER AND THINK ABOUT SHUFFLING THE ROSTER.
SNAP
YOU'RE STILL ON ABOUT THAT?
YEAH, THE WELL-BEING OF MY FRIENDS IS KINDA IMPORTANT TO ME.
NO.
THEN STOP TRYING TO--!

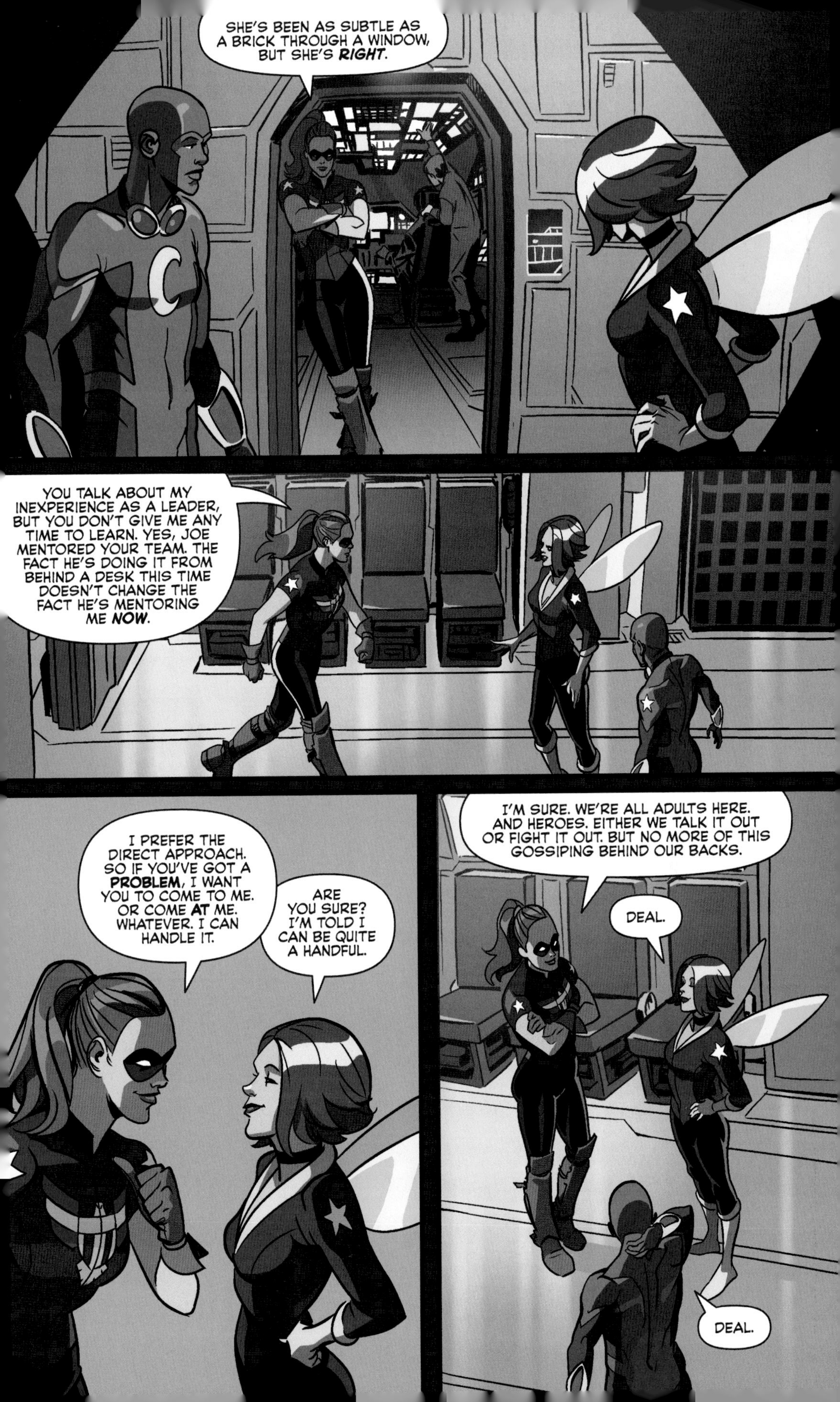
SHE'S BEEN AS SUBTLE AS A BRICK THROUGH A WINDOW, BUT SHE'S ***RIGHT***.
YOU TALK ABOUT MY INEXPERIENCE AS A LEADER, BUT YOU DON'T GIVE ME ANY TIME TO LEARN. YES, JOE MENTORED YOUR TEAM. THE FACT HE'S DOING IT FROM BEHIND A DESK THIS TIME DOESN'T CHANGE THE FACT HE'S MENTORING ME ***NOW***.
I PREFER THE DIRECT APPROACH. SO IF YOU'VE GOT A **PROBLEM**, I WANT YOU TO COME TO ME. OR COME **AT** ME. WHATEVER. I CAN HANDLE IT.
ARE YOU SURE? I'M TOLD I CAN BE QUITE A HANDFUL.
I'M SURE. WE'RE ALL ADULTS HERE. AND HEROES. EITHER WE TALK IT OUT OR FIGHT IT OUT. BUT NO MORE OF THIS GOSSIPING BEHIND OUR BACKS.
DEAL.
DEAL.

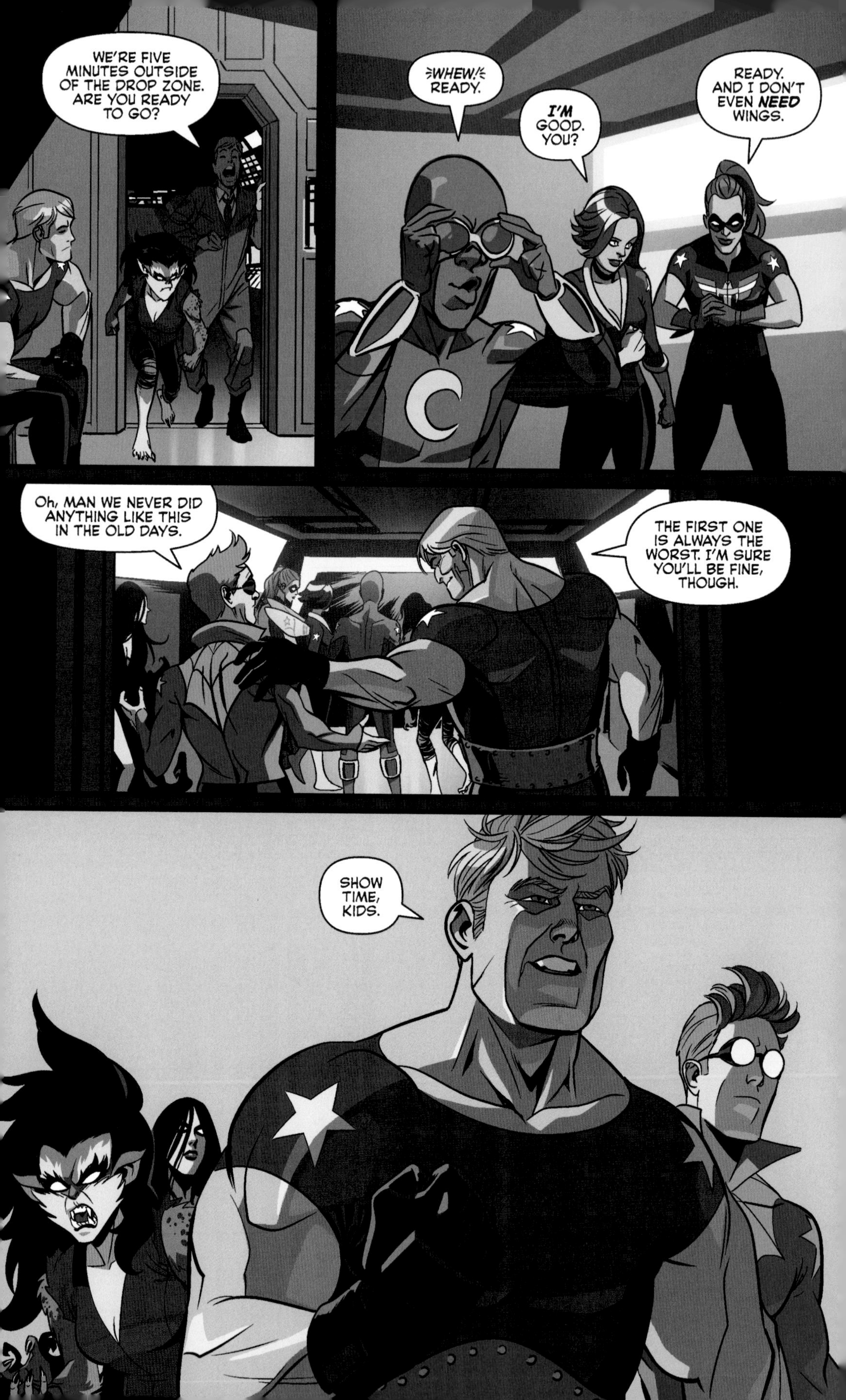
WE'RE FIVE MINUTES OUTSIDE OF THE DROP ZONE. ARE YOU READY TO GO?
WHEW! READY.
I'M GOOD. YOU?
READY. AND I DON'T EVEN NEED WINGS.
Oh, MAN WE NEVER DID ANYTHING LIKE THIS IN THE OLD DAYS.
THE FIRST ONE IS ALWAYS THE WORST. I'M SURE YOU'LL BE FINE, THOUGH.
SHOW TIME, KIDS.

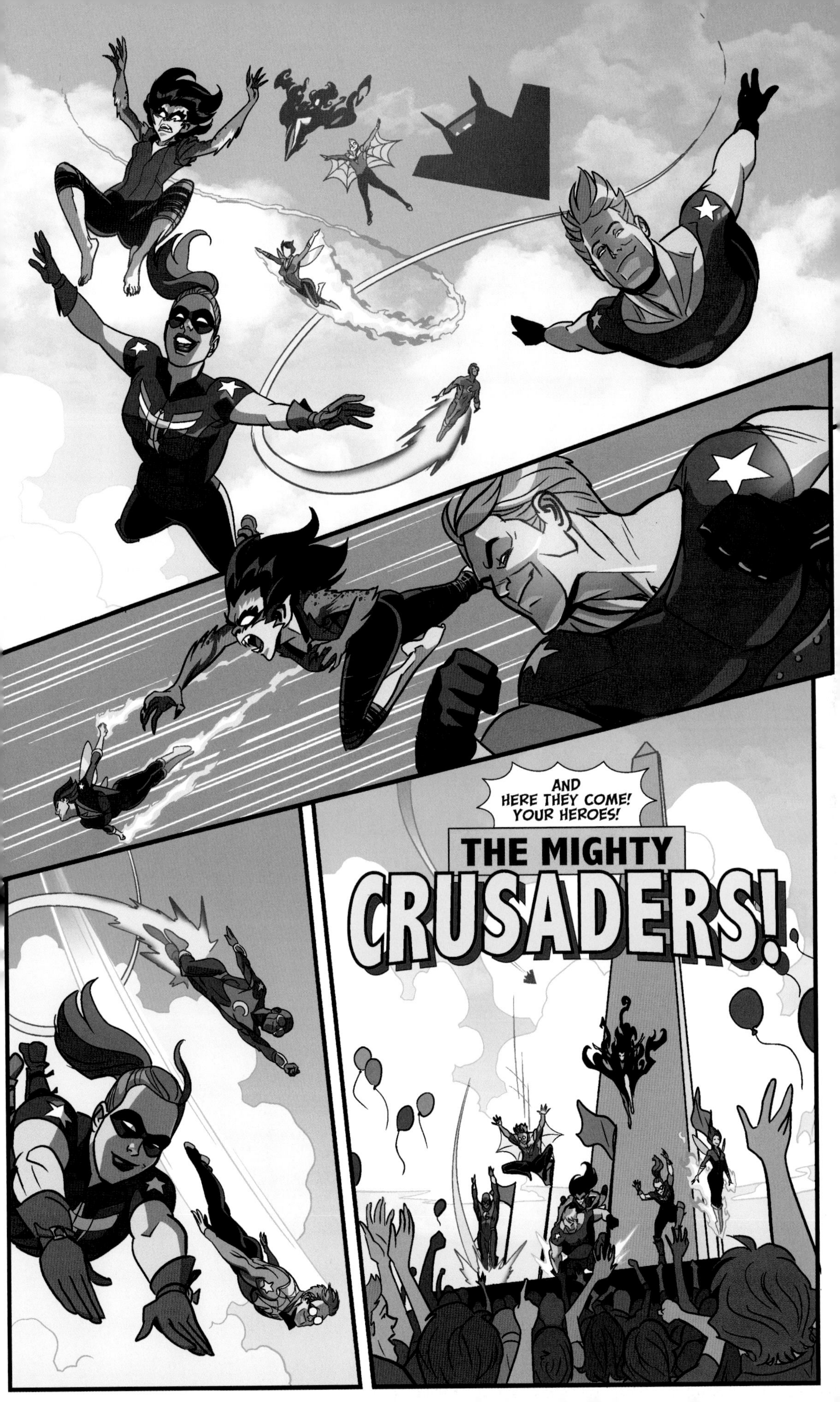

AND HERE THEY COME! YOUR HEROES!
THE MIGHTY CRUSADERS!

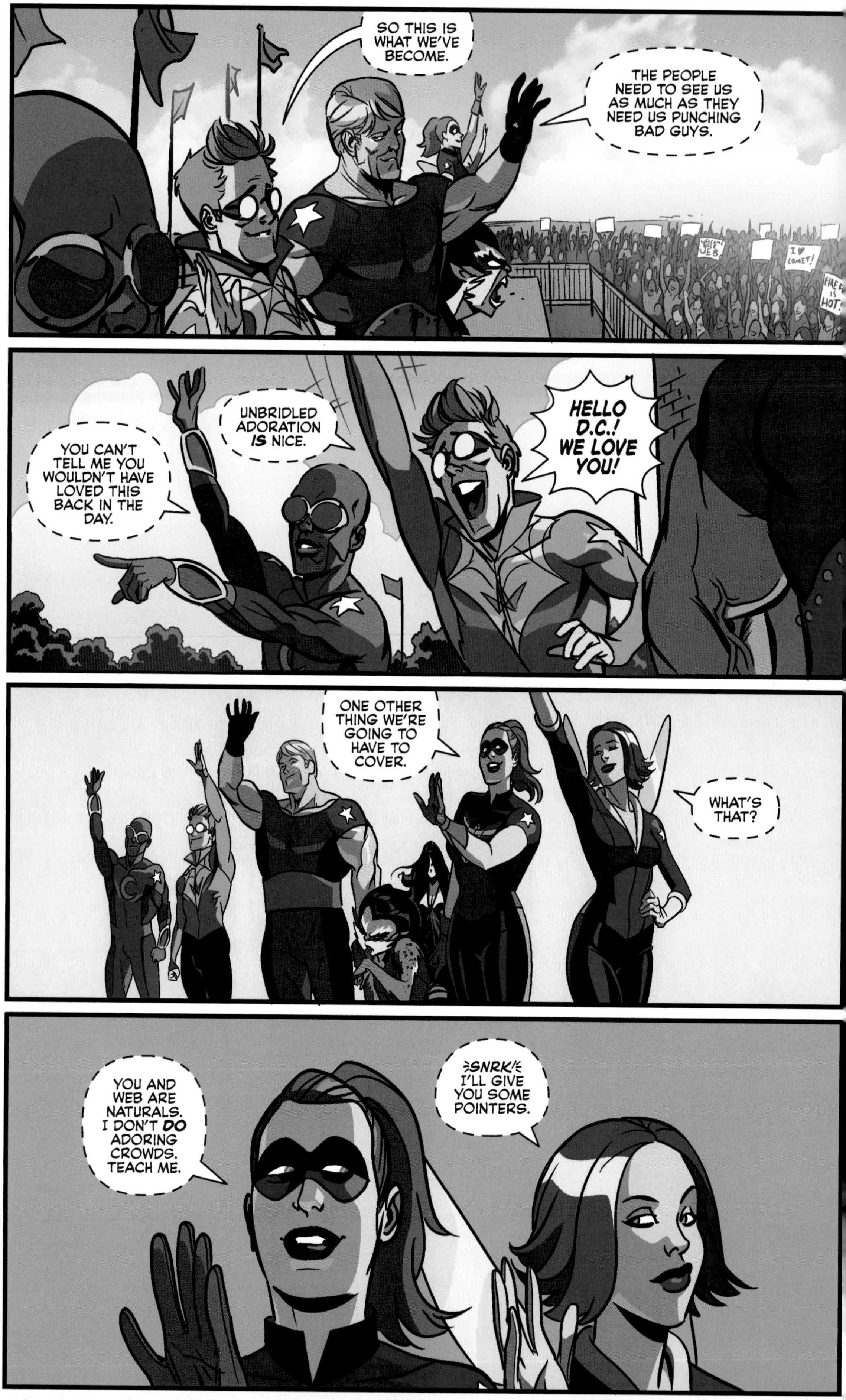
SO THIS IS WHAT WE'VE BECOME.
THE PEOPLE NEED TO SEE US AS MUCH AS THEY NEED US PUNCHING BAD GUYS.
YOU CAN'T TELL ME YOU WOULDN'T HAVE LOVED THIS BACK IN THE DAY.
UNBRIDLED ADORATION ***IS*** NICE.
HELLO D.C.! WE LOVE YOU!
ONE OTHER THING WE'RE GOING TO HAVE TO COVER.
WHAT'S THAT?
YOU AND WEB ARE NATURALS. I DON'T ***DO*** ADORING CROWDS. TEACH ME.
SNRK! I'LL GIVE YOU SOME POINTERS.

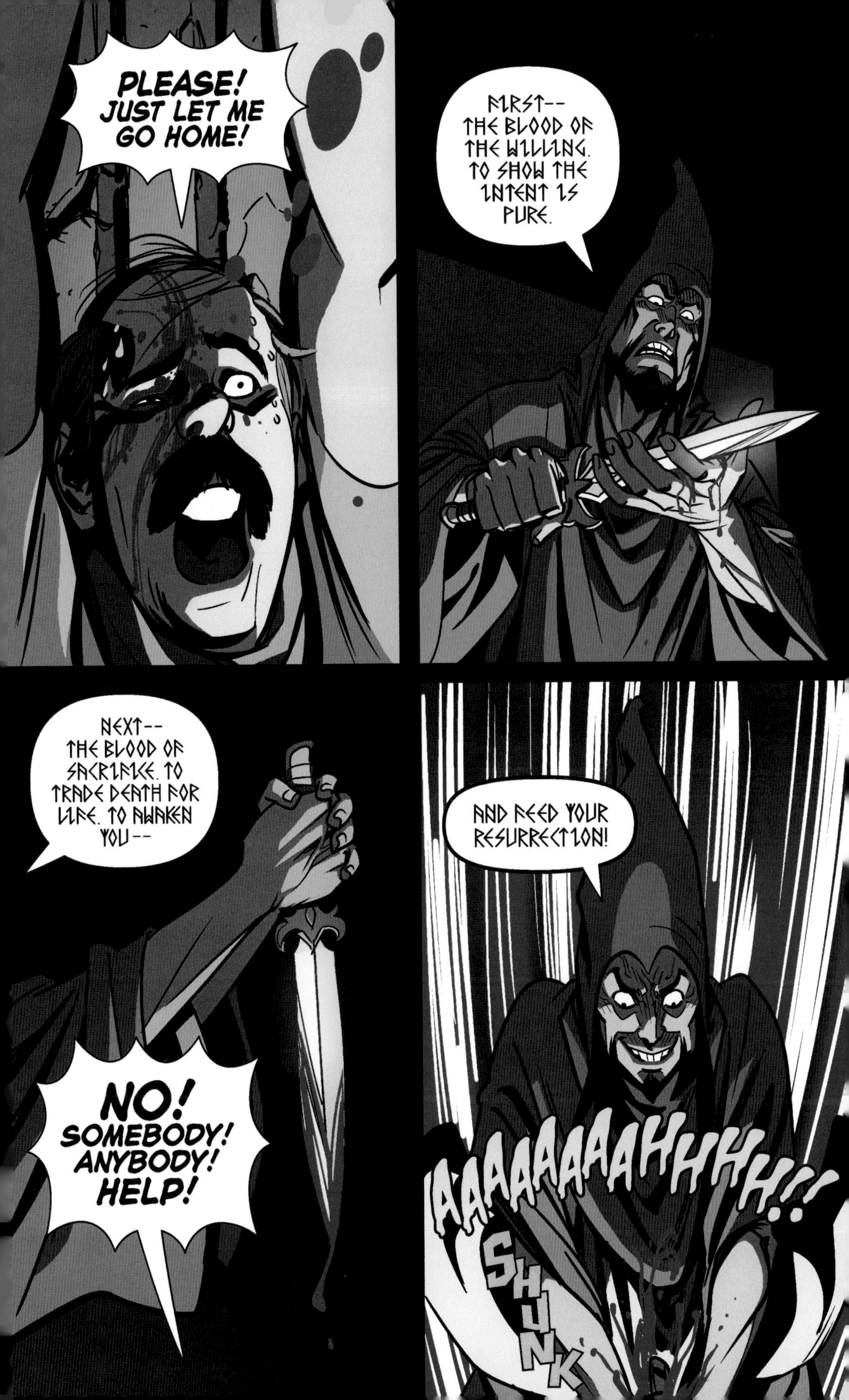
PLEASE! JUST LET ME GO HOME!
FIRST-- THE BLOOD OF THE WILLING. TO SHOW THE INTENT IS PURE.
NEXT-- THE BLOOD OF SACRIFICE. TO TRADE DEATH FOR LIFE. TO AWAKEN YOU--
NO! SOMEBODY! ANYBODY! HELP!
AND FEED YOUR RESURRECTION!
AAAAAAAAAHHHH!!!
SHUNK

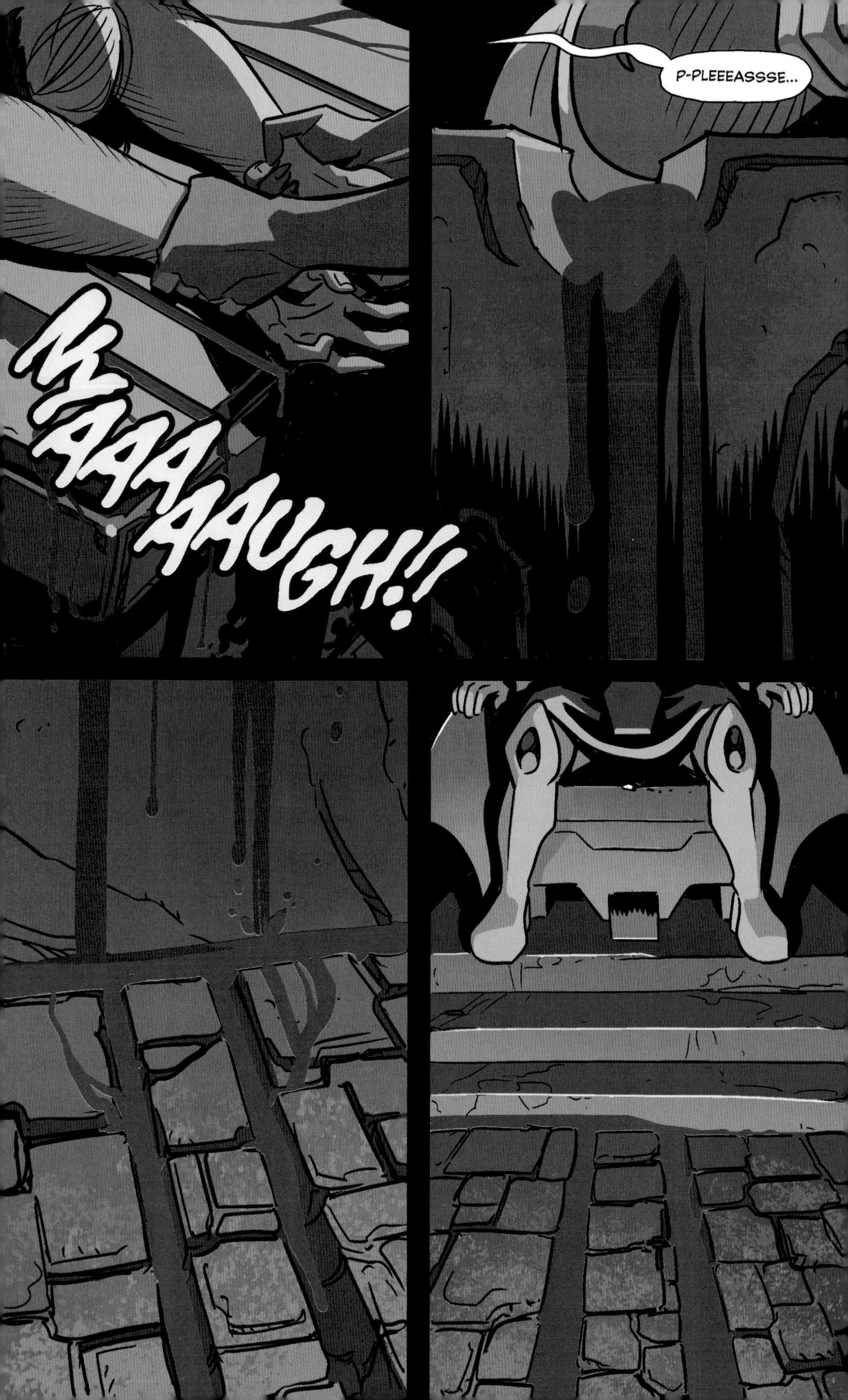
MAAAAAAUGH!!
P-PLEEEASSSE...

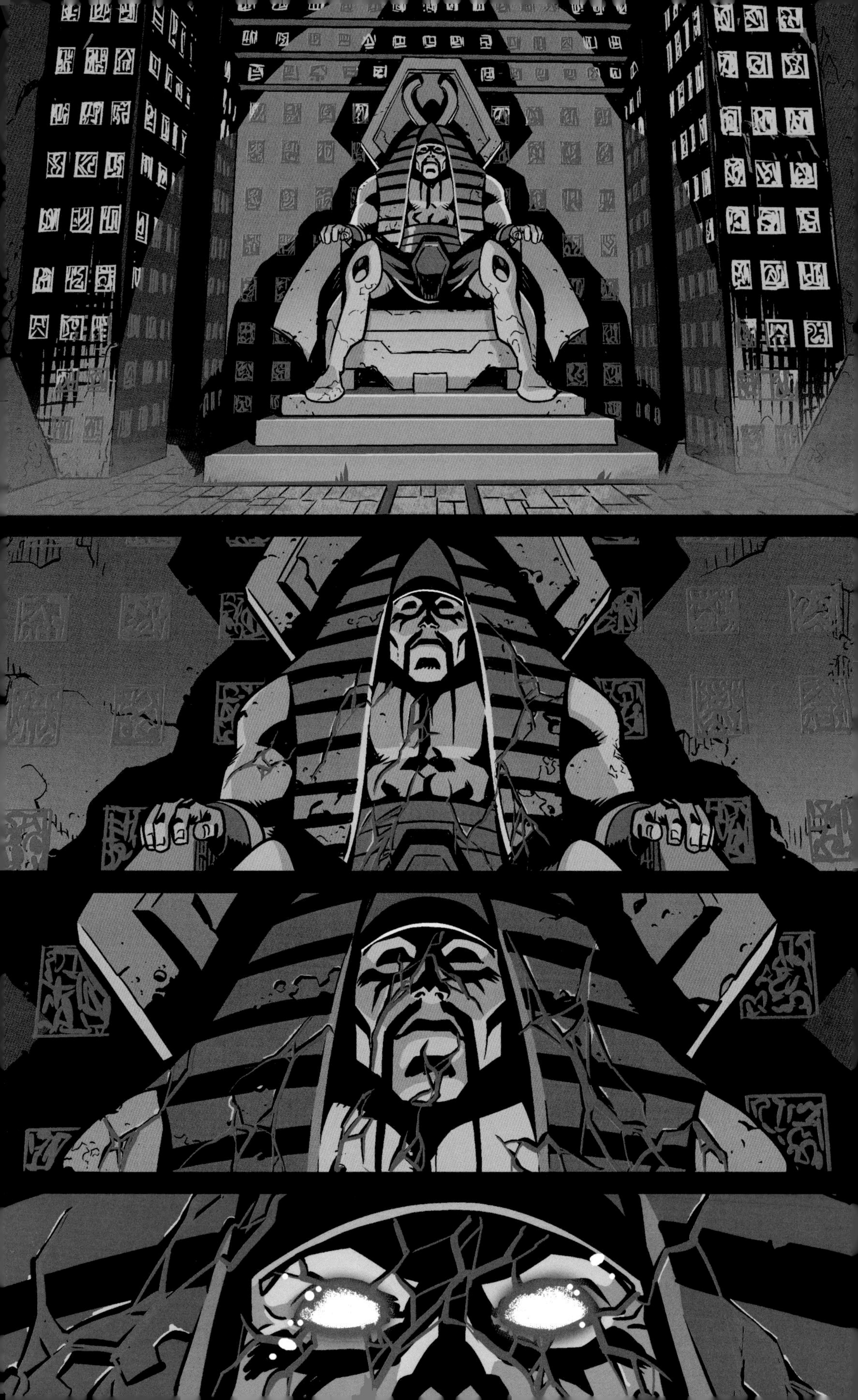

SO... PLANS FOR TONIGHT?

GIRLS' NIGHT WITH SHIELD. MIGHT NEED TO UNWIND AFTERWARDS, THOUGH...

WELL, I *DID* JUST BUY A KICKASS TV...

...IVY? WHAT IS IT?

BEEEEEEEEEE

CAR!

EEEEEEEEEEEEEEEEP!

KRUNCH

MIGHTY CRUSADERS!

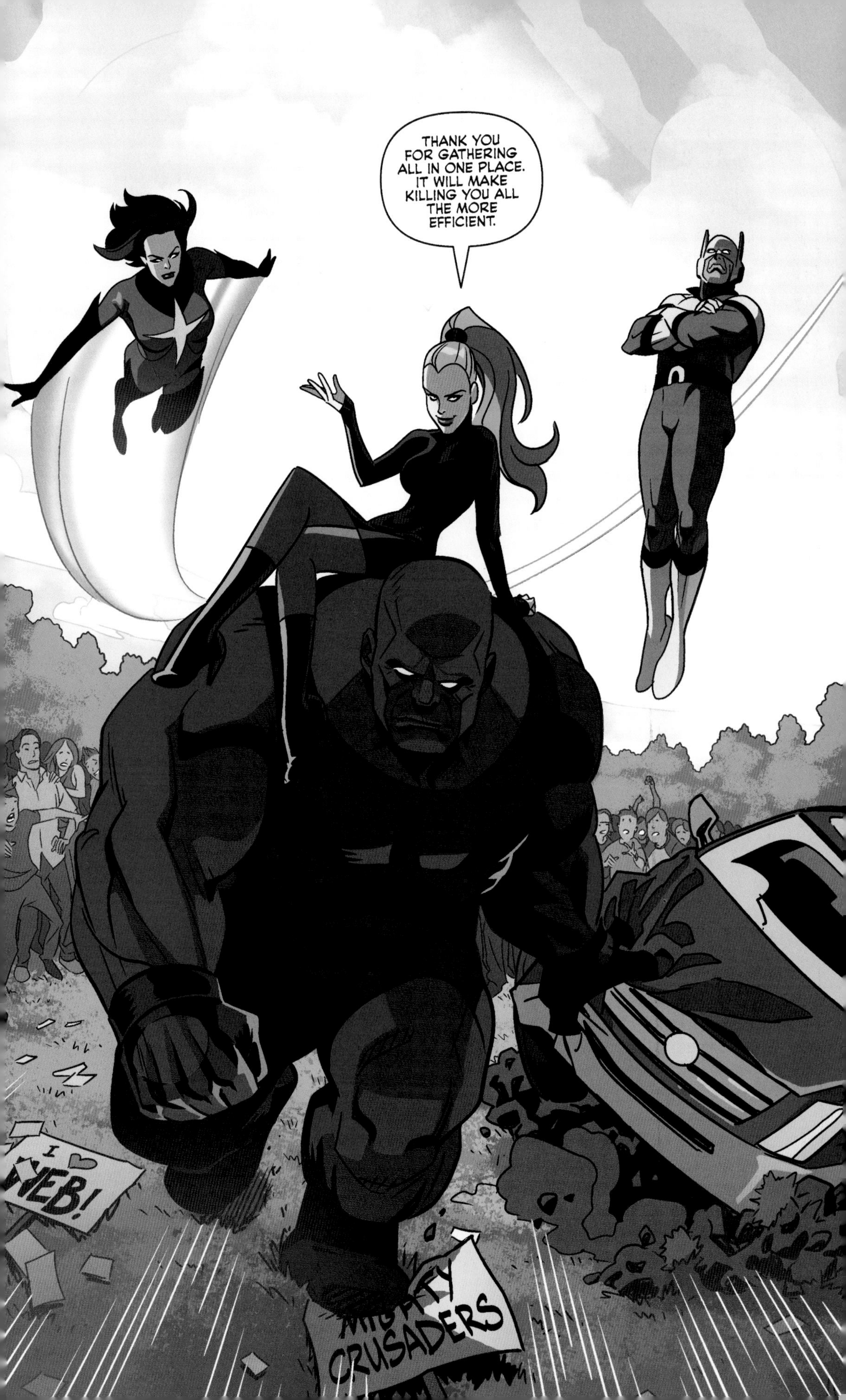
THANK YOU FOR GATHERING ALL IN ONE PLACE. IT WILL MAKE KILLING YOU ALL THE MORE EFFICIENT.
I ♥ WEB!
CRUSADERS

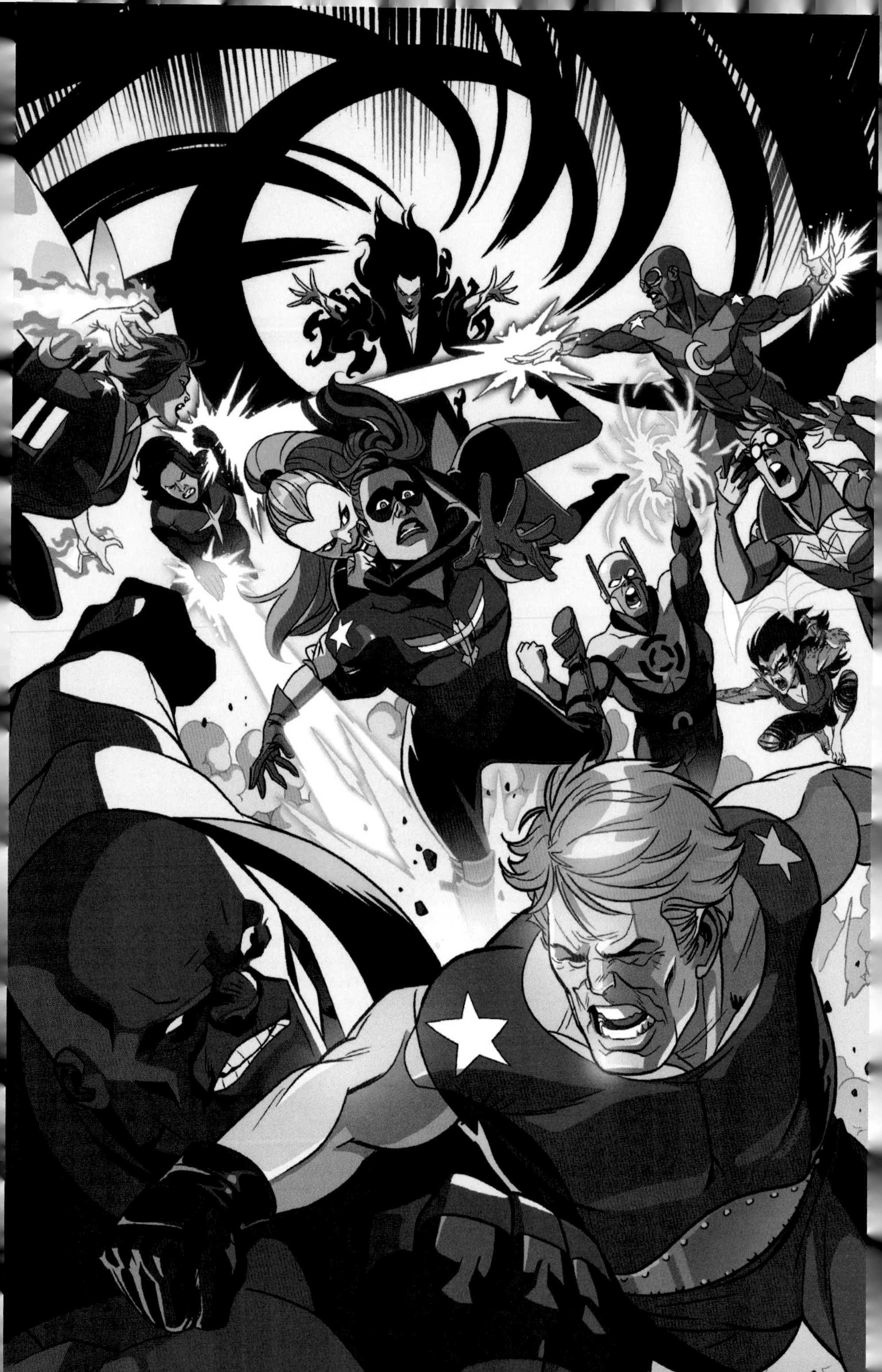

COVER ART • KELSEY SHANNON WITH MATT HERMS

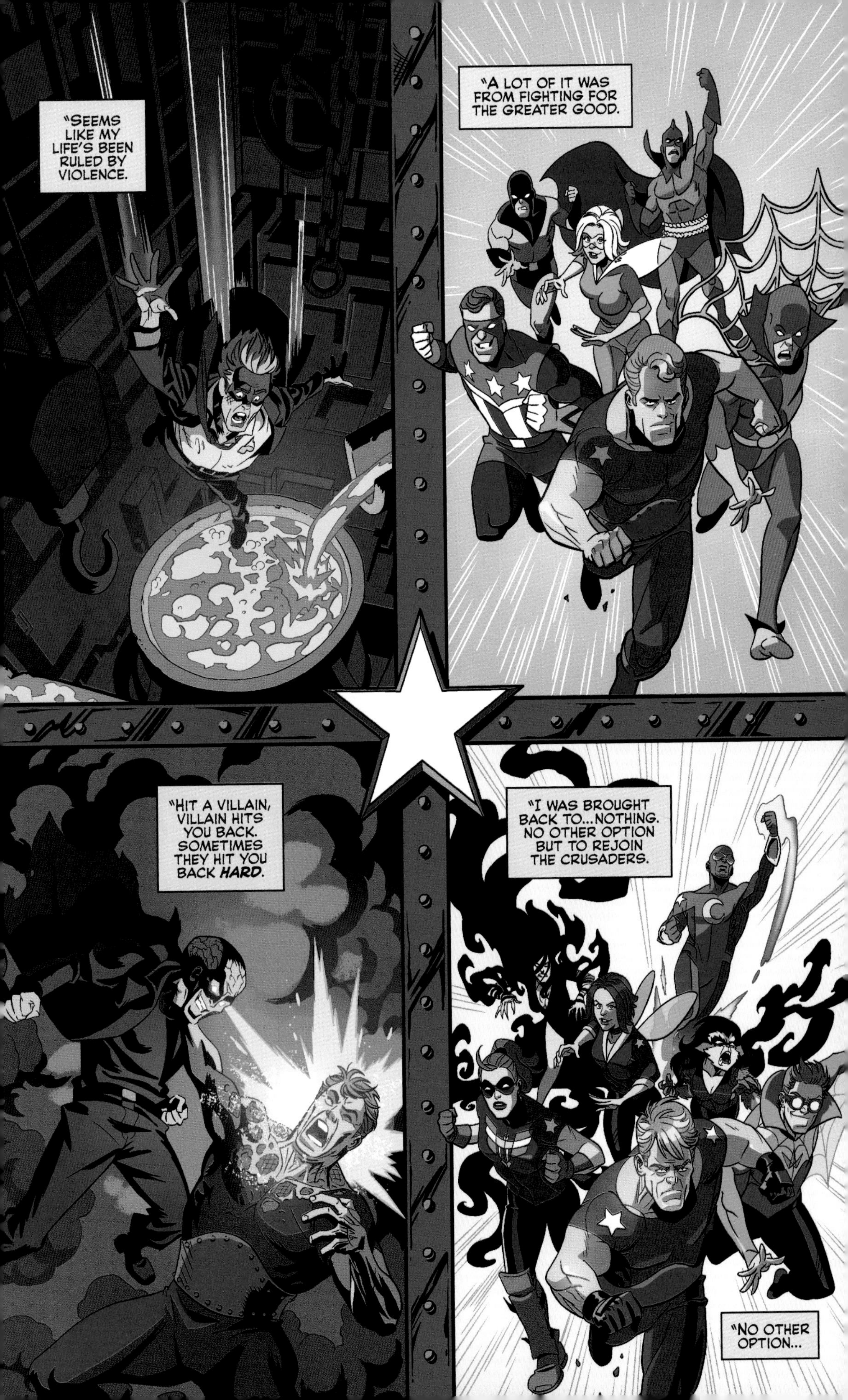
"SEEMS LIKE MY LIFE'S BEEN RULED BY VIOLENCE.
"A LOT OF IT WAS FROM FIGHTING FOR THE GREATER GOOD.
"HIT A VILLAIN, VILLAIN HITS YOU BACK. SOMETIMES THEY HIT YOU BACK ***HARD***.
"I WAS BROUGHT BACK TO...NOTHING. NO OTHER OPTION BUT TO REJOIN THE CRUSADERS.
"NO OTHER OPTION...

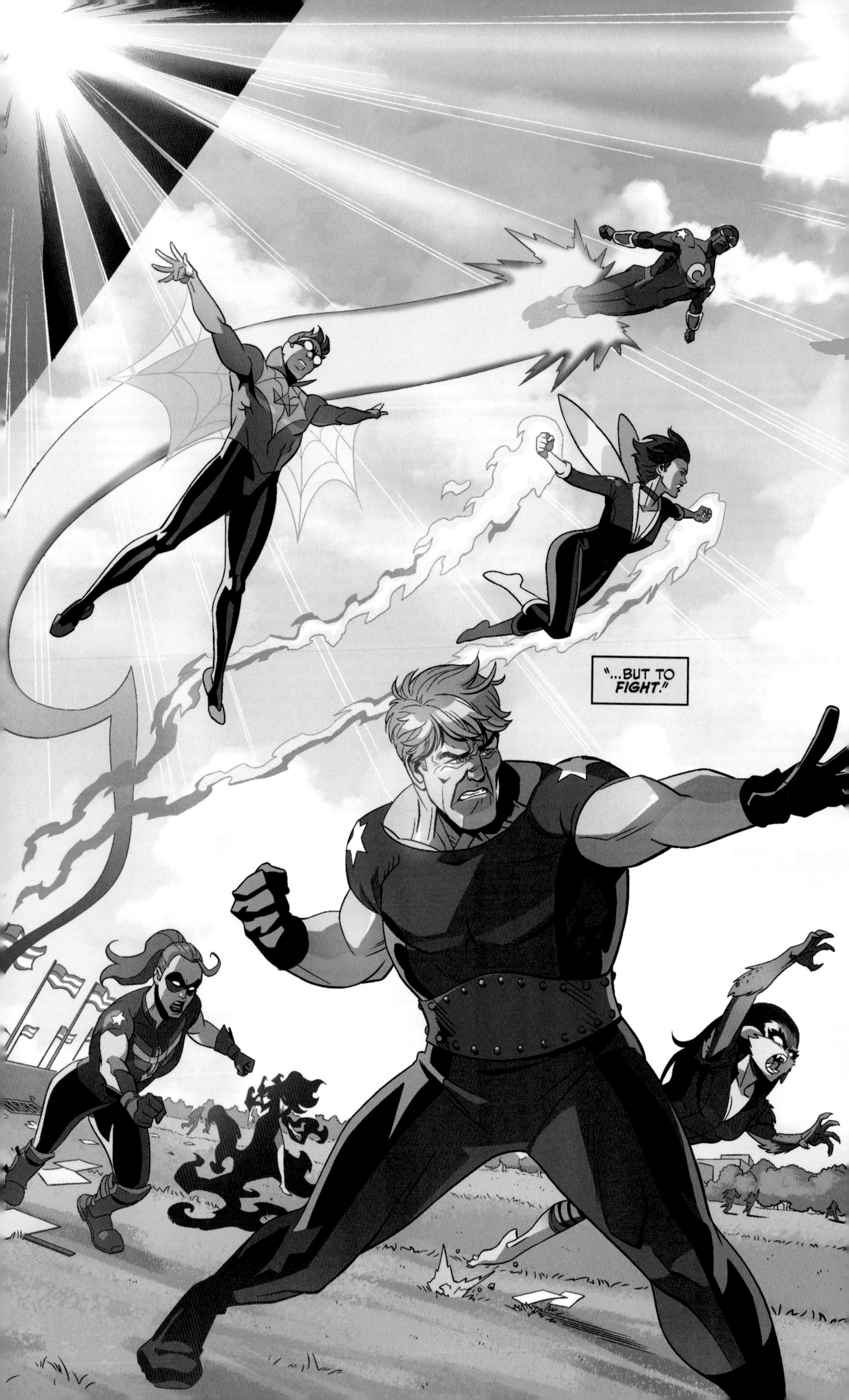
"...BUT TO FIGHT."

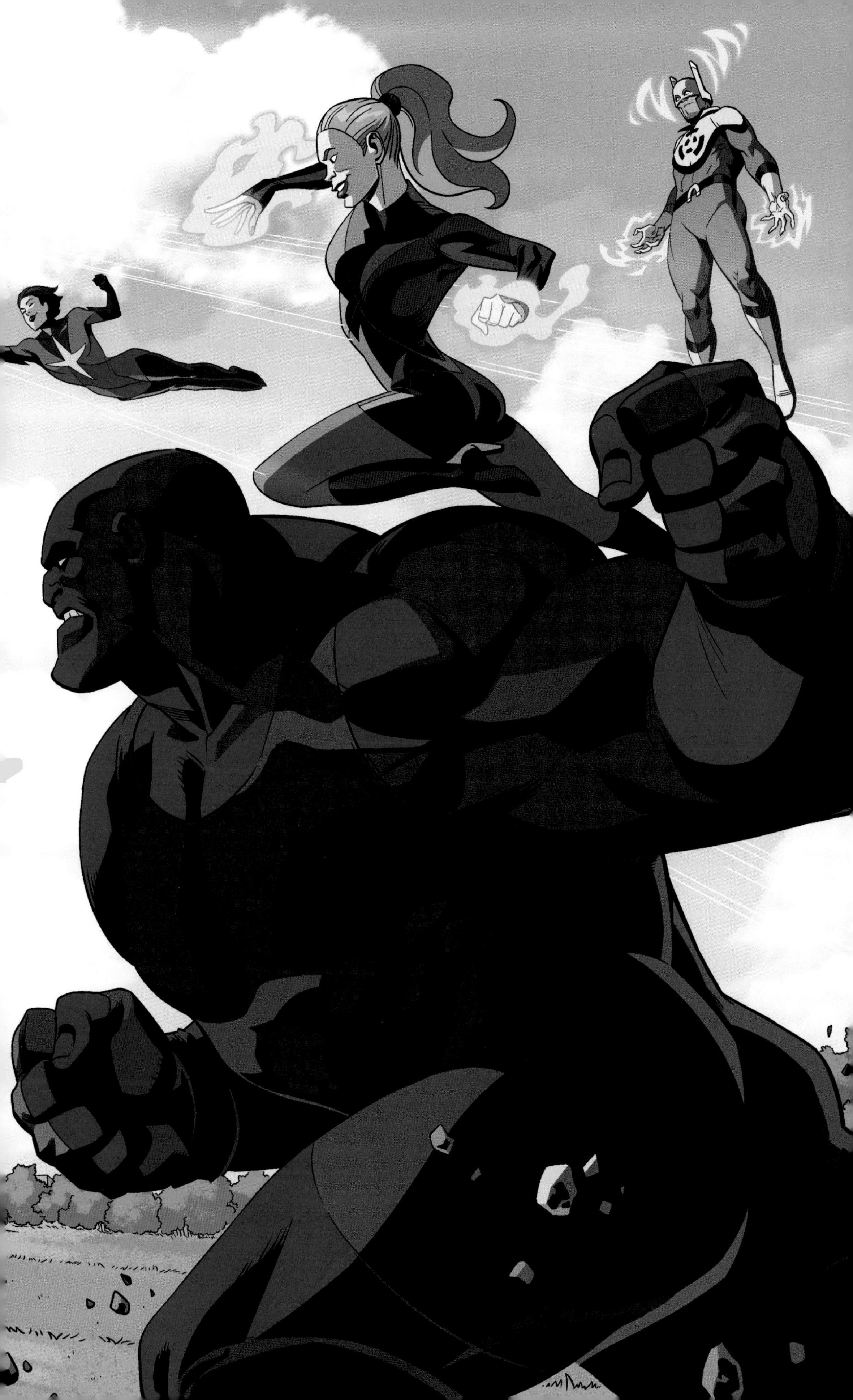

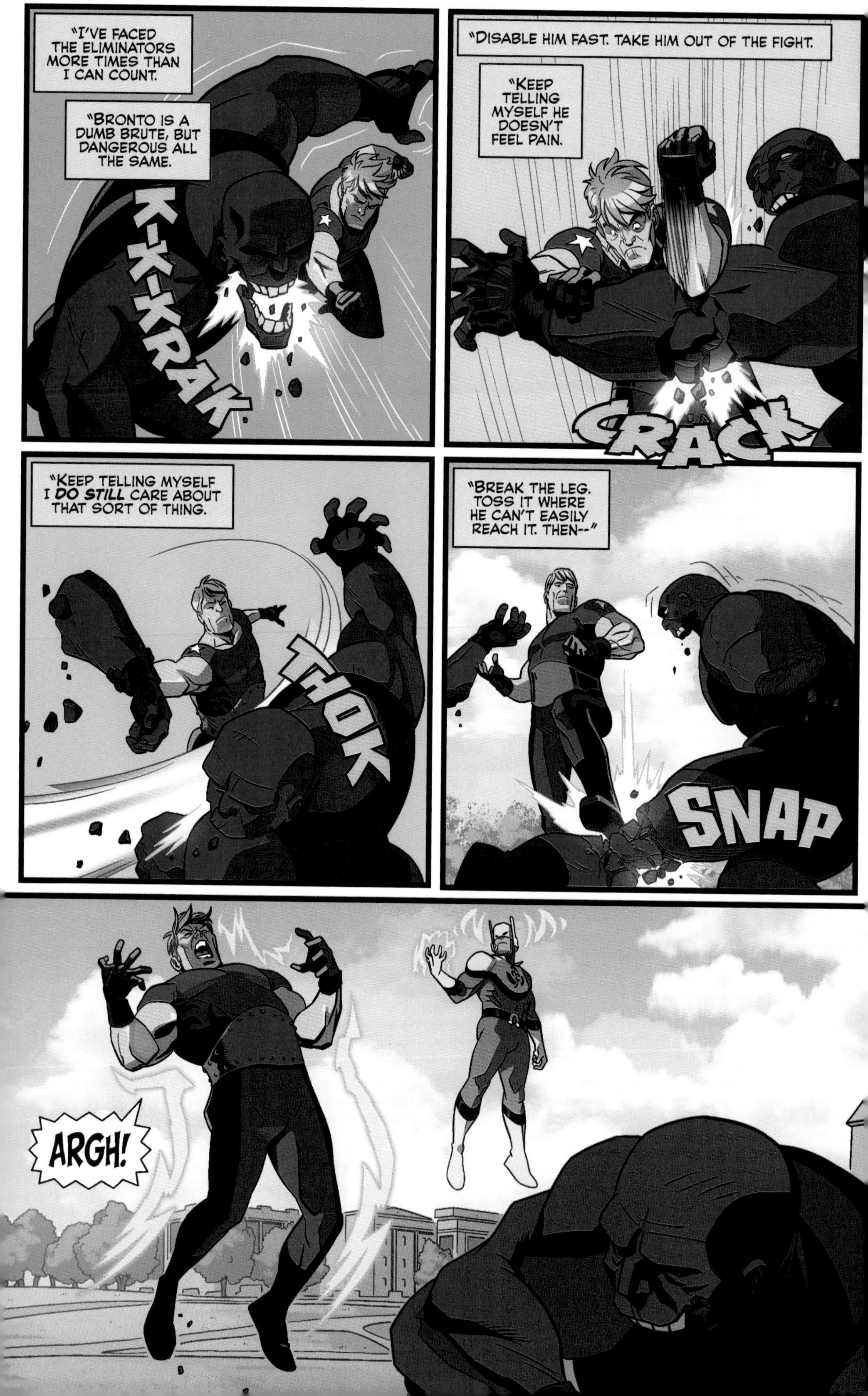

"I'VE FACED THE ELIMINATORS MORE TIMES THAN I CAN COUNT.
"BRONTO IS A DUMB BRUTE, BUT DANGEROUS ALL THE SAME.
K-K-KRAK
"DISABLE HIM FAST. TAKE HIM OUT OF THE FIGHT.
"KEEP TELLING MYSELF HE DOESN'T FEEL PAIN.
CRACK
"KEEP TELLING MYSELF I DO STILL CARE ABOUT THAT SORT OF THING.
THOK
"BREAK THE LEG. TOSS IT WHERE HE CAN'T EASILY REACH IT. THEN--"
SNAP
ARGH!

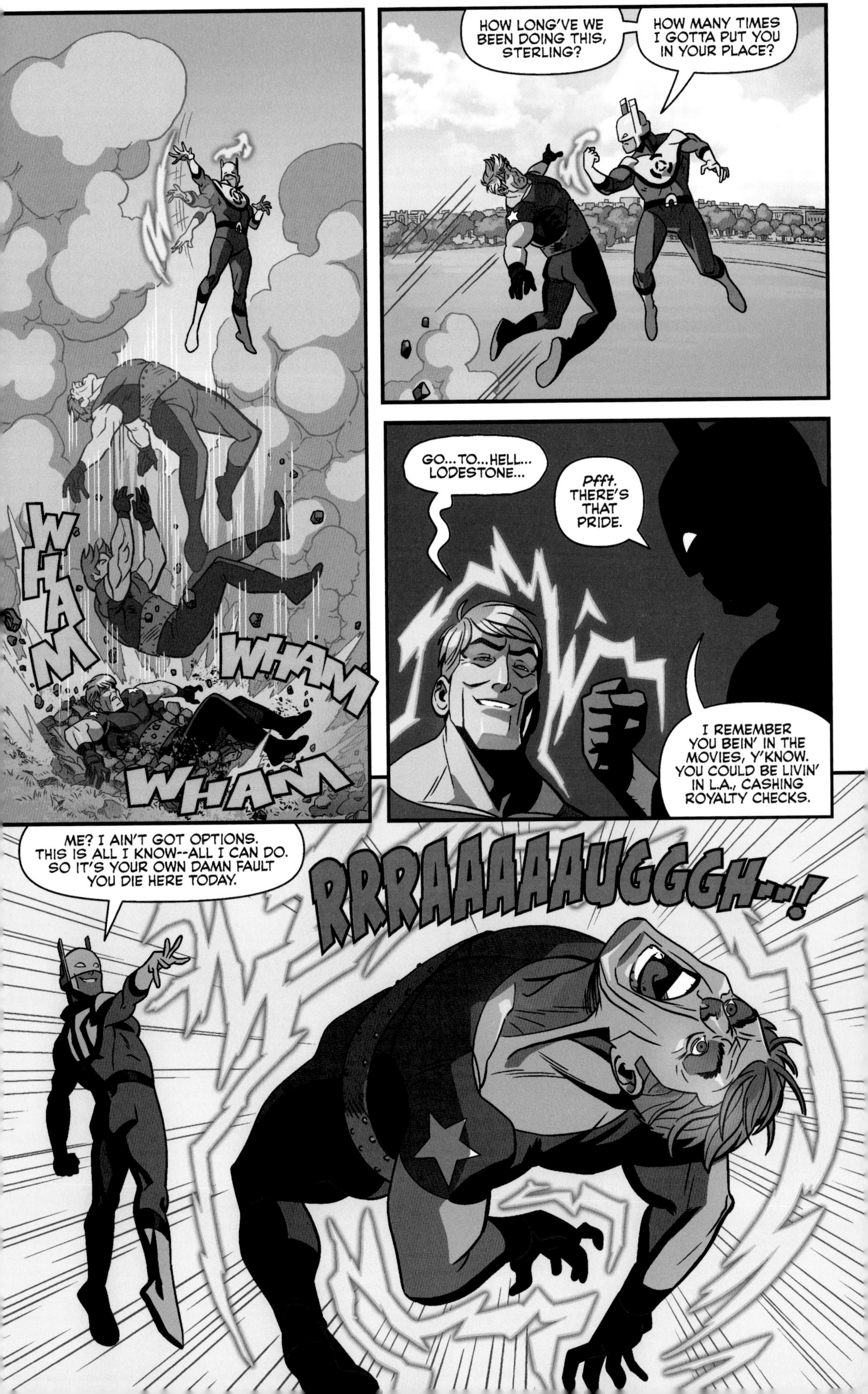
WHAM
WHAM
WHAM
HOW LONG'VE WE BEEN DOING THIS, STERLING?
HOW MANY TIMES I GOTTA PUT YOU IN YOUR PLACE?
GO...TO...HELL... LODESTONE...
Pfft. THERE'S THAT PRIDE.
I REMEMBER YOU BEIN' IN THE MOVIES, Y'KNOW. YOU COULD BE LIVIN' IN L.A., CASHING ROYALTY CHECKS.
ME? I AIN'T GOT OPTIONS. THIS IS ALL I KNOW--ALL I CAN DO. SO IT'S YOUR OWN DAMN FAULT YOU DIE HERE TODAY.
RRRAAAAAAUGGGH--!

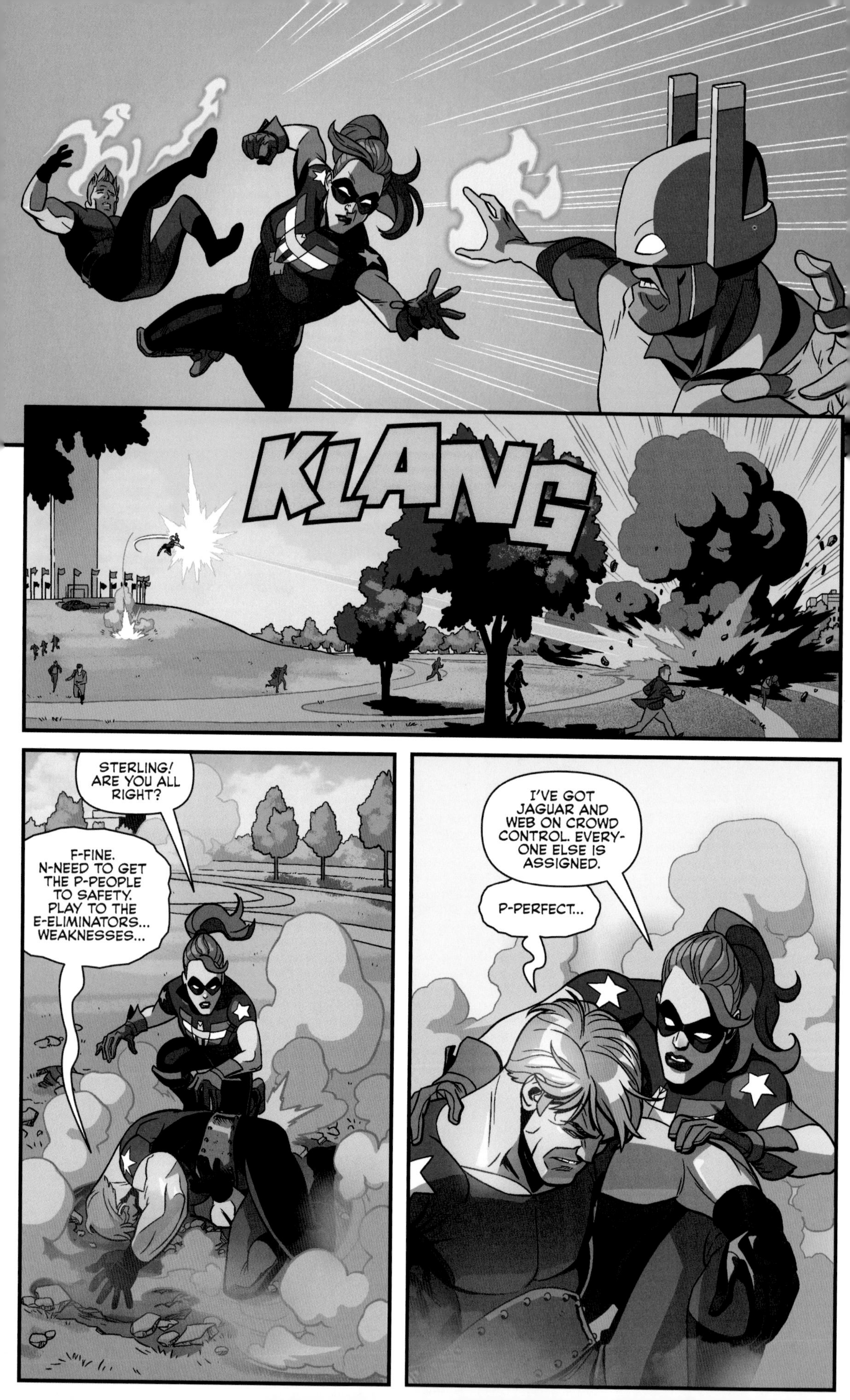
KLANG
STERLING! ARE YOU ALL RIGHT?
F-FINE. N-NEED TO GET THE P-PEOPLE TO SAFETY. PLAY TO THE E-ELIMINATORS... WEAKNESSES...
I'VE GOT JAGUAR AND WEB ON CROWD CONTROL. EVERY-ONE ELSE IS ASSIGNED.
P-PERFECT...

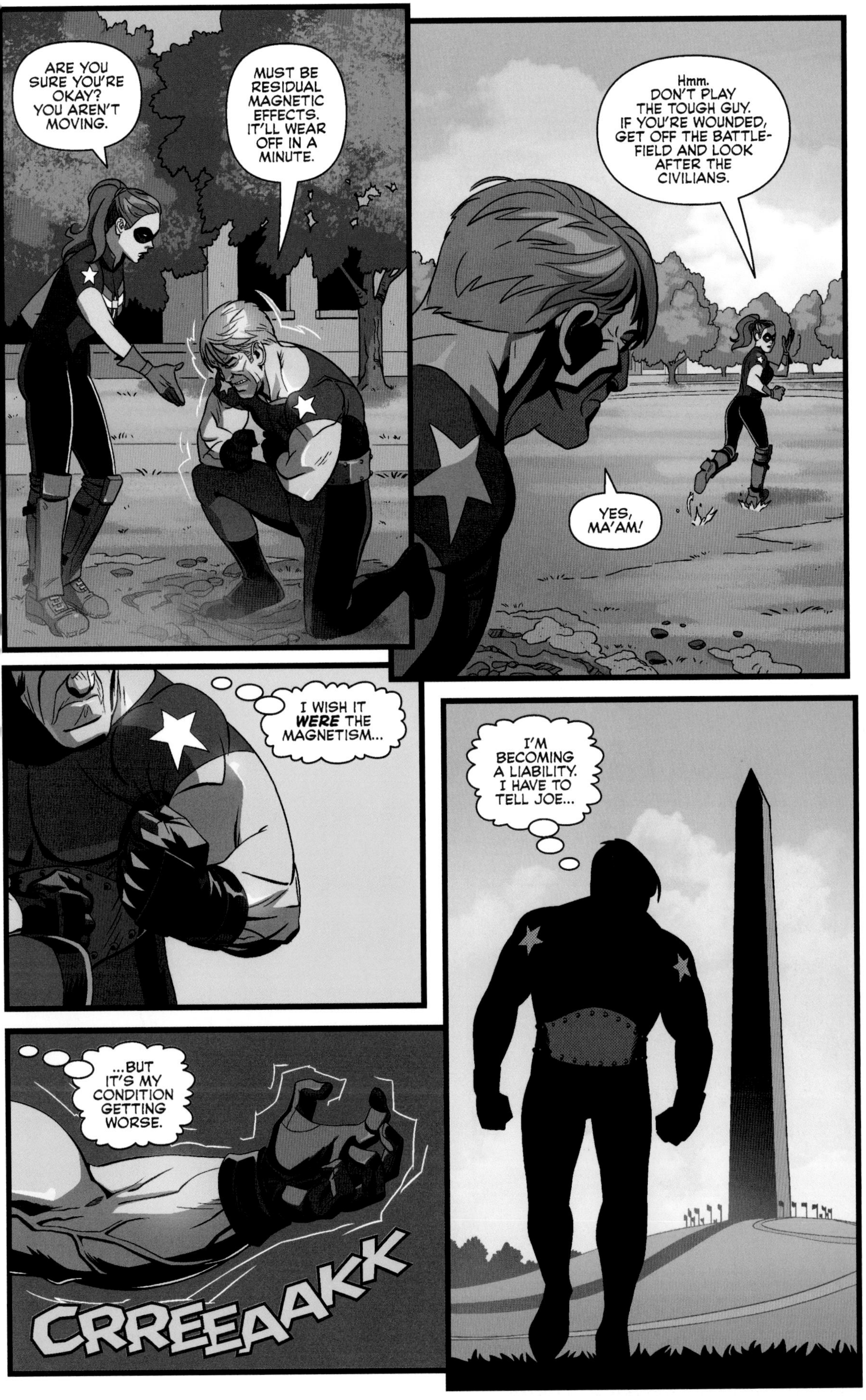
ARE YOU SURE YOU'RE OKAY? YOU AREN'T MOVING.
MUST BE RESIDUAL MAGNETIC EFFECTS. IT'LL WEAR OFF IN A MINUTE.
Hmm. DON'T PLAY THE TOUGH GUY. IF YOU'RE WOUNDED, GET OFF THE BATTLE-FIELD AND LOOK AFTER THE CIVILIANS.
YES, MA'AM!
I WISH IT *WERE* THE MAGNETISM...
...BUT IT'S MY CONDITION GETTING WORSE.
CRREEAAKK
I'M BECOMING A LIABILITY. I HAVE TO TELL JOE...

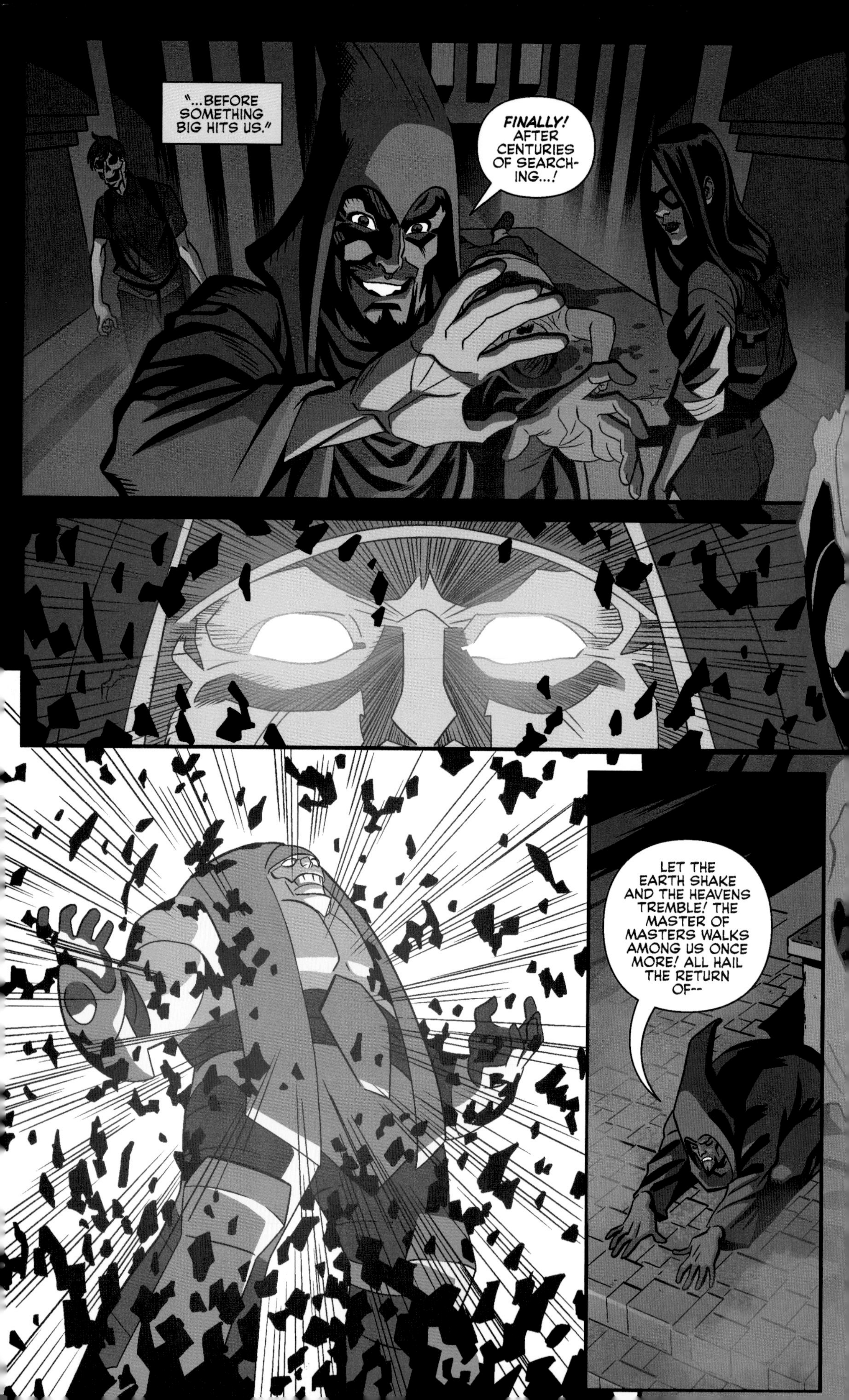
"...BEFORE SOMETHING BIG HITS US."
FINALLY! AFTER CENTURIES OF SEARCH-ING...!
LET THE EARTH SHAKE AND THE HEAVENS TREMBLE! THE MASTER OF MASTERS WALKS AMONG US ONCE MORE! ALL HAIL THE RETURN OF--

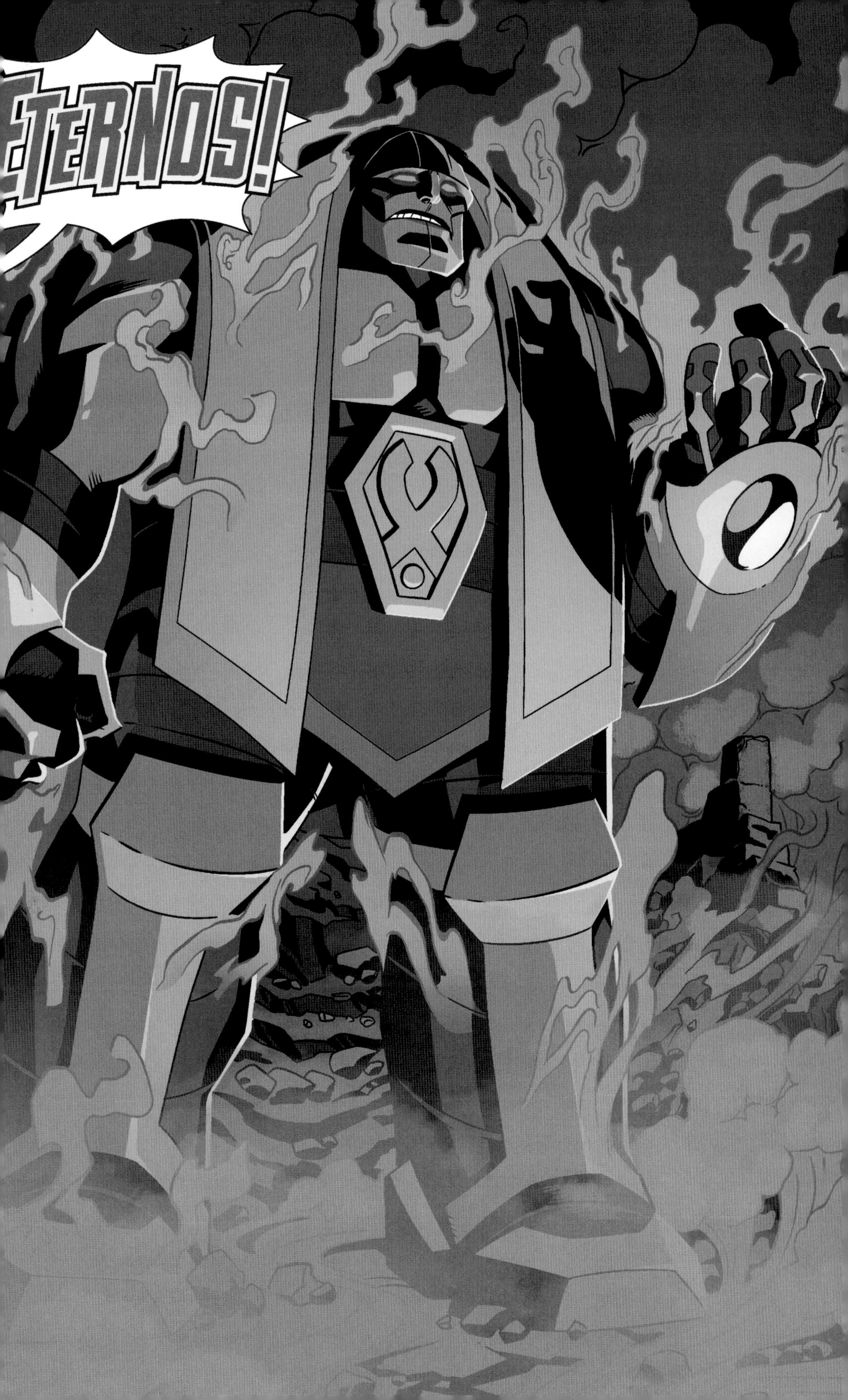
TERNOS!

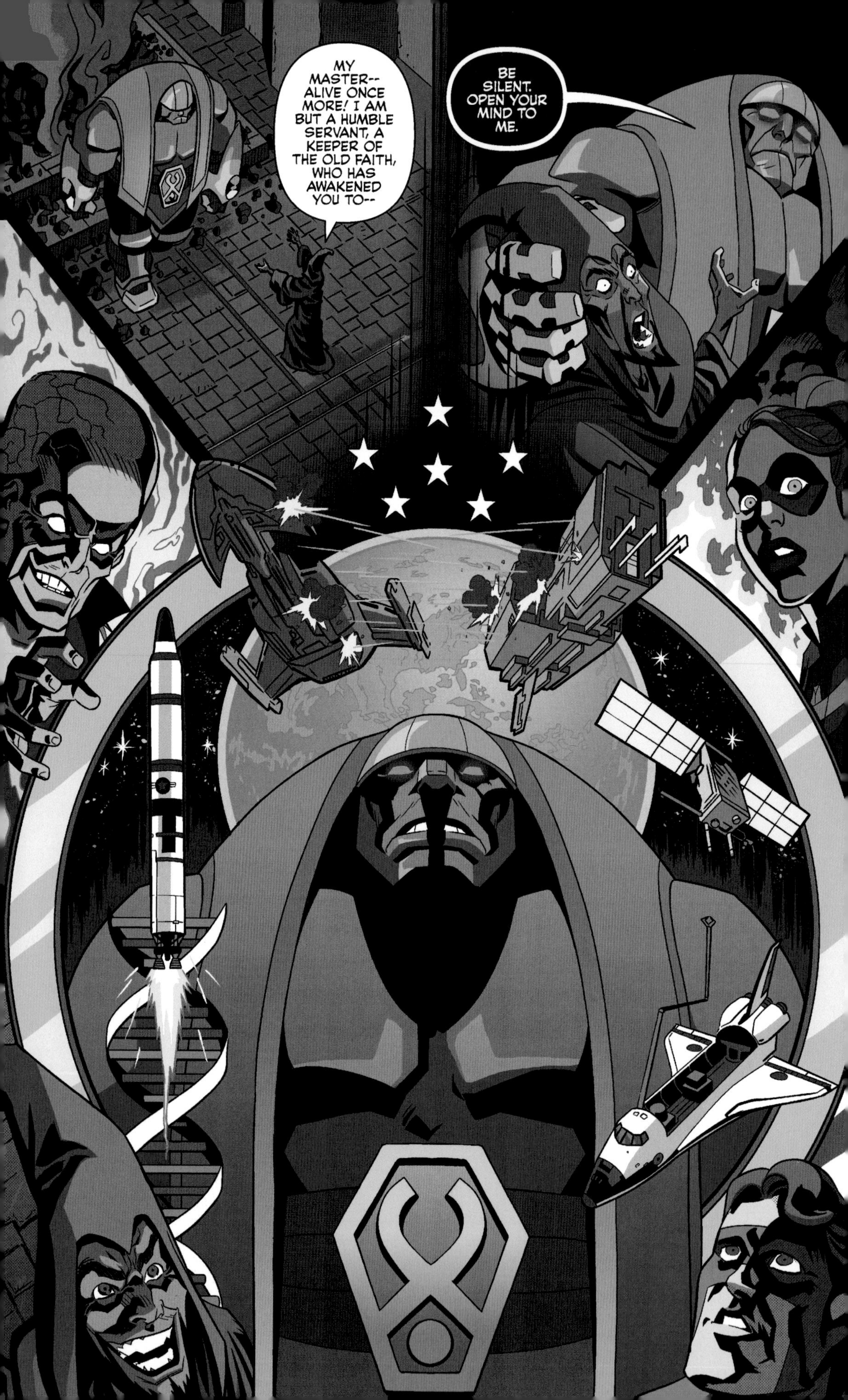
MY MASTER-- ALIVE ONCE MORE! I AM BUT A HUMBLE SERVANT, A KEEPER OF THE OLD FAITH, WHO HAS AWAKENED YOU TO--
BE SILENT. OPEN YOUR MIND TO ME.

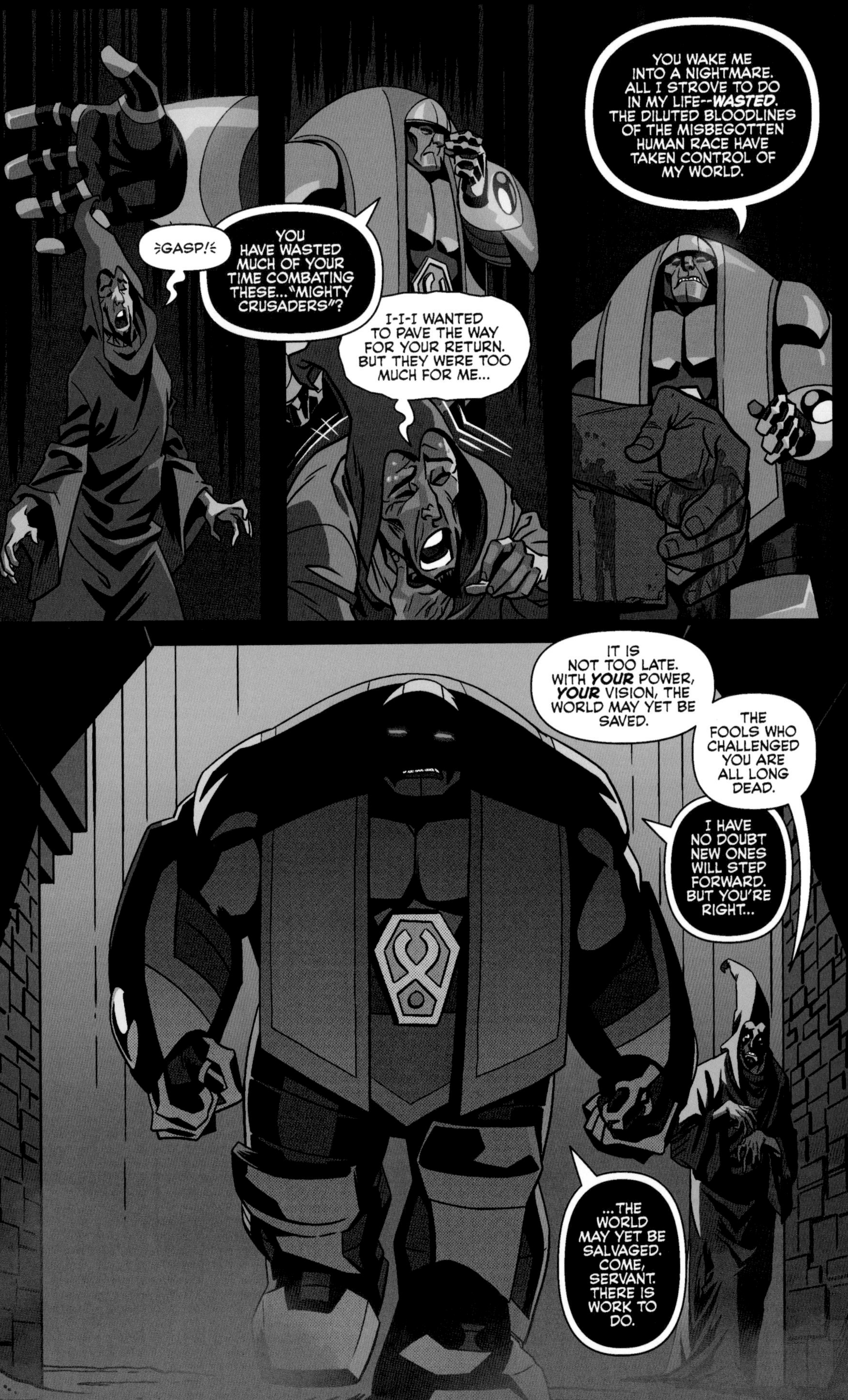

GASP!
YOU HAVE WASTED MUCH OF YOUR TIME COMBATING THESE..."MIGHTY CRUSADERS"?
I-I-I WANTED TO PAVE THE WAY FOR YOUR RETURN. BUT THEY WERE TOO MUCH FOR ME...
YOU WAKE ME INTO A NIGHTMARE. ALL I STROVE TO DO IN MY LIFE--WASTED. THE DILUTED BLOODLINES OF THE MISBEGOTTEN HUMAN RACE HAVE TAKEN CONTROL OF MY WORLD.
IT IS NOT TOO LATE. WITH YOUR POWER, YOUR VISION, THE WORLD MAY YET BE SAVED.
THE FOOLS WHO CHALLENGED YOU ARE ALL LONG DEAD.
I HAVE NO DOUBT NEW ONES WILL STEP FORWARD. BUT YOU'RE RIGHT...
...THE WORLD MAY YET BE SALVAGED. COME, SERVANT. THERE IS WORK TO DO.

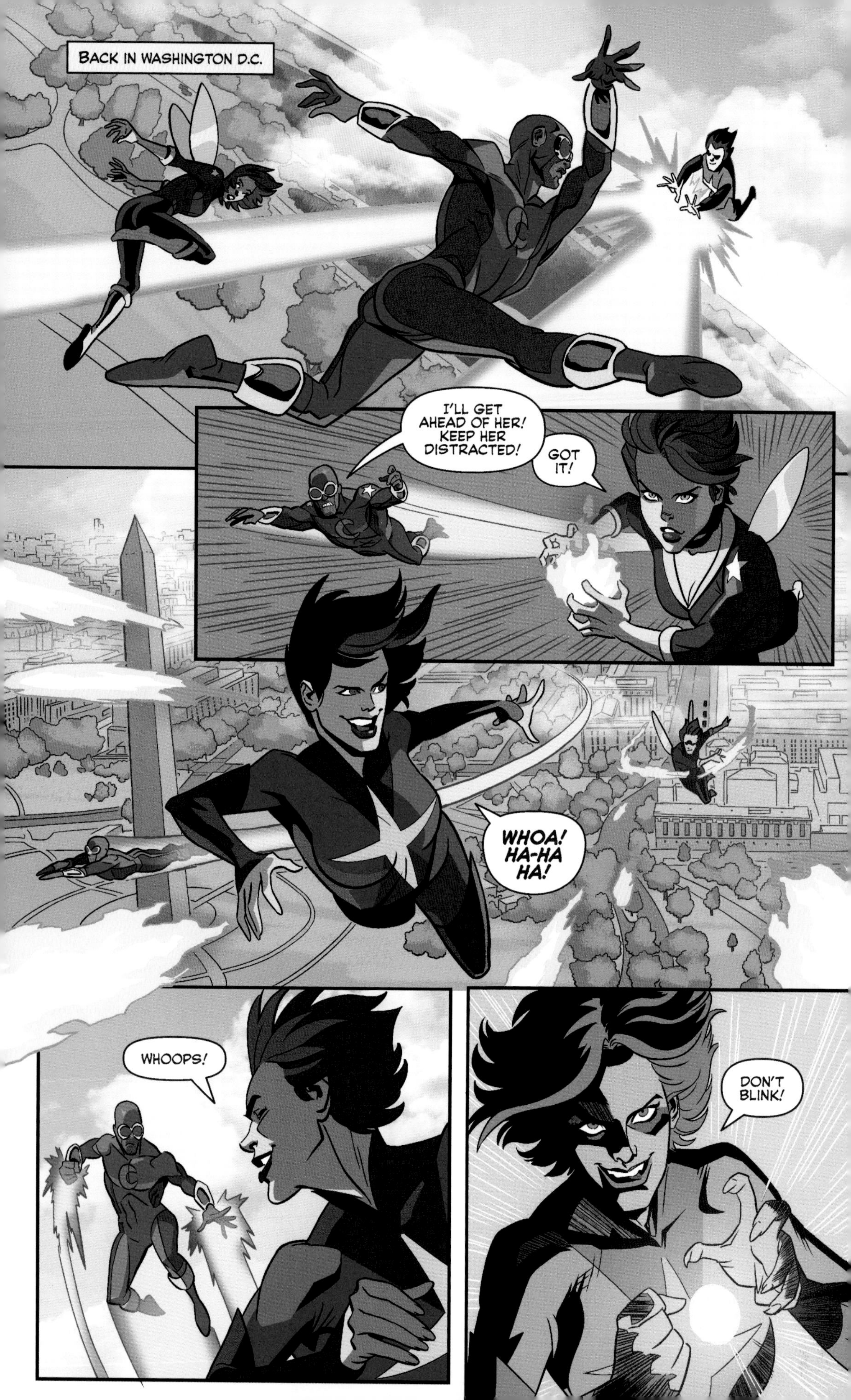
BACK IN WASHINGTON D.C.
I'LL GET AHEAD OF HER! KEEP HER DISTRACTED!
GOT IT!
WHOA! HA-HA HA!
WHOOPS!
DON'T BLINK!

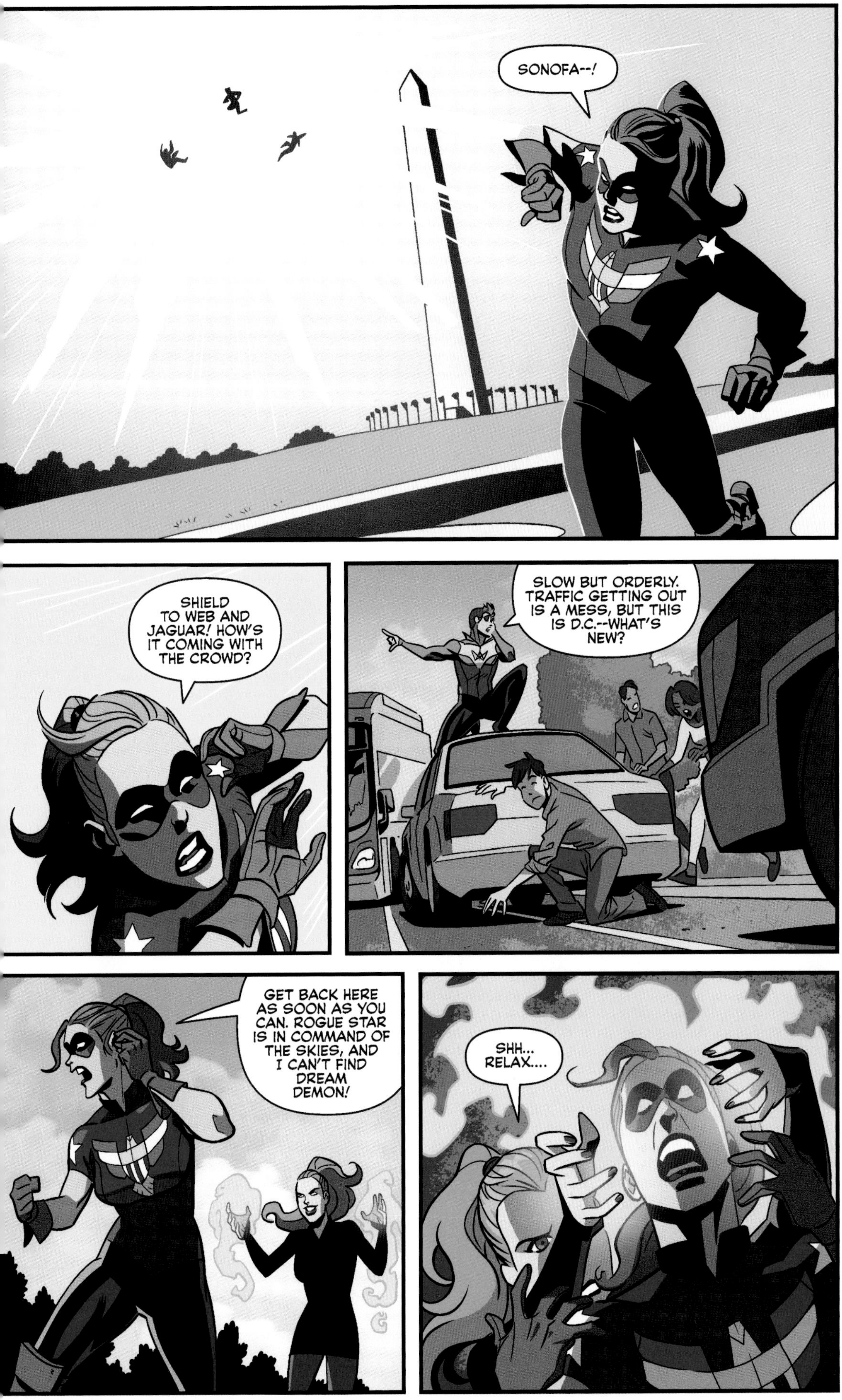
SONOFA--!
SHIELD TO WEB AND JAGUAR! HOW'S IT COMING WITH THE CROWD?
SLOW BUT ORDERLY. TRAFFIC GETTING OUT IS A MESS, BUT THIS IS D.C.--WHAT'S NEW?
GET BACK HERE AS SOON AS YOU CAN. ROGUE STAR IS IN COMMAND OF THE SKIES, AND I CAN'T FIND DREAM DEMON!
SHH... RELAX....

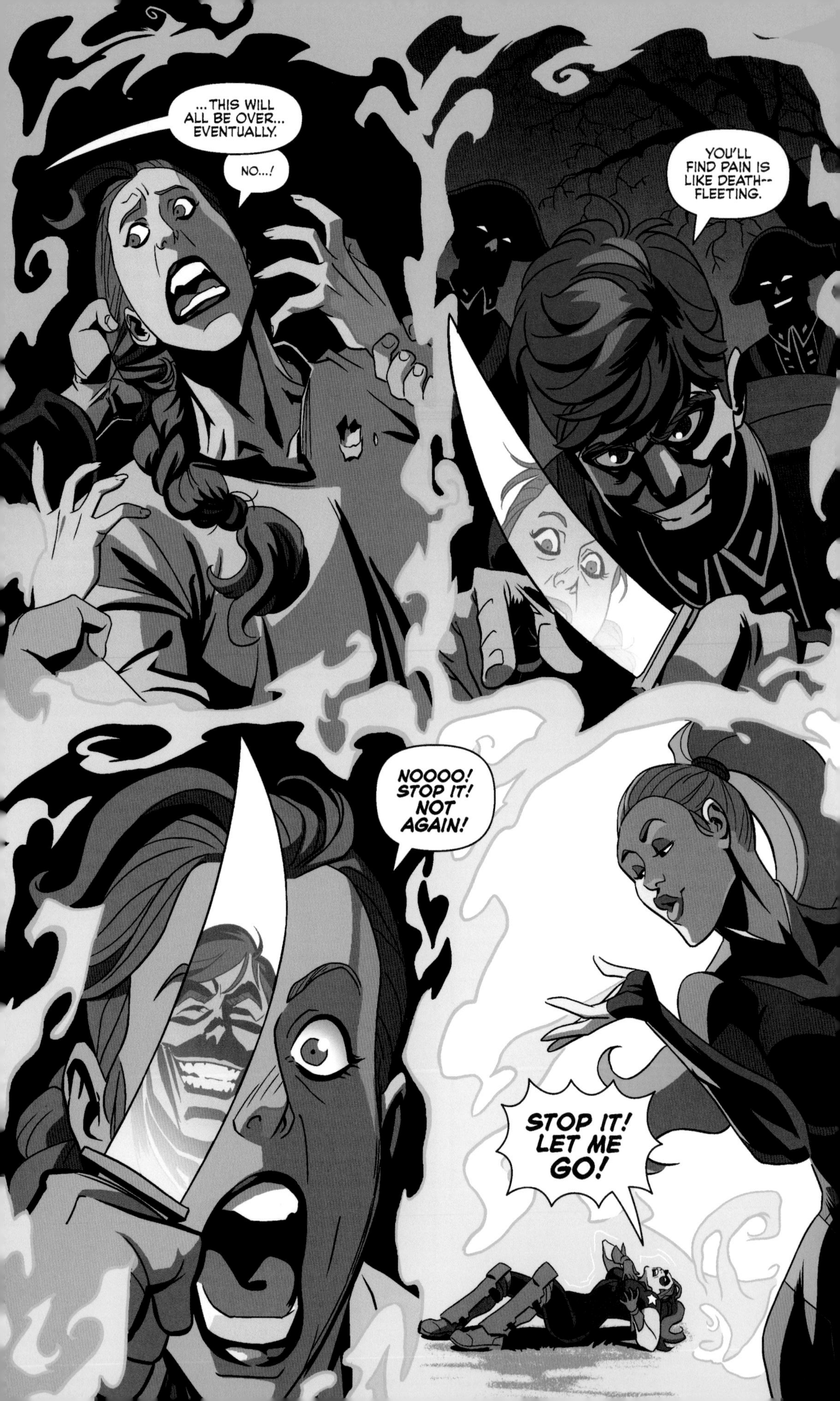
...THIS WILL ALL BE OVER... EVENTUALLY.
NO...!
YOU'LL FIND PAIN IS LIKE DEATH--FLEETING.
NOOOO! STOP IT! NOT AGAIN!
STOP IT! LET ME GO!

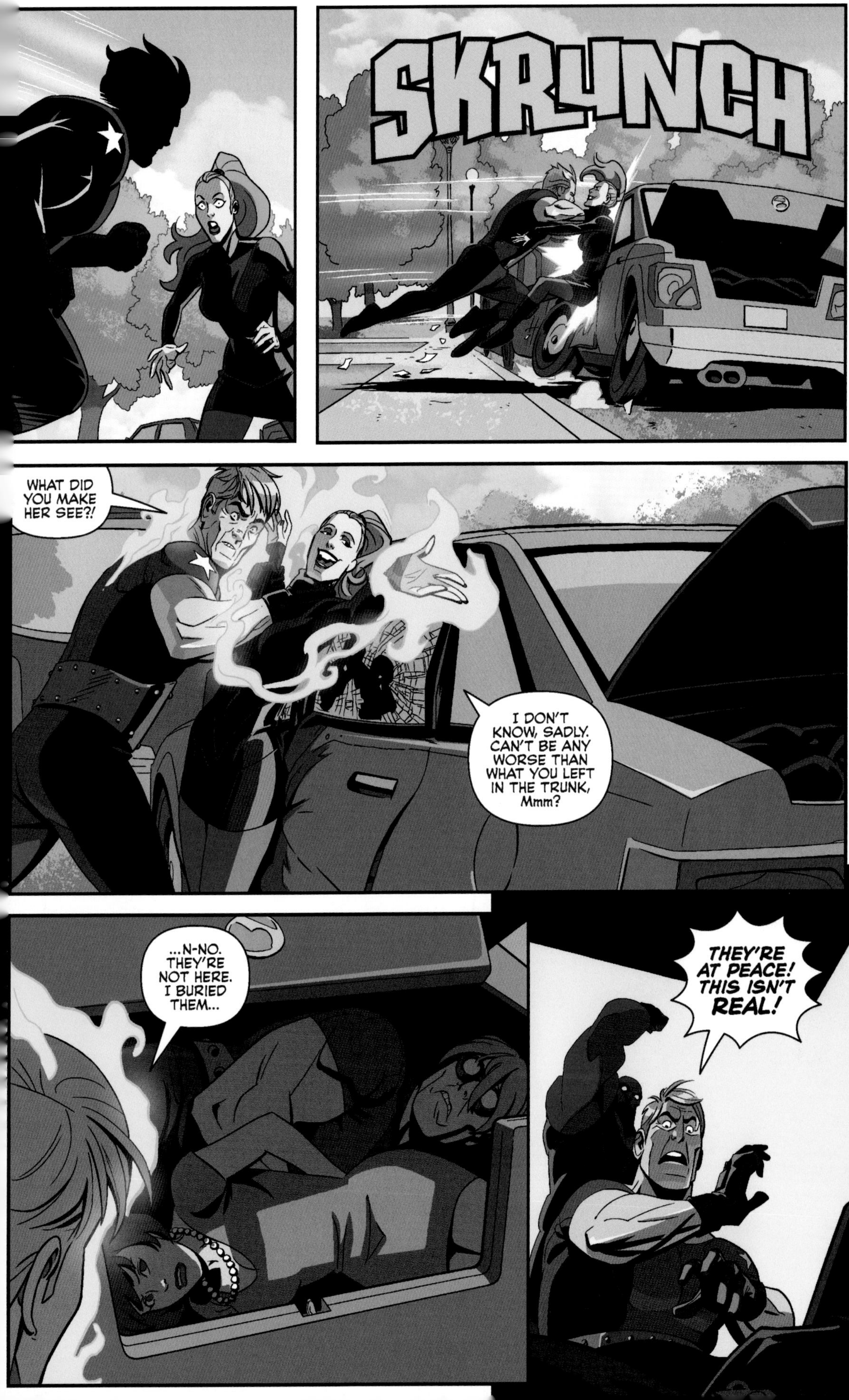
SKRUNCH
WHAT DID YOU MAKE HER SEE?!
I DON'T KNOW, SADLY. CAN'T BE ANY WORSE THAN WHAT YOU LEFT IN THE TRUNK, Mmm?
...N-NO. THEY'RE NOT HERE. I BURIED THEM...
THEY'RE AT PEACE! THIS ISN'T REAL!

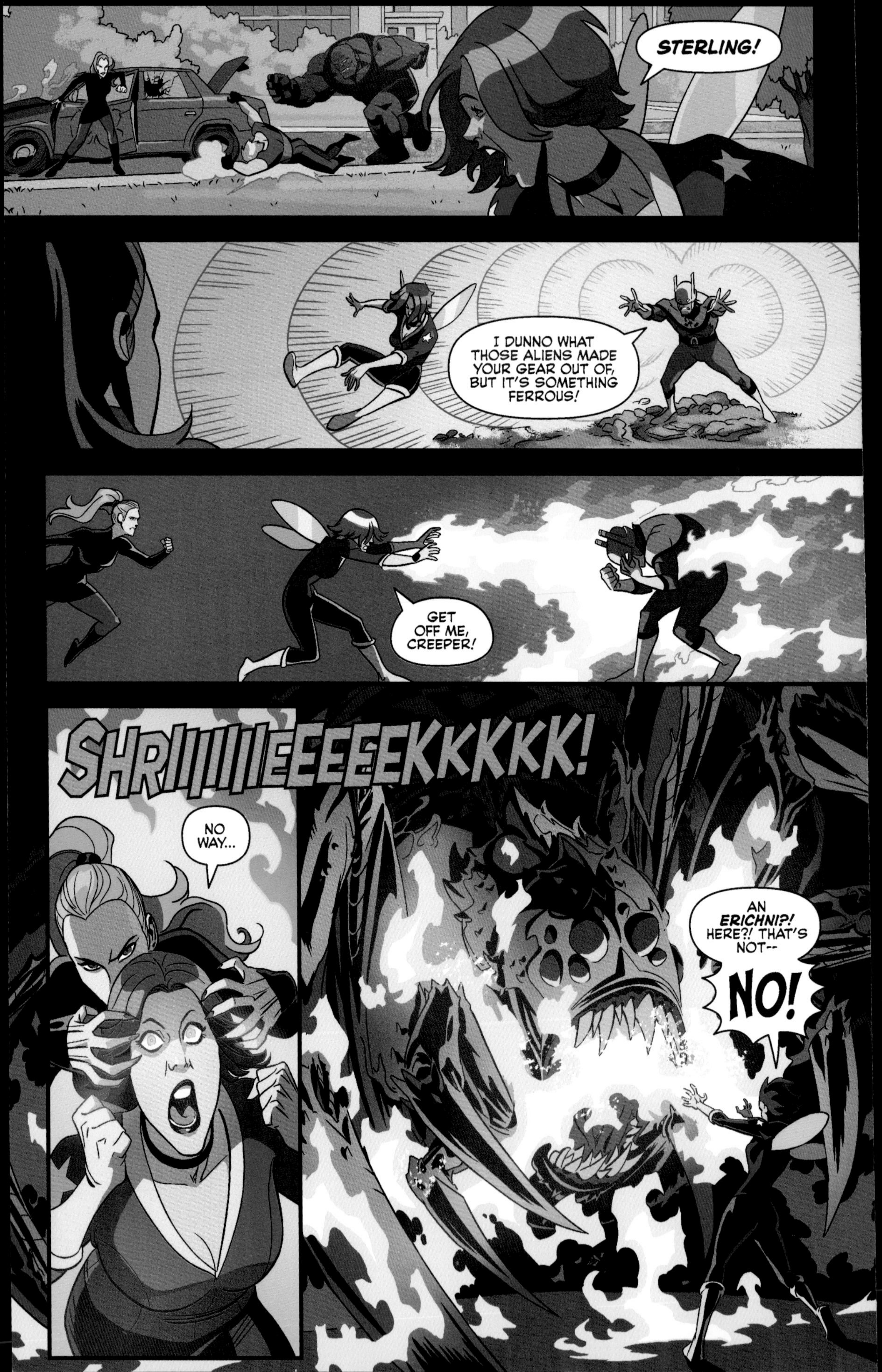
STERLING!
I DUNNO WHAT THOSE ALIENS MADE YOUR GEAR OUT OF, BUT IT'S SOMETHING FERROUS!
GET OFF ME, CREEPER!
SHRIIIIIIEEEEEKKKKK!
NO WAY...
AN ERICHNI?! HERE?! THAT'S NOT--
NO!

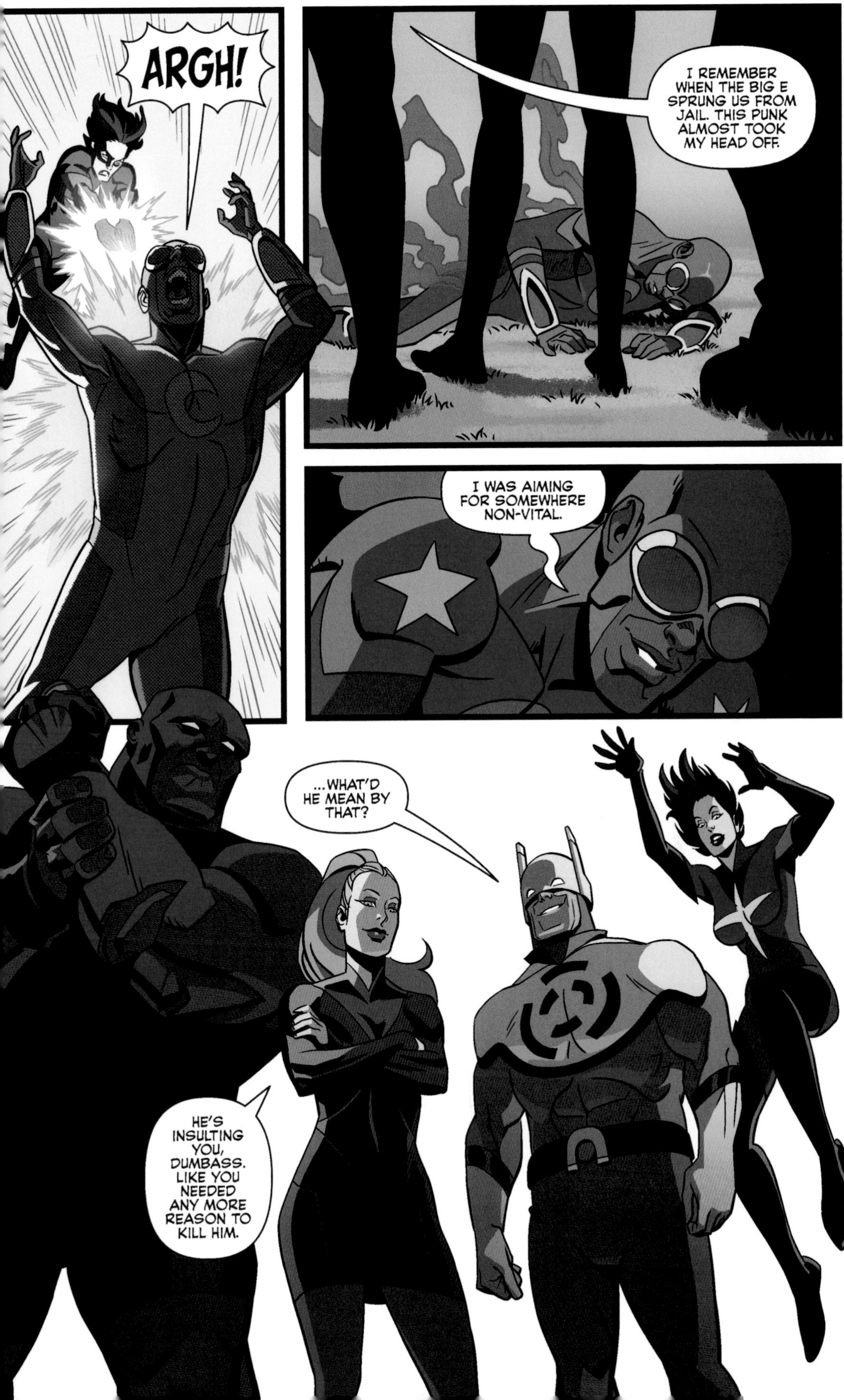
ARGH!
I REMEMBER WHEN THE BIG E SPRUNG US FROM JAIL. THIS PUNK ALMOST TOOK MY HEAD OFF.
I WAS AIMING FOR SOMEWHERE NON-VITAL.
...WHAT'D HE MEAN BY THAT?
HE'S INSULTING YOU, DUMBASS. LIKE YOU NEEDED ANY MORE REASON TO KILL HIM.

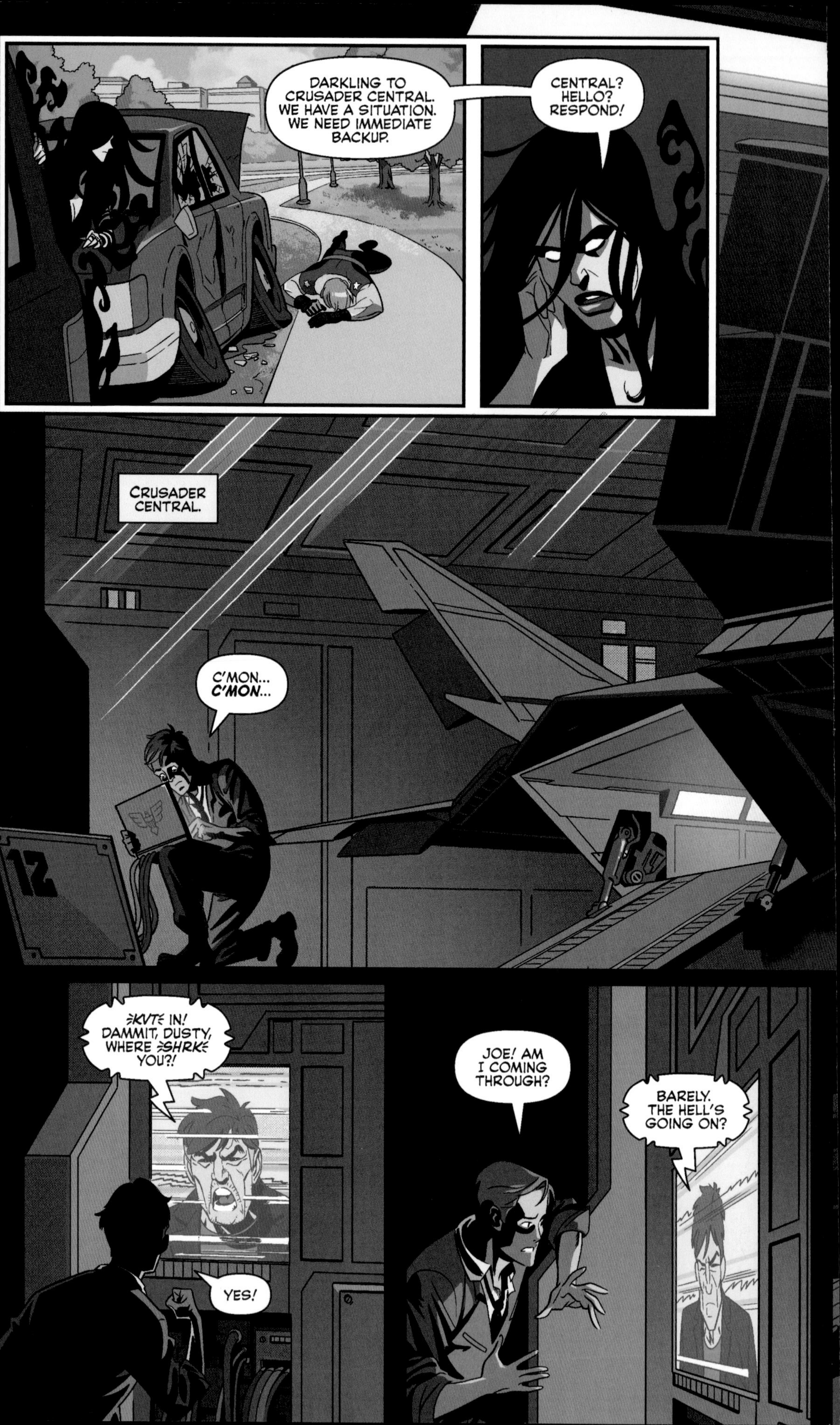
DARKLING TO CRUSADER CENTRAL. WE HAVE A SITUATION. WE NEED IMMEDIATE BACKUP.
CENTRAL? HELLO? RESPOND!
CRUSADER CENTRAL.
C'MON... C'MON...
KVT IN! DAMMIT, DUSTY, WHERE SHRK YOU?!
YES!
JOE! AM I COMING THROUGH?
BARELY. THE HELL'S GOING ON?

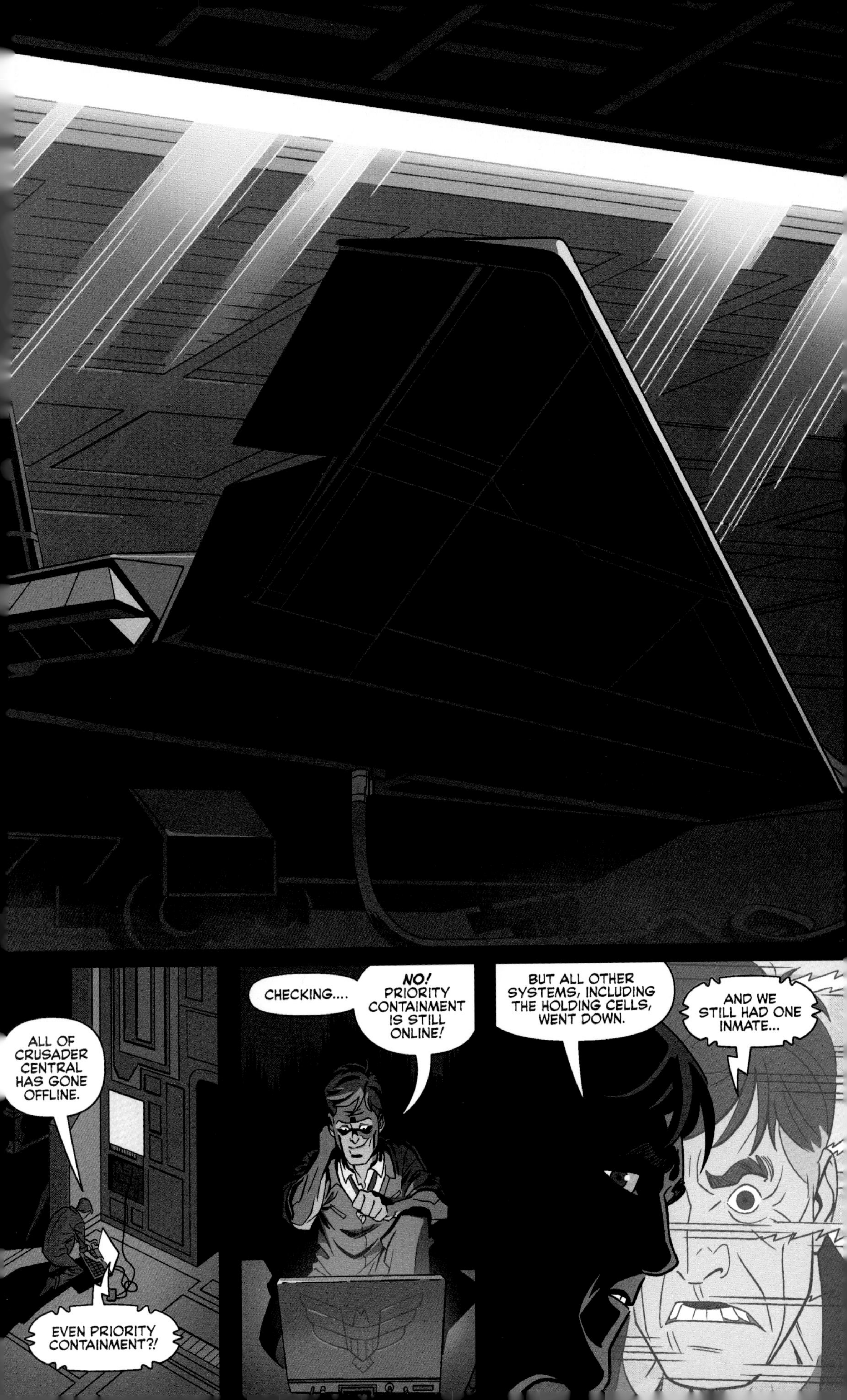
ALL OF CRUSADER CENTRAL HAS GONE OFFLINE.
EVEN PRIORITY CONTAINMENT?!
CHECKING....
NO! PRIORITY CONTAINMENT IS STILL ONLINE!
BUT ALL OTHER SYSTEMS, INCLUDING THE HOLDING CELLS, WENT DOWN.
AND WE STILL HAD ONE INMATE...

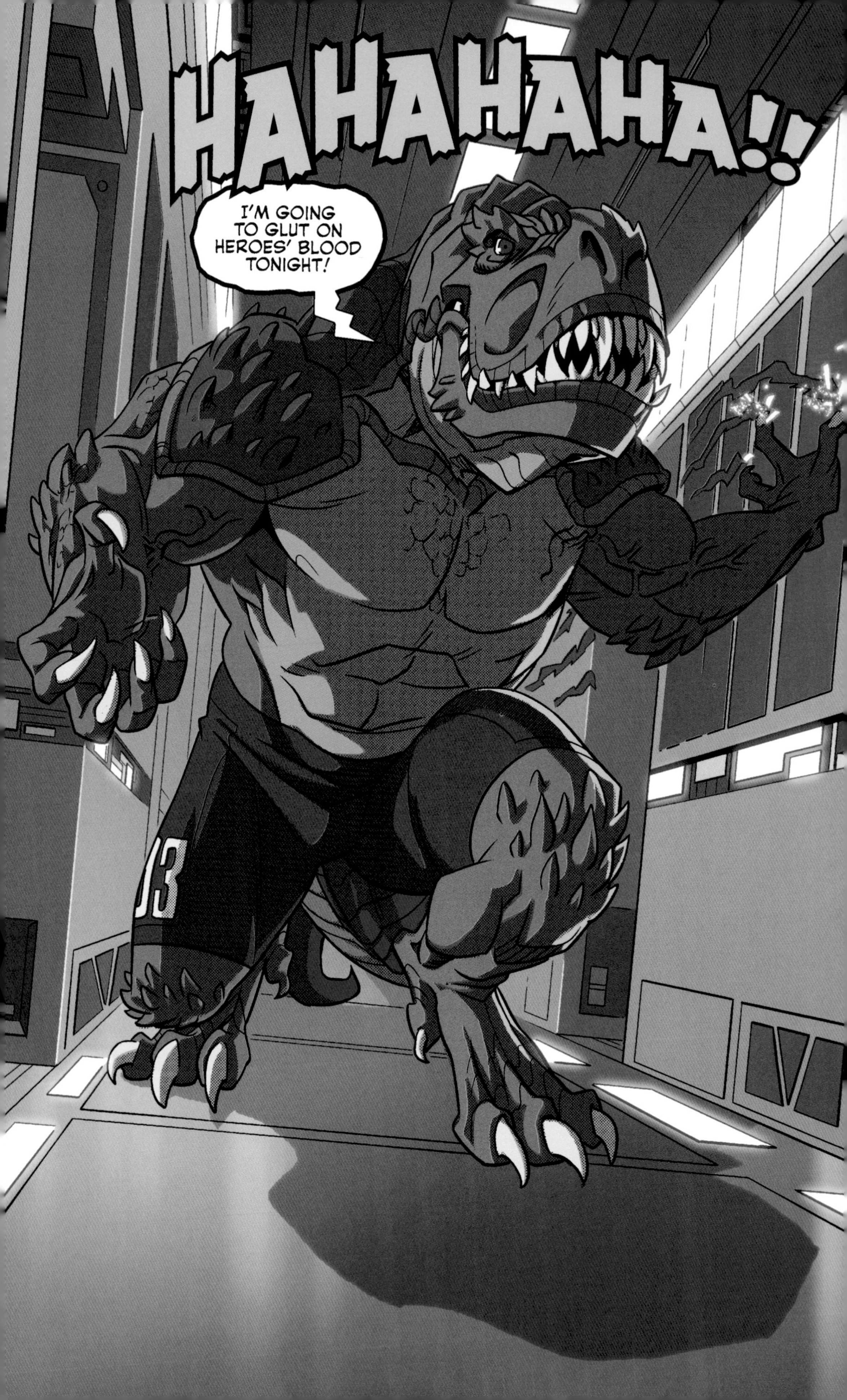
HAHAHAHA!!
I'M GOING TO GLUT ON HEROES' BLOOD TONIGHT!
03

ISSUE FOUR

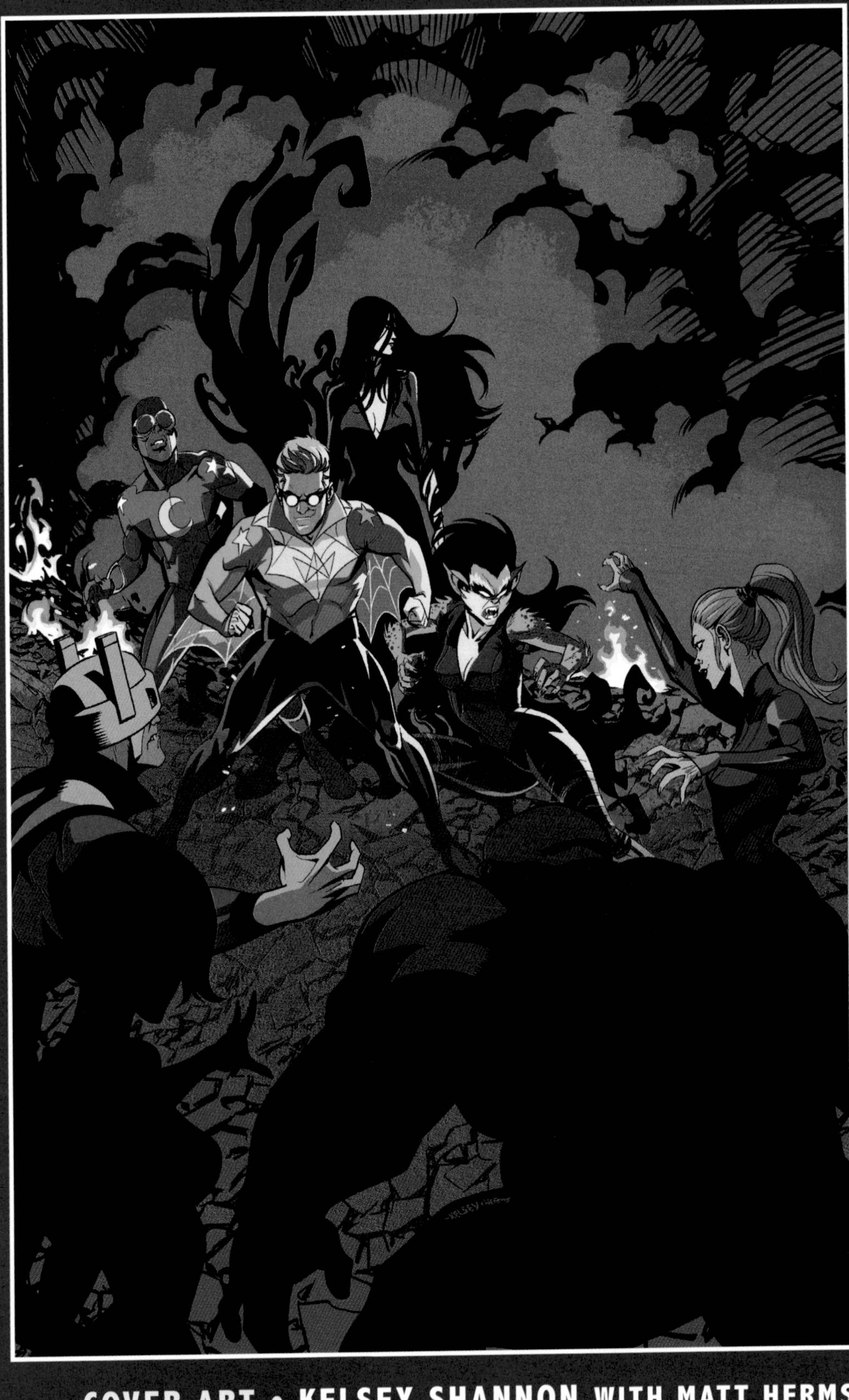

COVER ART • KELSEY SHANNON WITH MATT HERMS

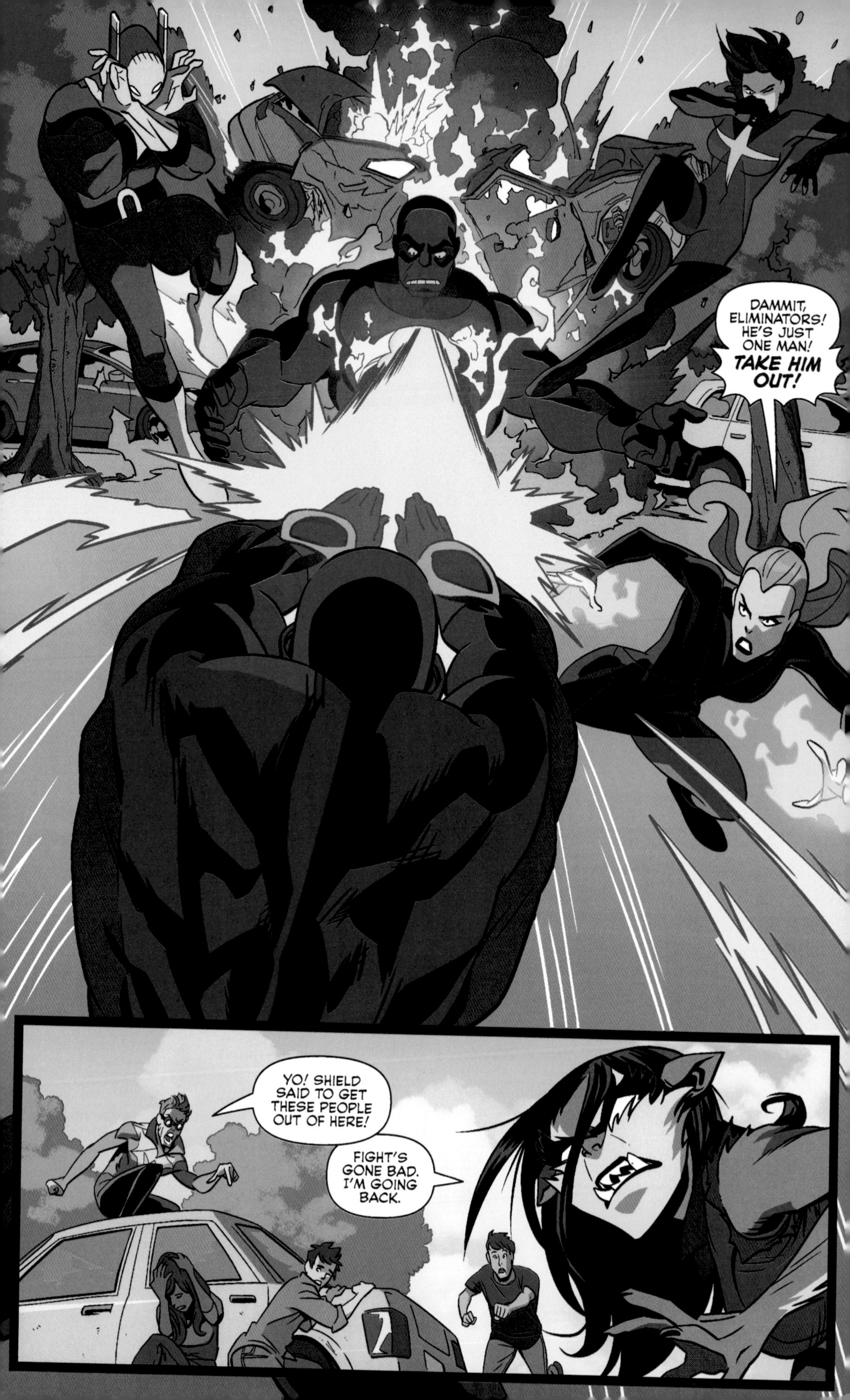
DAMMIT, ELIMINATORS! HE'S JUST ONE MAN! **TAKE HIM OUT!**
YO! SHIELD SAID TO GET THESE PEOPLE OUT OF HERE!
FIGHT'S GONE BAD. I'M GOING BACK.

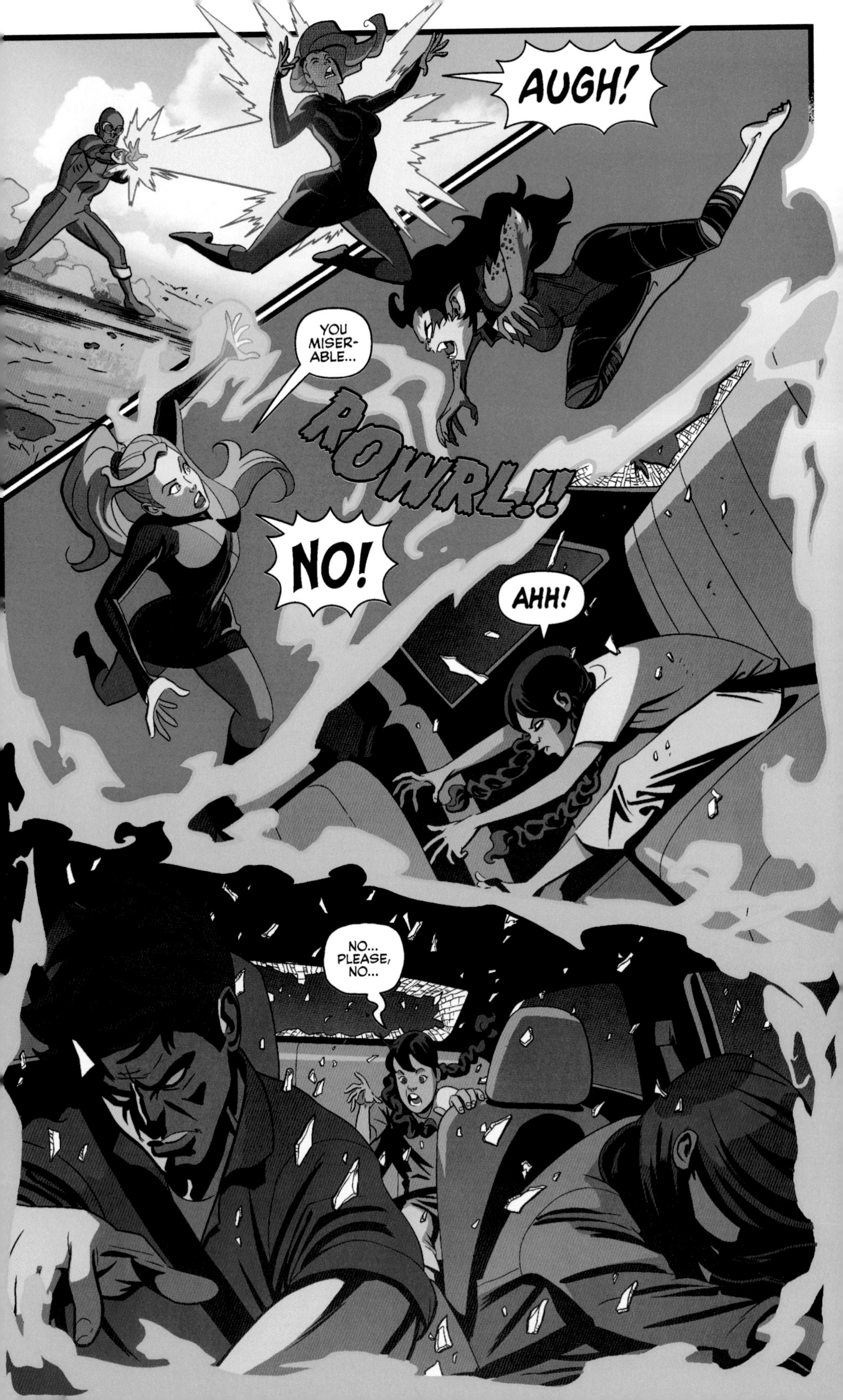

AUGH!
YOU MISERABLE...
ROWRL!!
NO!
AHH!
NO... PLEASE, NO...

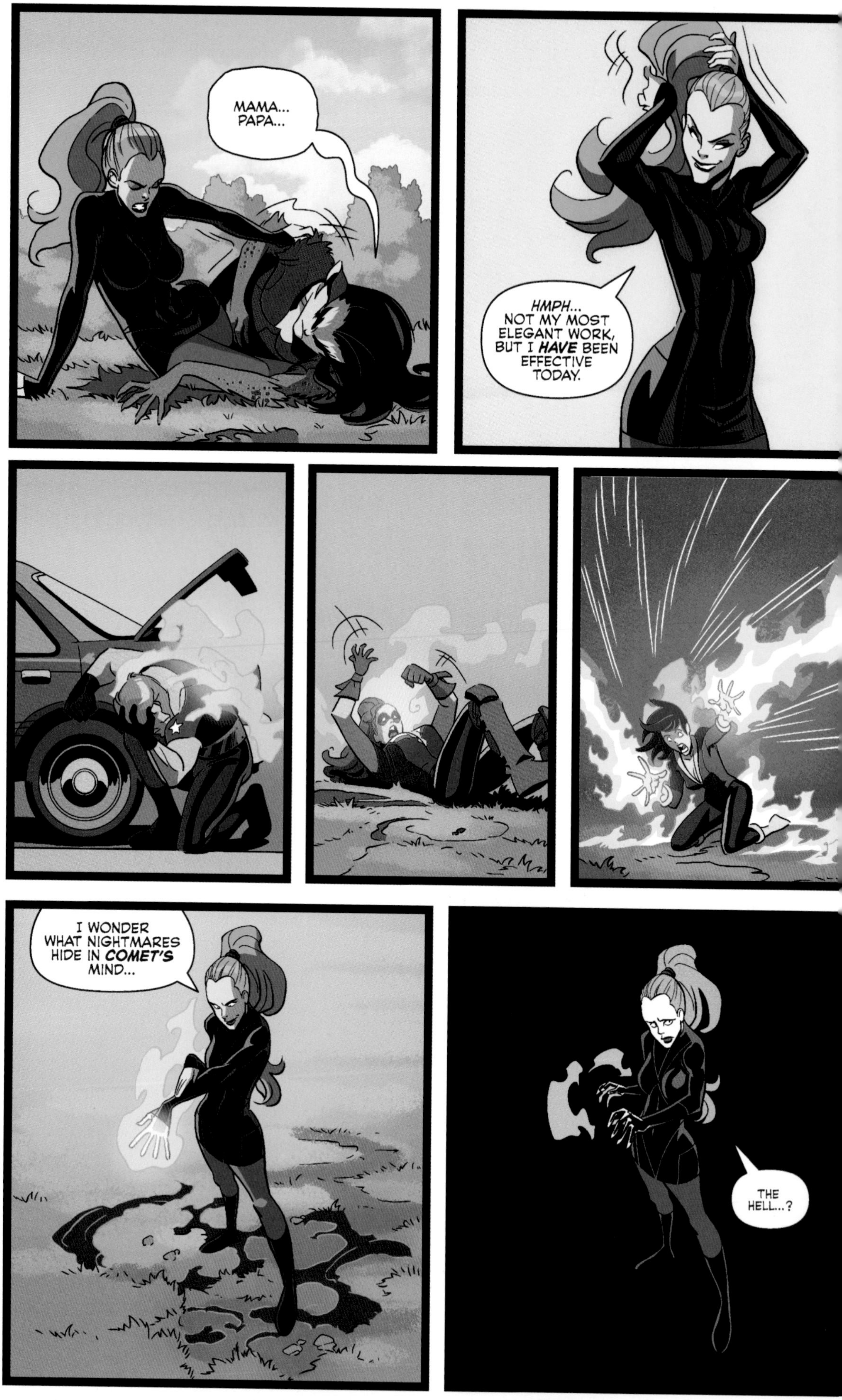
MAMA... PAPA...
HMPH... NOT MY MOST ELEGANT WORK, BUT I HAVE BEEN EFFECTIVE TODAY.
I WONDER WHAT NIGHTMARES HIDE IN COMET'S MIND...
THE HELL...?

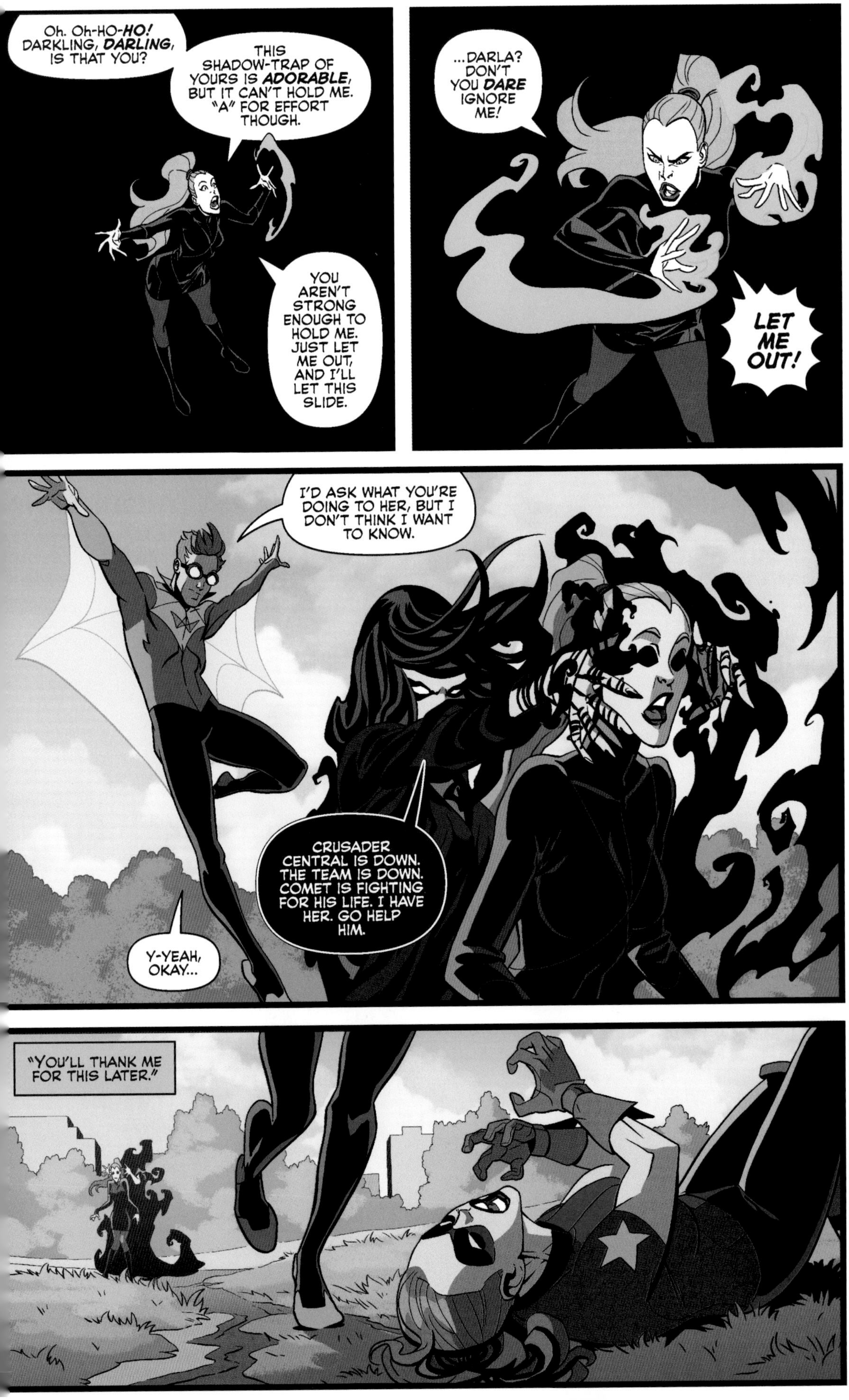
Oh. Oh-HO-**HO!** DARKLING, **DARLING,** IS THAT YOU?
THIS SHADOW-TRAP OF YOURS IS **ADORABLE,** BUT IT CAN'T HOLD ME. "A" FOR EFFORT THOUGH.
YOU AREN'T STRONG ENOUGH TO HOLD ME. JUST LET ME OUT, AND I'LL LET THIS SLIDE.
...DARLA? DON'T YOU **DARE** IGNORE ME!
LET ME OUT!
I'D ASK WHAT YOU'RE DOING TO HER, BUT I DON'T THINK I WANT TO KNOW.
CRUSADER CENTRAL IS DOWN. THE TEAM IS DOWN. COMET IS FIGHTING FOR HIS LIFE. I HAVE HER. GO HELP HIM.
Y-YEAH, OKAY...
"YOU'LL THANK ME FOR THIS LATER."

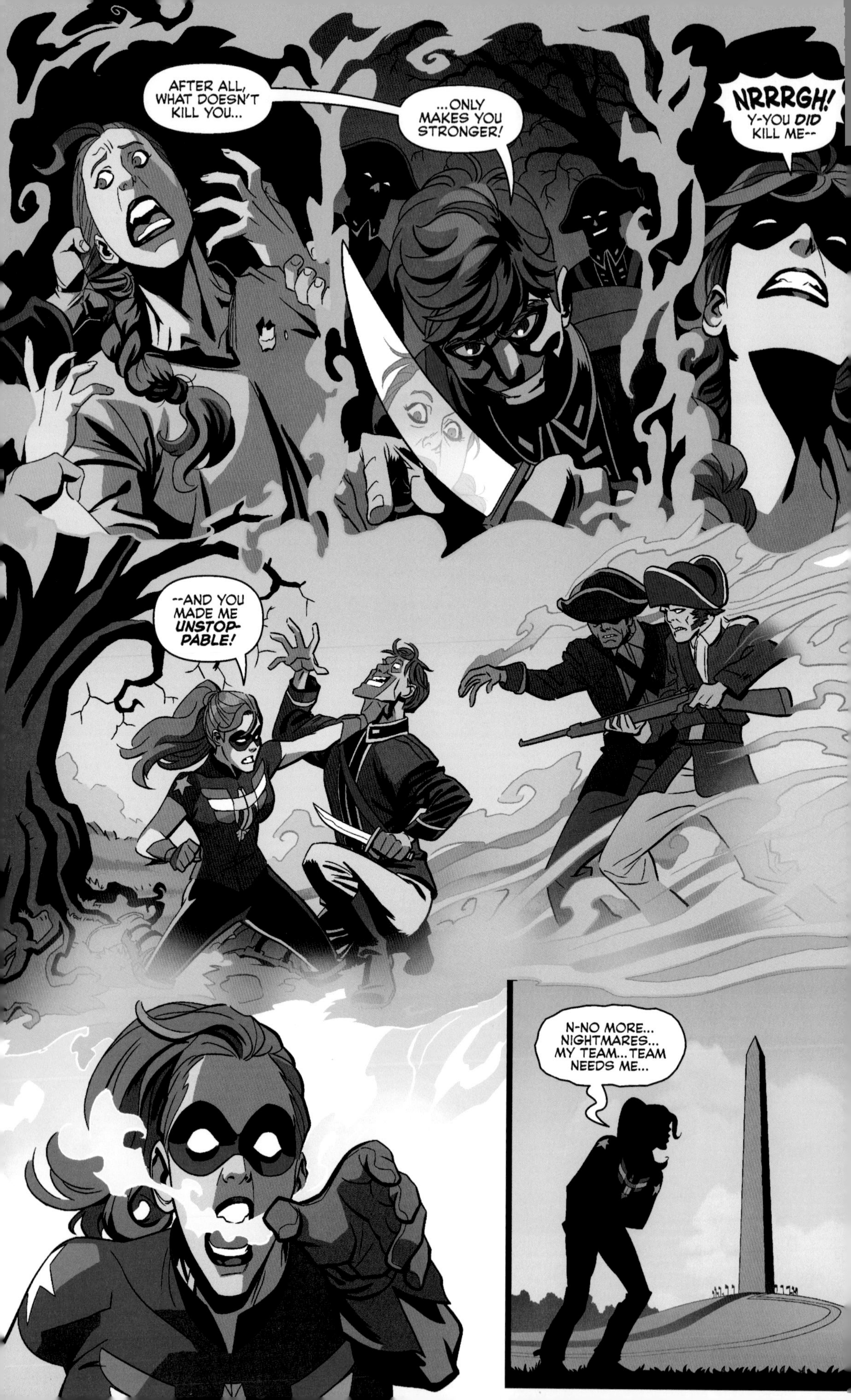
AFTER ALL, WHAT DOESN'T KILL YOU...
...ONLY MAKES YOU STRONGER!
NRRRGH! Y-YOU DID KILL ME--
--AND YOU MADE ME UNSTOP-PABLE!
N-NO MORE... NIGHTMARES... MY TEAM...TEAM NEEDS ME...

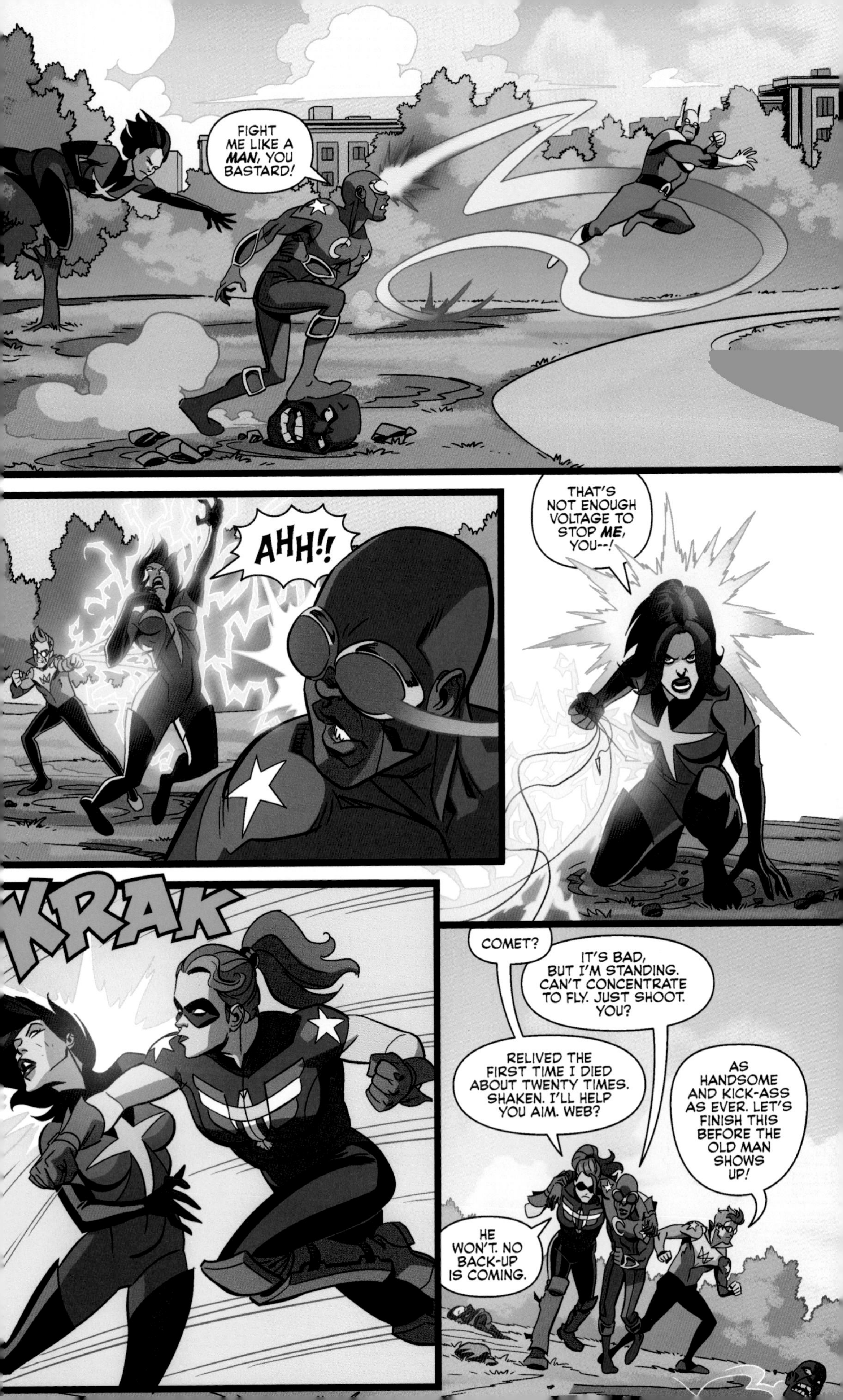

FIGHT ME LIKE A MAN, YOU BASTARD!
AHH!!
THAT'S NOT ENOUGH VOLTAGE TO STOP ME, YOU--!
KRAK
COMET?
IT'S BAD, BUT I'M STANDING. CAN'T CONCENTRATE TO FLY. JUST SHOOT. YOU?
RELIVED THE FIRST TIME I DIED ABOUT TWENTY TIMES. SHAKEN. I'LL HELP YOU AIM. WEB?
AS HANDSOME AND KICK-ASS AS EVER. LET'S FINISH THIS BEFORE THE OLD MAN SHOWS UP!
HE WON'T. NO BACK-UP IS COMING.

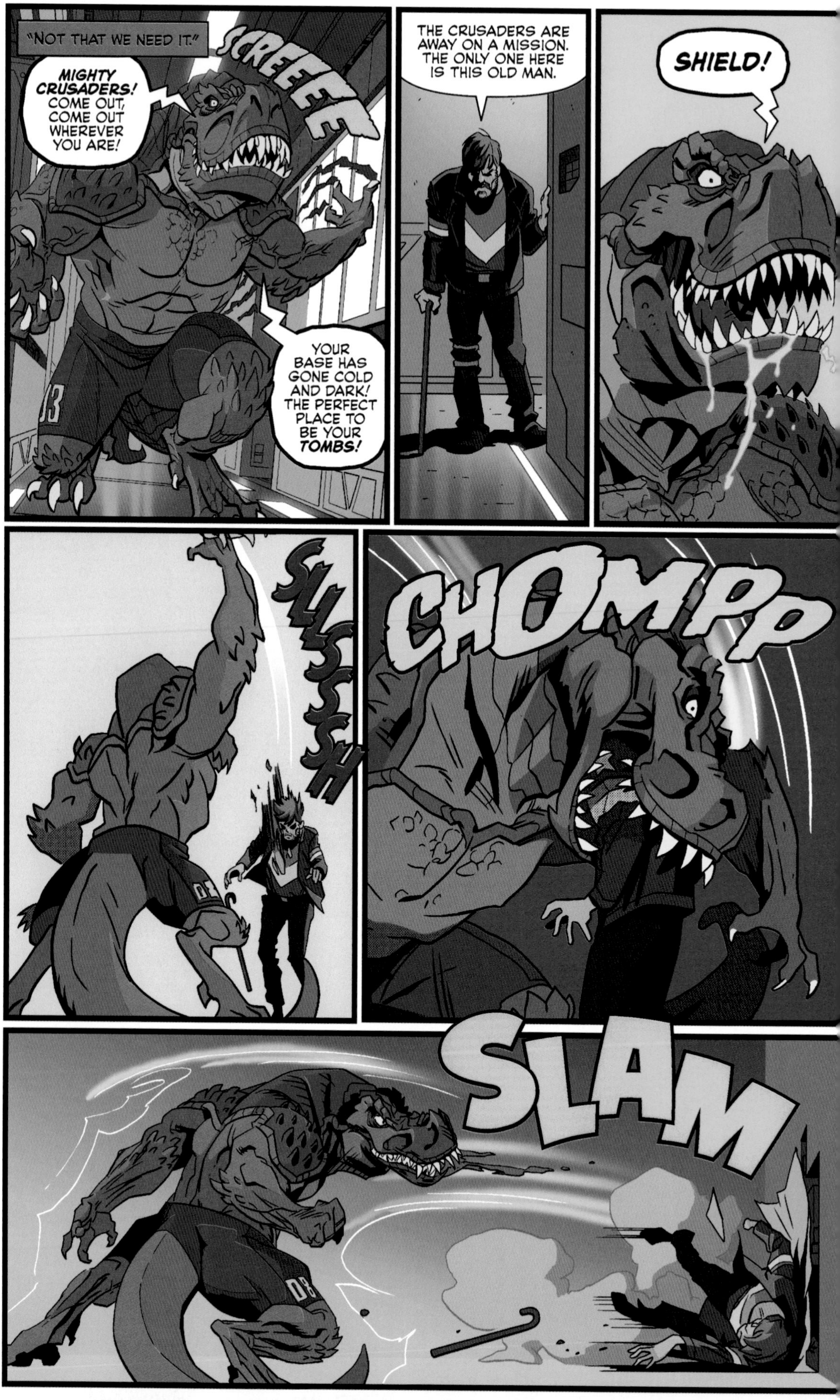

"NOT THAT WE NEED IT."
SCREEEEE
MIGHTY CRUSADERS! COME OUT, COME OUT WHEREVER YOU ARE!
YOUR BASE HAS GONE COLD AND DARK! THE PERFECT PLACE TO BE YOUR TOMBS!
THE CRUSADERS ARE AWAY ON A MISSION. THE ONLY ONE HERE IS THIS OLD MAN.
SHIELD!
SLISSSH
CHOMPP
SLAM

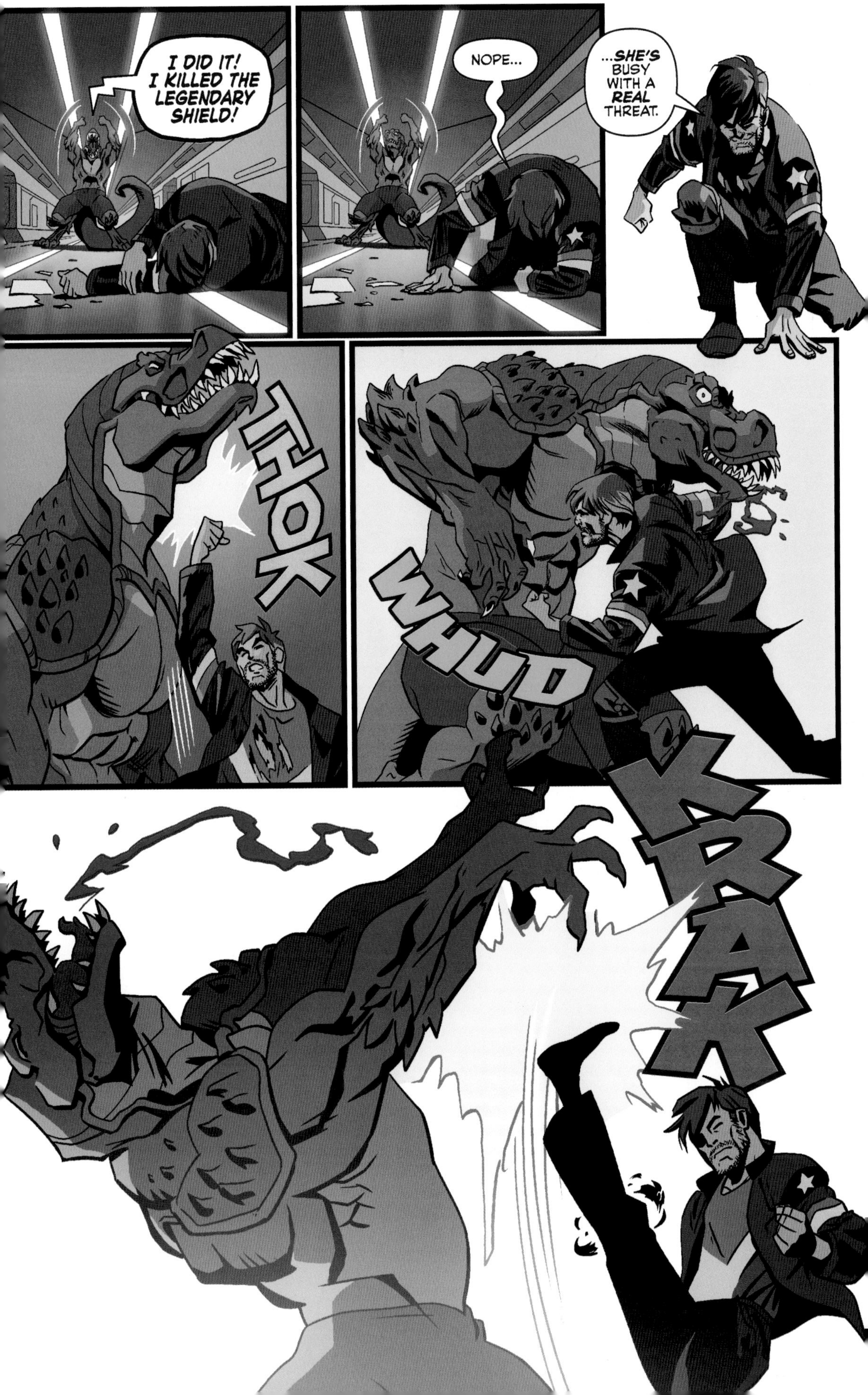
I DID IT! I KILLED THE LEGENDARY SHIELD!
NOPE...
...SHE'S BUSY WITH A REAL THREAT.
THOK
WHUD
KRAK

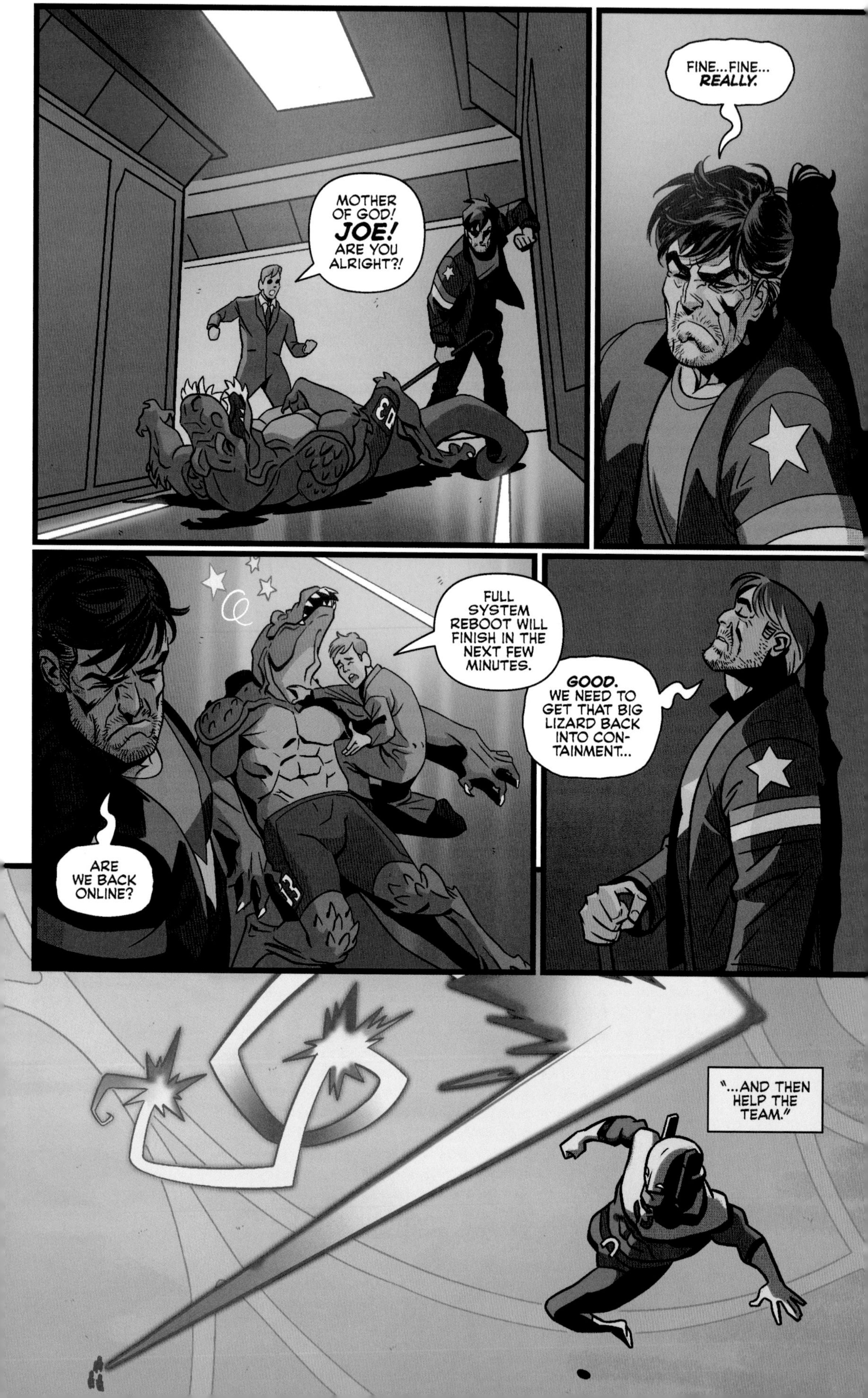
MOTHER OF GOD! JOE! ARE YOU ALRIGHT?!
FINE...FINE... REALLY.
ARE WE BACK ONLINE?
FULL SYSTEM REBOOT WILL FINISH IN THE NEXT FEW MINUTES.
GOOD. WE NEED TO GET THAT BIG LIZARD BACK INTO CON-TAINMENT...
"...AND THEN HELP THE TEAM."

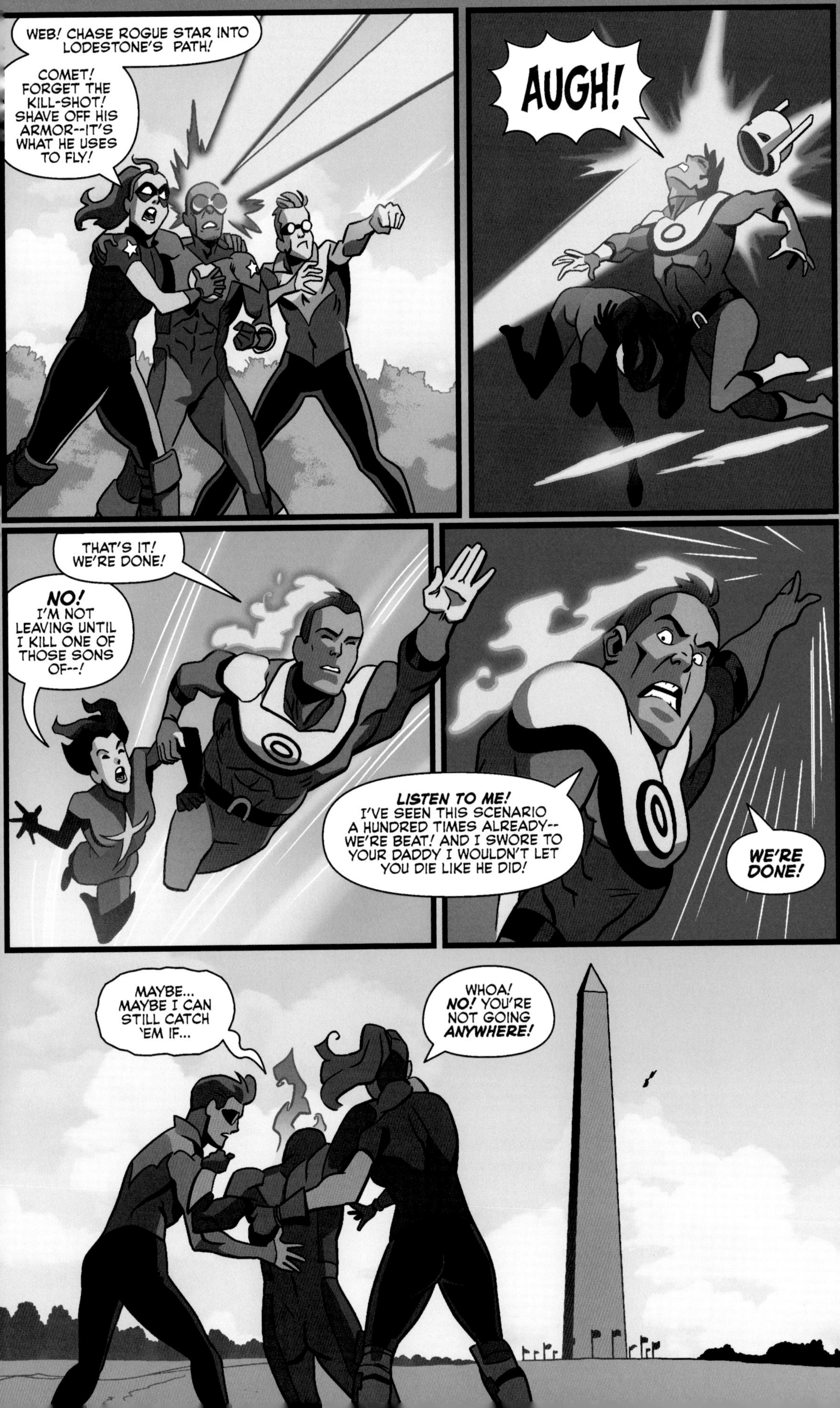
WEB! CHASE ROGUE STAR INTO LODESTONE'S PATH!
COMET! FORGET THE KILL-SHOT! SHAVE OFF HIS ARMOR--IT'S WHAT HE USES TO FLY!
AUGH!
THAT'S IT! WE'RE DONE!
NO! I'M NOT LEAVING UNTIL I KILL ONE OF THOSE SONS OF--!
LISTEN TO ME! I'VE SEEN THIS SCENARIO A HUNDRED TIMES ALREADY--WE'RE BEAT! AND I SWORE TO YOUR DADDY I WOULDN'T LET YOU DIE LIKE HE DID!
WE'RE DONE!
MAYBE... MAYBE I CAN STILL CATCH 'EM IF...
WHOA! NO! YOU'RE NOT GOING ANYWHERE!

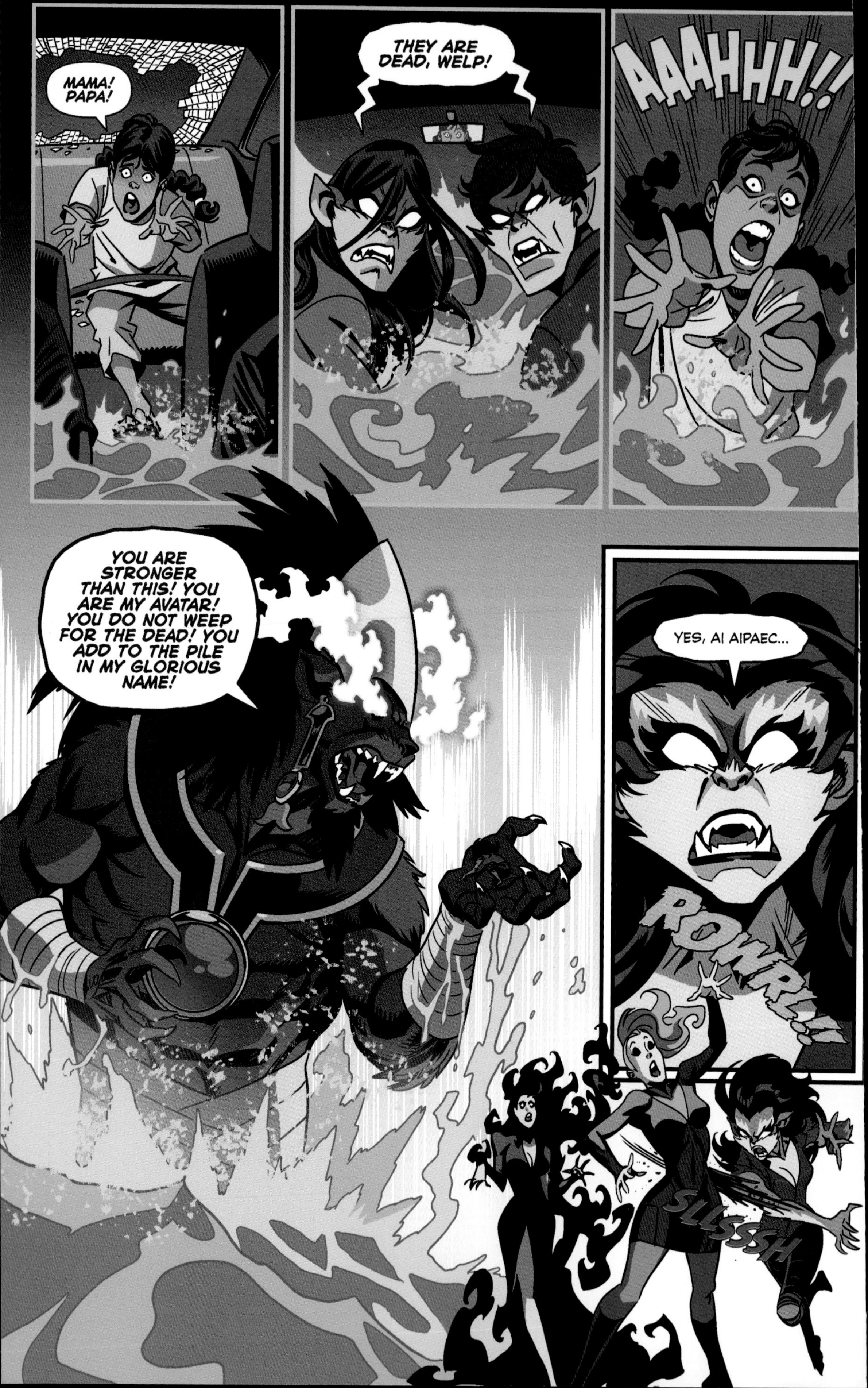
MAMA! PAPA!
THEY ARE DEAD, WELP!
AAAHHH!!
YOU ARE STRONGER THAN THIS! YOU ARE MY AVATAR! YOU DO NOT WEEP FOR THE DEAD! YOU ADD TO THE PILE IN MY GLORIOUS NAME!
YES, AI AIPAEC...
ROWRL!
SLISSSH

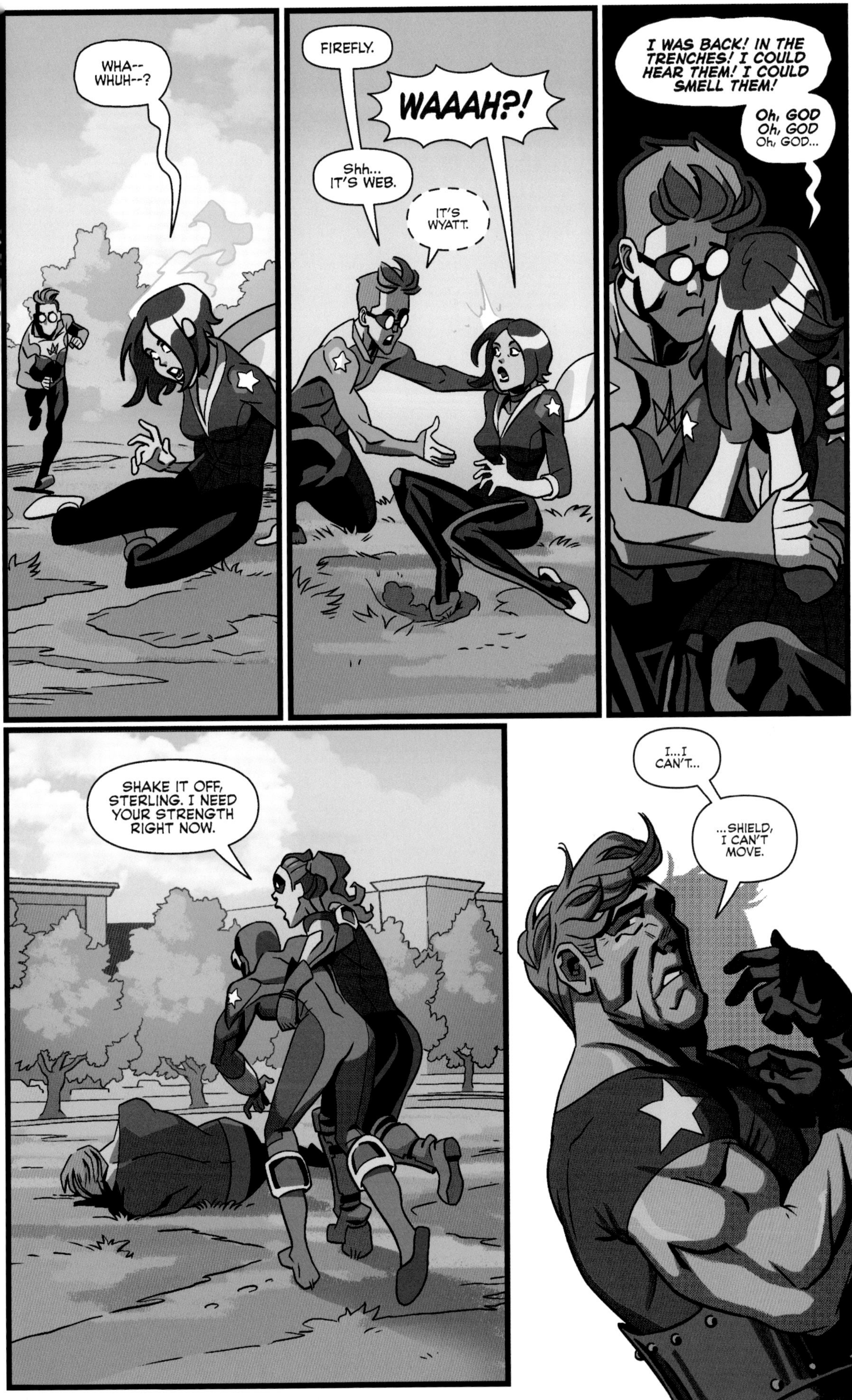
WHA--
WHUH--?
FIREFLY.
WAAAH?!
Shh... IT'S WEB.
IT'S WYATT.
I WAS BACK! IN THE TRENCHES! I COULD HEAR THEM! I COULD SMELL THEM!
Oh, GOD
Oh, GOD
Oh, GOD...
SHAKE IT OFF, STERLING. I NEED YOUR STRENGTH RIGHT NOW.
I...I CAN'T...
...SHIELD, I CAN'T MOVE.

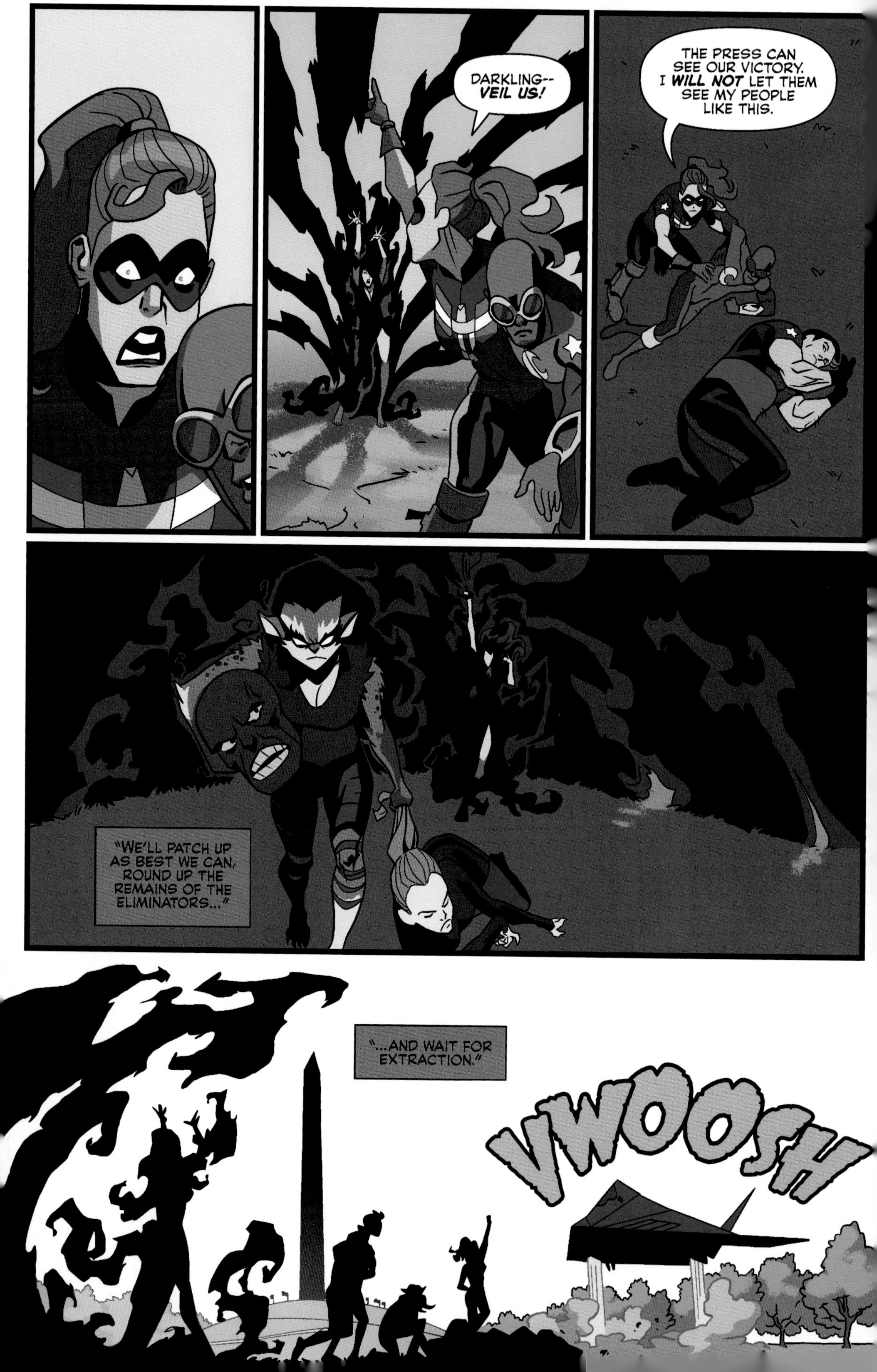
DARKLING--
VEIL US!
THE PRESS CAN SEE OUR VICTORY. I WILL NOT LET THEM SEE MY PEOPLE LIKE THIS.
"WE'LL PATCH UP AS BEST WE CAN, ROUND UP THE REMAINS OF THE ELIMINATORS..."
"...AND WAIT FOR EXTRACTION."
VWOOSH

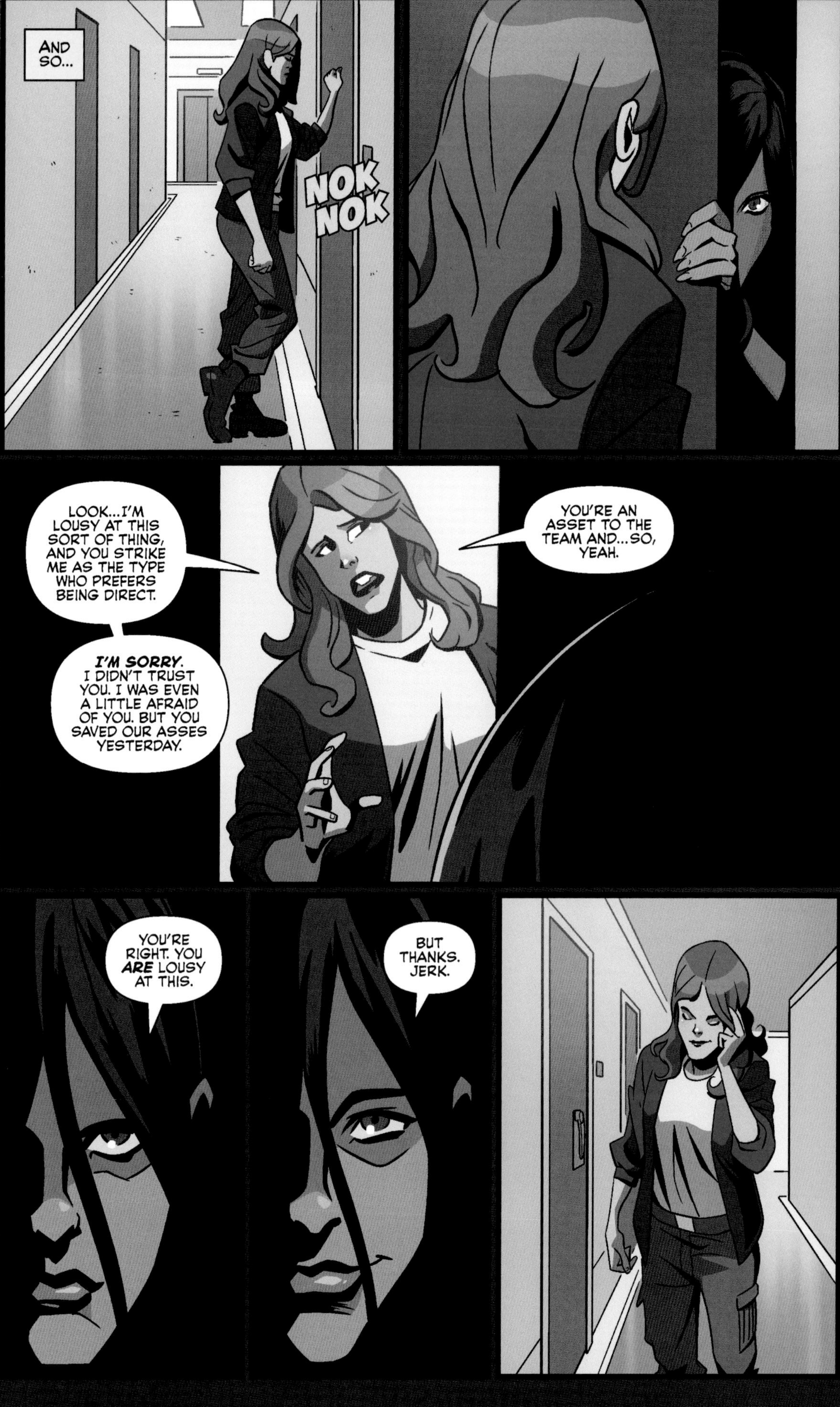
AND SO...
NOK NOK
LOOK...I'M LOUSY AT THIS SORT OF THING, AND YOU STRIKE ME AS THE TYPE WHO PREFERS BEING DIRECT.
I'M SORRY. I DIDN'T TRUST YOU. I WAS EVEN A LITTLE AFRAID OF YOU. BUT YOU SAVED OUR ASSES YESTERDAY.
YOU'RE AN ASSET TO THE TEAM AND...SO, YEAH.
YOU'RE RIGHT. YOU *ARE* LOUSY AT THIS.
BUT THANKS. *JERK*.

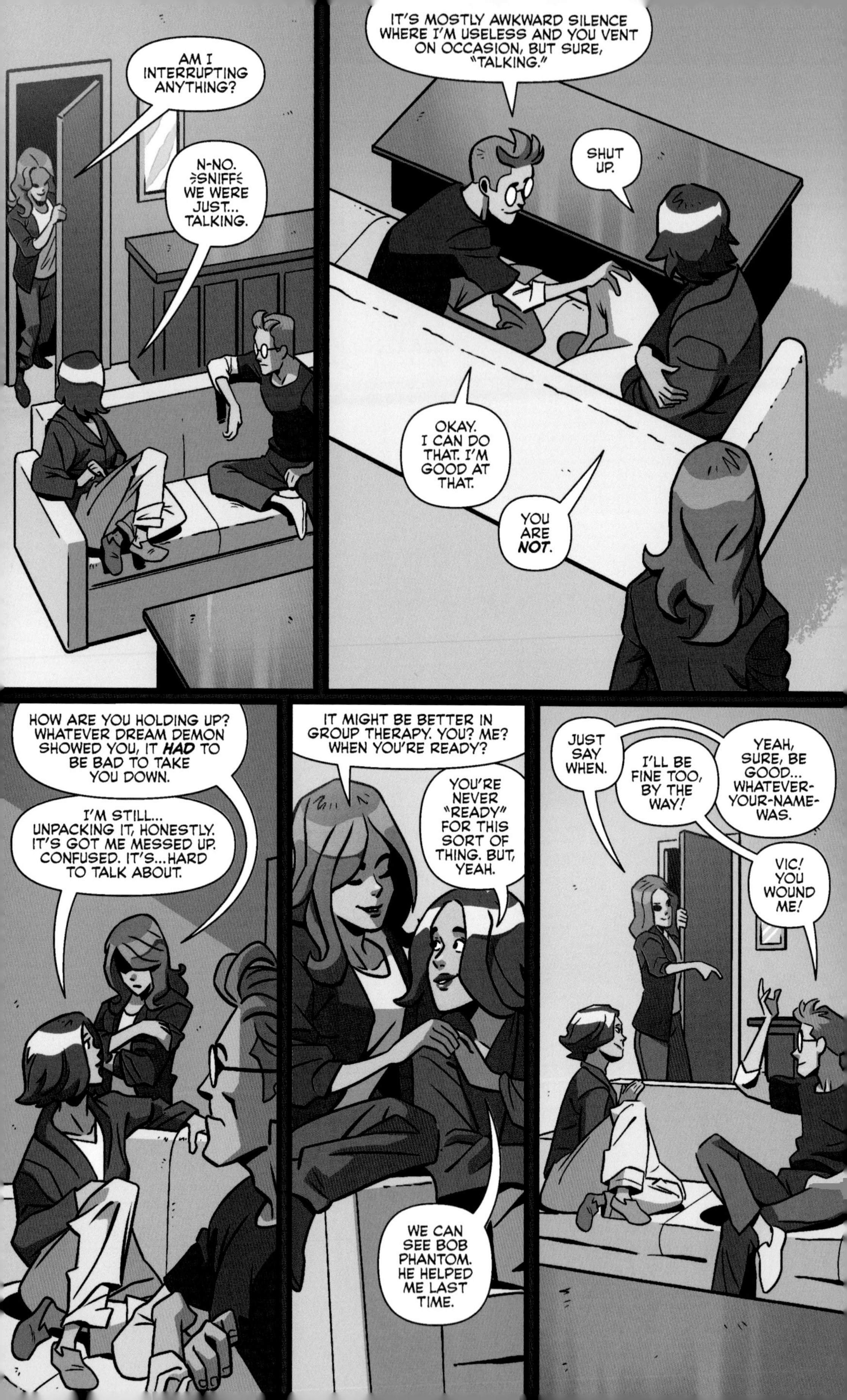

AM I INTERRUPTING ANYTHING?
N-NO. *SNIFF* WE WERE JUST... TALKING.
IT'S MOSTLY AWKWARD SILENCE WHERE I'M USELESS AND YOU VENT ON OCCASION, BUT SURE, "TALKING."
SHUT UP.
OKAY. I CAN DO THAT. I'M GOOD AT THAT.
YOU ARE ***NOT***.
HOW ARE YOU HOLDING UP? WHATEVER DREAM DEMON SHOWED YOU, IT ***HAD*** TO BE BAD TO TAKE YOU DOWN.
I'M STILL... UNPACKING IT, HONESTLY. IT'S GOT ME MESSED UP. CONFUSED. IT'S...HARD TO TALK ABOUT.
IT MIGHT BE BETTER IN GROUP THERAPY. YOU? ME? WHEN YOU'RE READY?
YOU'RE NEVER "READY" FOR THIS SORT OF THING. BUT, YEAH.
WE CAN SEE BOB PHANTOM. HE HELPED ME LAST TIME.
JUST SAY WHEN.
YEAH, SURE, BE GOOD... WHATEVER-YOUR-NAME-WAS.
I'LL BE FINE TOO, BY THE WAY!
VIC! YOU WOUND ME!

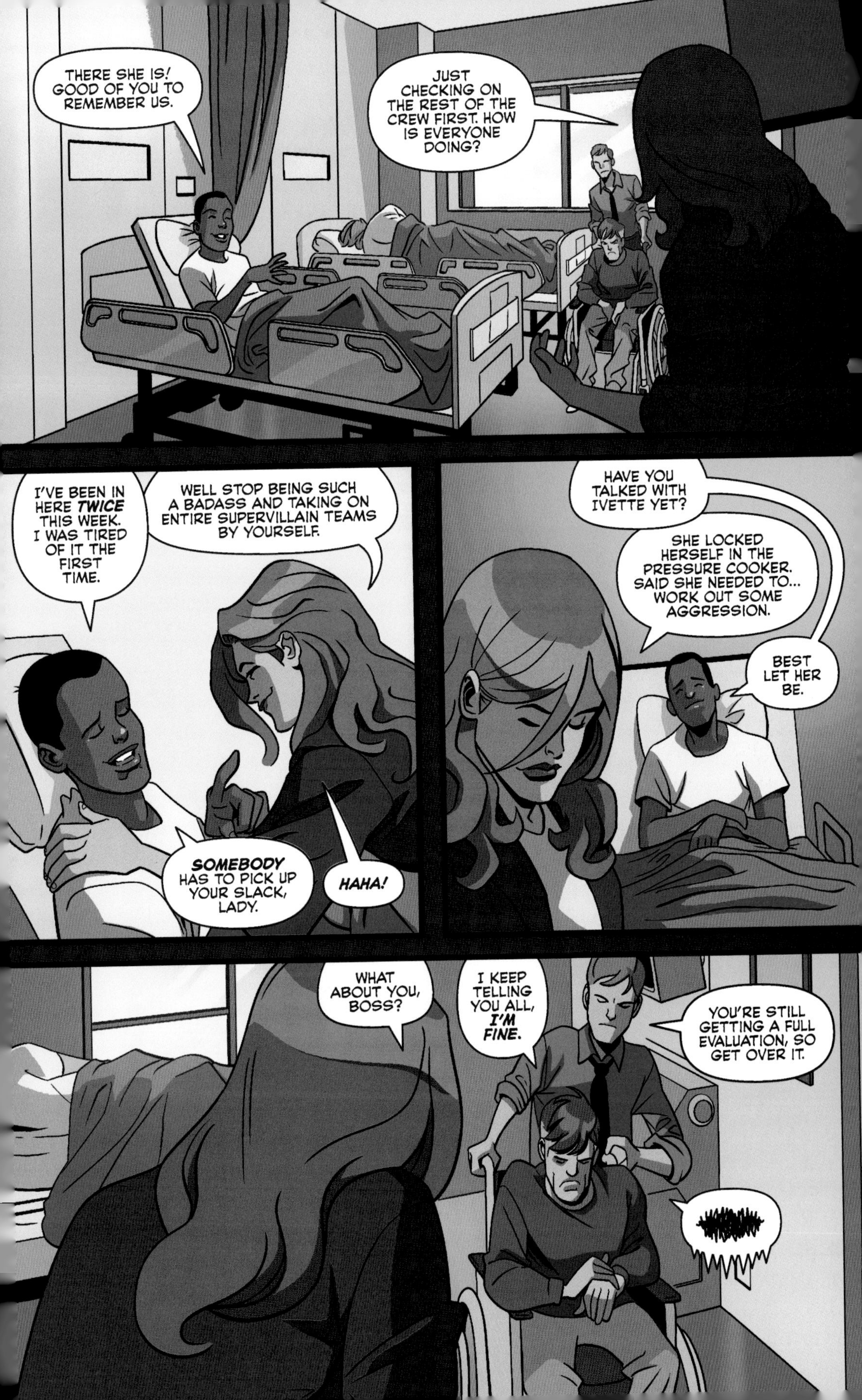
THERE SHE IS! GOOD OF YOU TO REMEMBER US.
JUST CHECKING ON THE REST OF THE CREW FIRST. HOW IS EVERYONE DOING?
I'VE BEEN IN HERE *TWICE* THIS WEEK. I WAS TIRED OF IT THE FIRST TIME.
WELL STOP BEING SUCH A BADASS AND TAKING ON ENTIRE SUPERVILLAIN TEAMS BY YOURSELF.
SOMEBODY HAS TO PICK UP YOUR SLACK, LADY.
HAHA!
HAVE YOU TALKED WITH IVETTE YET?
SHE LOCKED HERSELF IN THE PRESSURE COOKER. SAID SHE NEEDED TO... WORK OUT SOME AGGRESSION.
BEST LET HER BE.
WHAT ABOUT YOU, BOSS?
I KEEP TELLING YOU ALL, *I'M FINE*.
YOU'RE STILL GETTING A FULL EVALUATION, SO GET OVER IT.

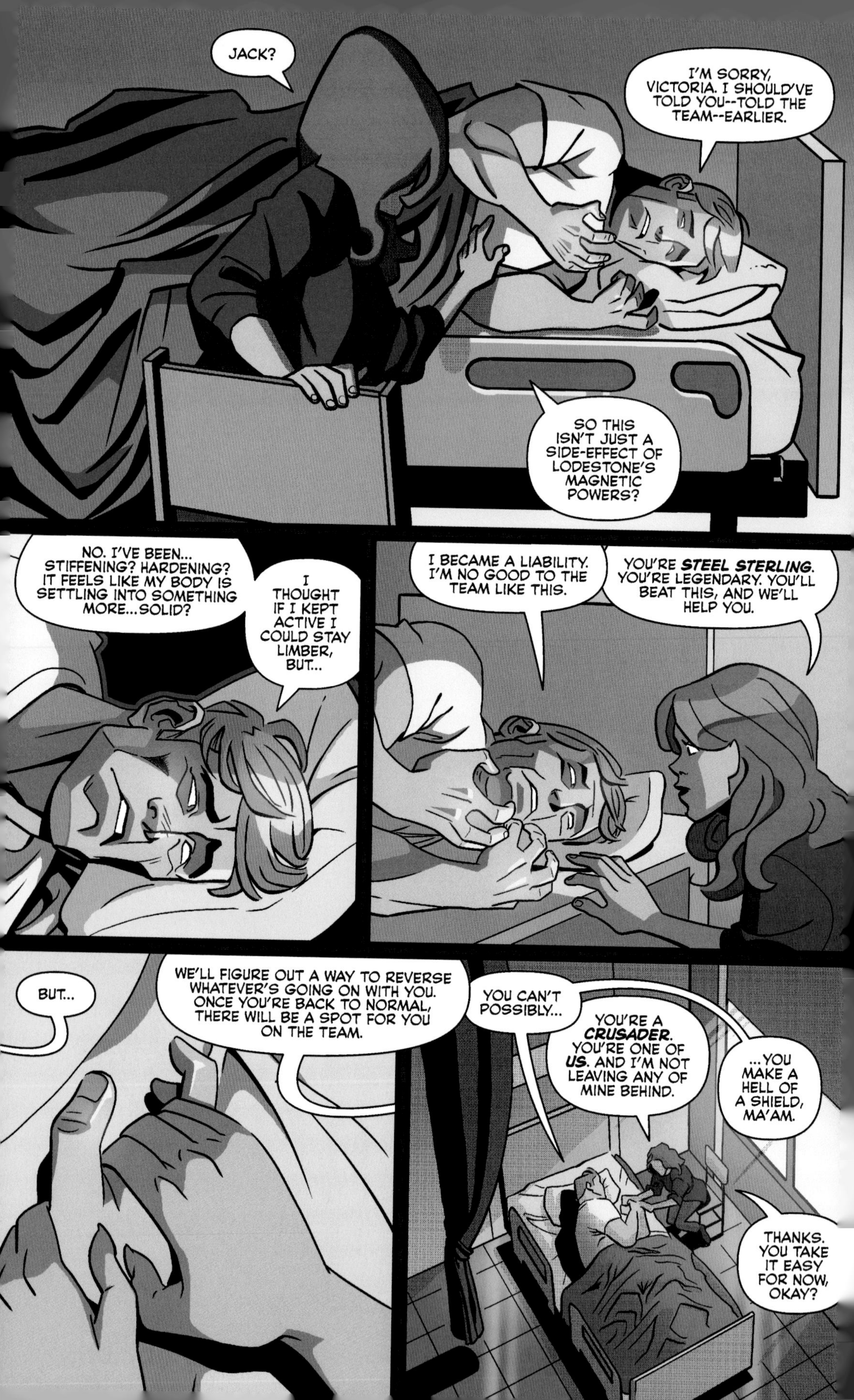
JACK?
I'M SORRY, VICTORIA. I SHOULD'VE TOLD YOU--TOLD THE TEAM--EARLIER.
SO THIS ISN'T JUST A SIDE-EFFECT OF LODESTONE'S MAGNETIC POWERS?
NO. I'VE BEEN... STIFFENING? HARDENING? IT FEELS LIKE MY BODY IS SETTLING INTO SOMETHING MORE...SOLID?
I THOUGHT IF I KEPT ACTIVE I COULD STAY LIMBER, BUT...
I BECAME A LIABILITY. I'M NO GOOD TO THE TEAM LIKE THIS.
YOU'RE STEEL STERLING. YOU'RE LEGENDARY. YOU'LL BEAT THIS, AND WE'LL HELP YOU.
BUT...
WE'LL FIGURE OUT A WAY TO REVERSE WHATEVER'S GOING ON WITH YOU. ONCE YOU'RE BACK TO NORMAL, THERE WILL BE A SPOT FOR YOU ON THE TEAM.
YOU CAN'T POSSIBLY...
YOU'RE A CRUSADER. YOU'RE ONE OF US. AND I'M NOT LEAVING ANY OF MINE BEHIND.
...YOU MAKE A HELL OF A SHIELD, MA'AM.
THANKS. YOU TAKE IT EASY FOR NOW, OKAY?

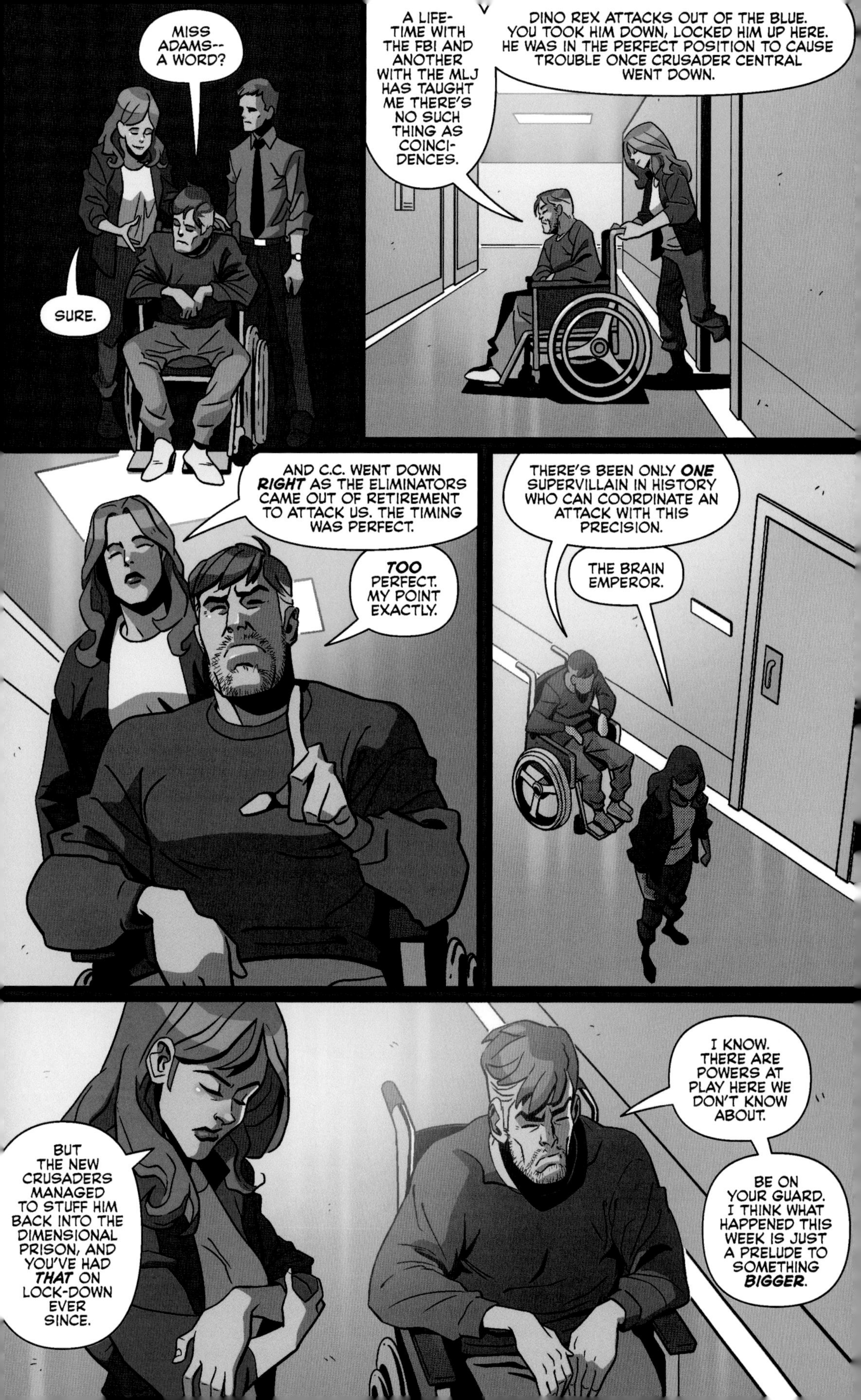
MISS ADAMS-- A WORD?
SURE.
A LIFETIME WITH THE FBI AND ANOTHER WITH THE MLJ HAS TAUGHT ME THERE'S NO SUCH THING AS COINCIDENCES.
DINO REX ATTACKS OUT OF THE BLUE. YOU TOOK HIM DOWN, LOCKED HIM UP HERE. HE WAS IN THE PERFECT POSITION TO CAUSE TROUBLE ONCE CRUSADER CENTRAL WENT DOWN.
AND C.C. WENT DOWN RIGHT AS THE ELIMINATORS CAME OUT OF RETIREMENT TO ATTACK US. THE TIMING WAS PERFECT.
TOO PERFECT. MY POINT EXACTLY.
THERE'S BEEN ONLY ONE SUPERVILLAIN IN HISTORY WHO CAN COORDINATE AN ATTACK WITH THIS PRECISION.
THE BRAIN EMPEROR.
BUT THE NEW CRUSADERS MANAGED TO STUFF HIM BACK INTO THE DIMENSIONAL PRISON, AND YOU'VE HAD THAT ON LOCK-DOWN EVER SINCE.
I KNOW. THERE ARE POWERS AT PLAY HERE WE DON'T KNOW ABOUT.
BE ON YOUR GUARD. I THINK WHAT HAPPENED THIS WEEK IS JUST A PRELUDE TO SOMETHING BIGGER.

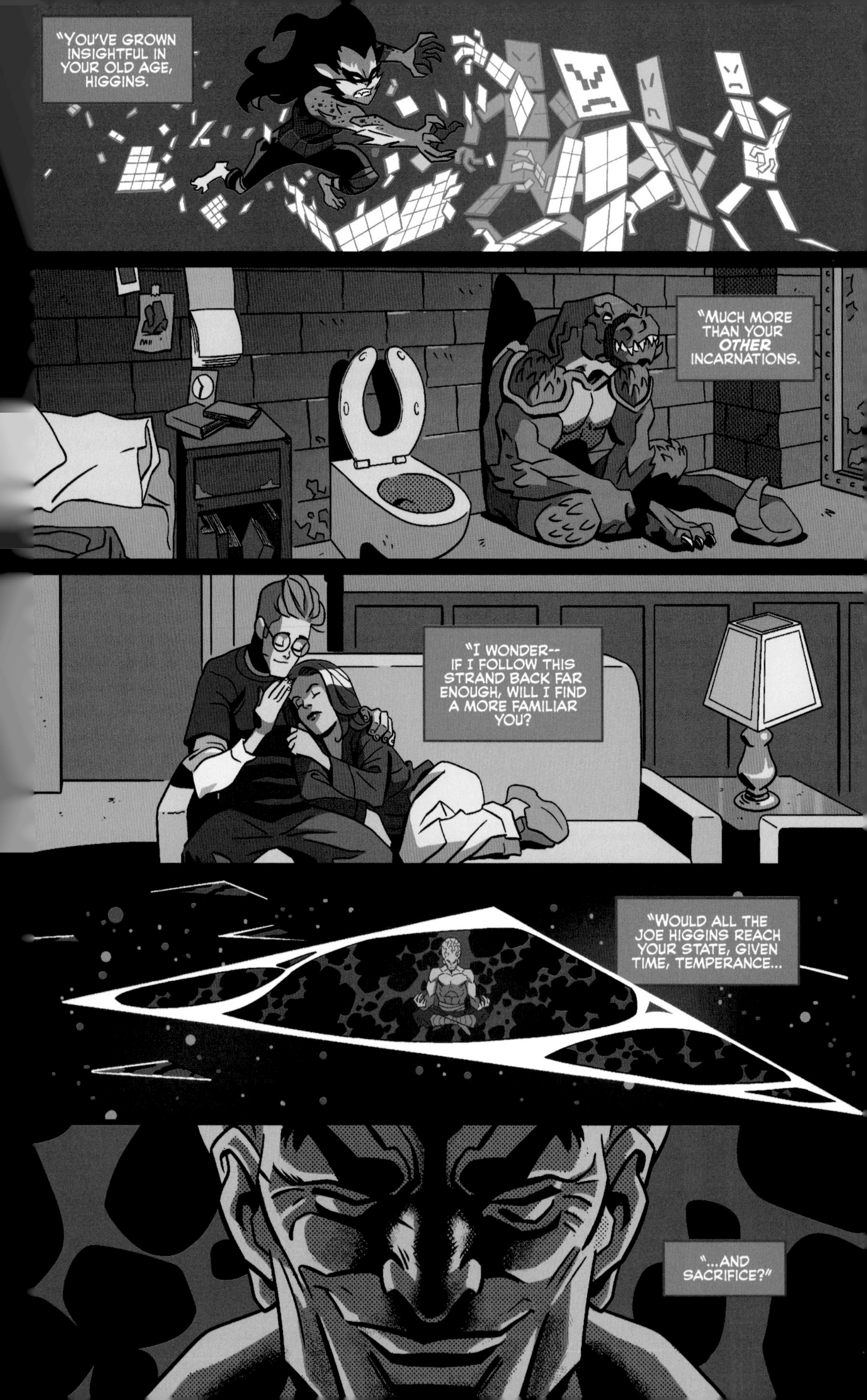
"YOU'VE GROWN INSIGHTFUL IN YOUR OLD AGE, HIGGINS.
"MUCH MORE THAN YOUR *OTHER* INCARNATIONS.
"I WONDER-- IF I FOLLOW THIS STRAND BACK FAR ENOUGH, WILL I FIND A MORE FAMILIAR YOU?
"WOULD ALL THE JOE HIGGINS REACH YOUR STATE, GIVEN TIME, TEMPERANCE...
"...AND SACRIFICE?"

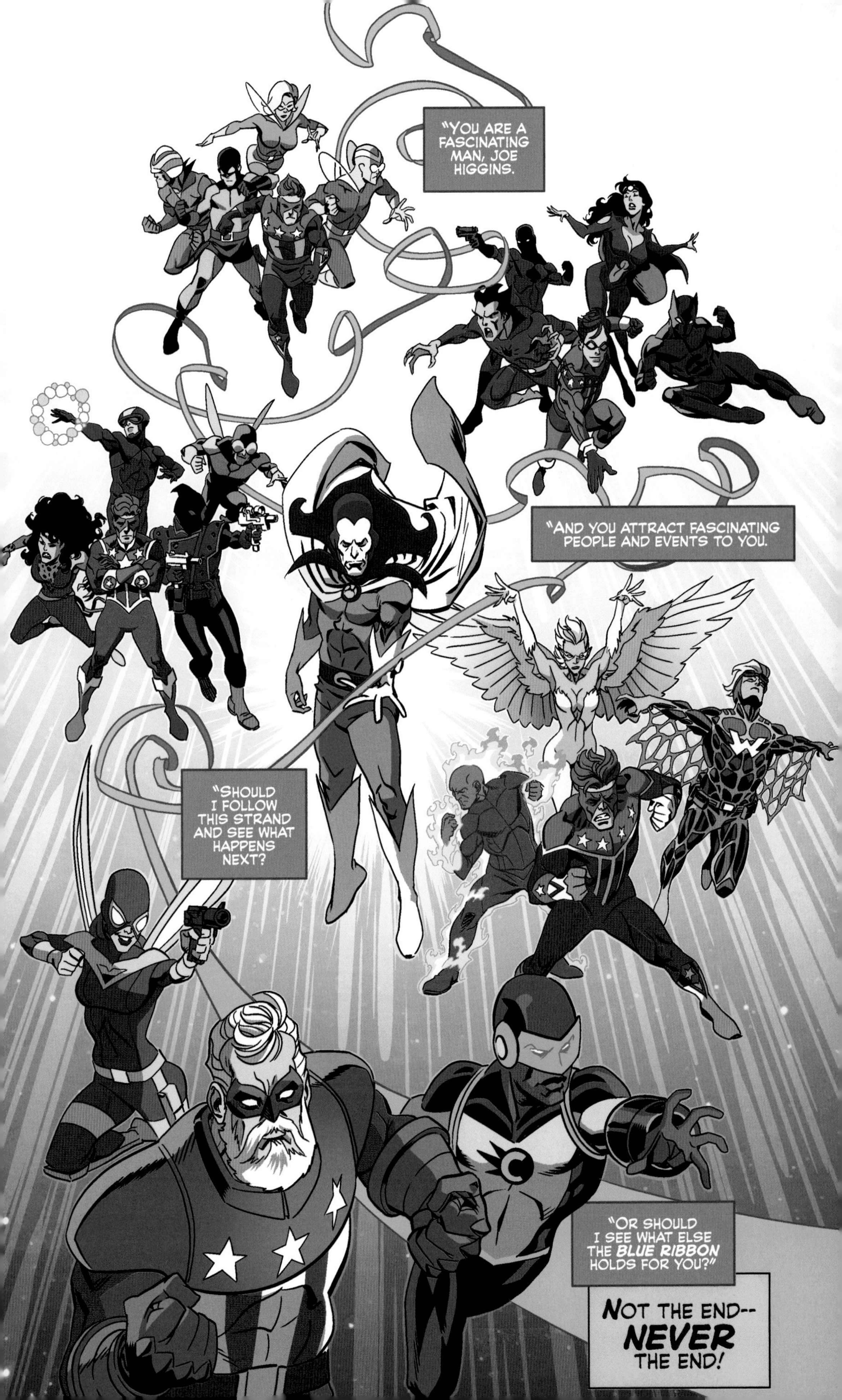
"YOU ARE A FASCINATING MAN, JOE HIGGINS.
"AND YOU ATTRACT FASCINATING PEOPLE AND EVENTS TO YOU.
"SHOULD I FOLLOW THIS STRAND AND SEE WHAT HAPPENS NEXT?
"OR SHOULD I SEE WHAT ELSE THE BLUE RIBBON HOLDS FOR YOU?"
NOT THE END-- NEVER THE END!

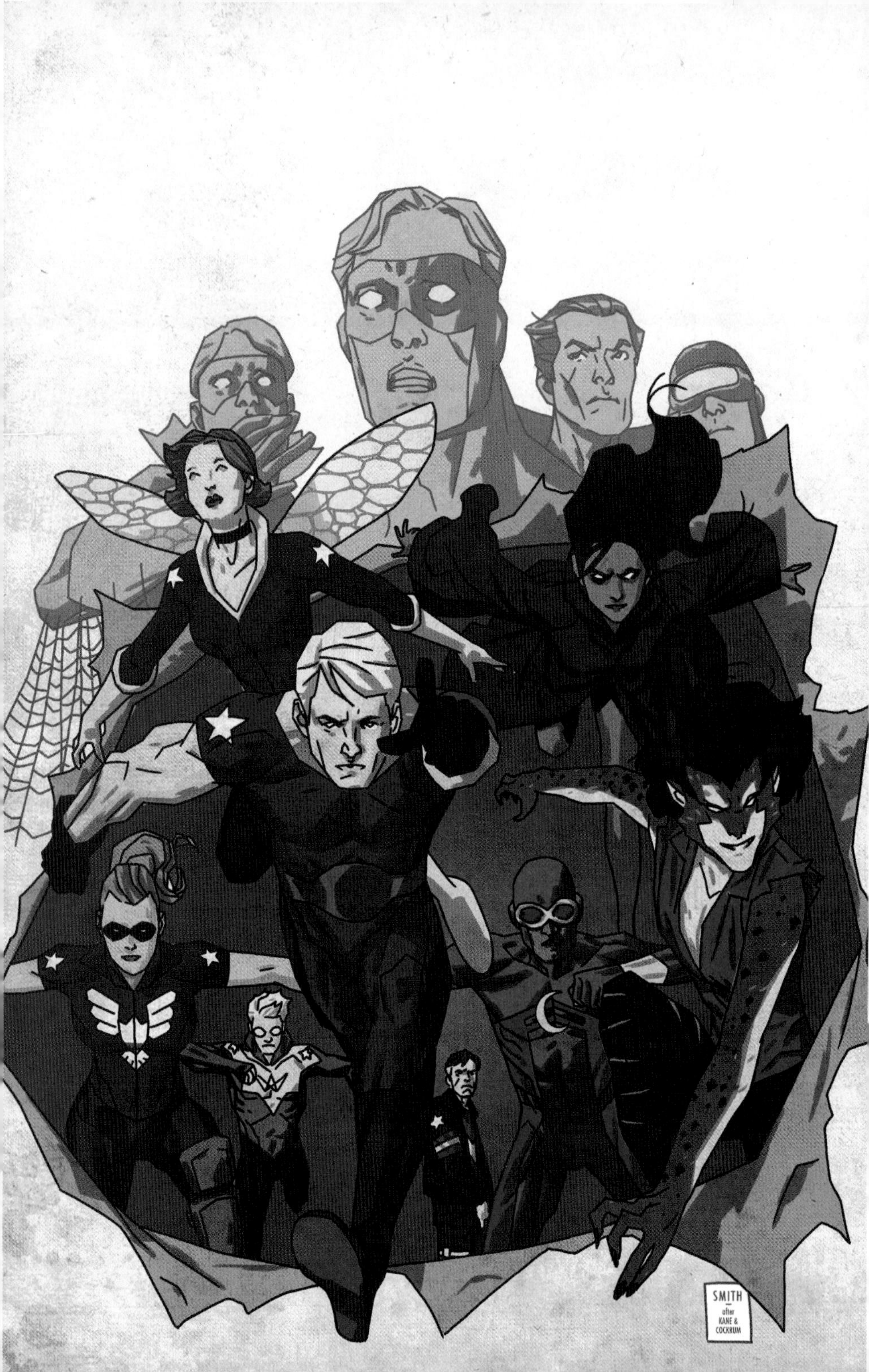
SMITH
after
KANE &
COCKRUM

ISSUE 1 VARIANT ART • MATTHEW DOW SMITH

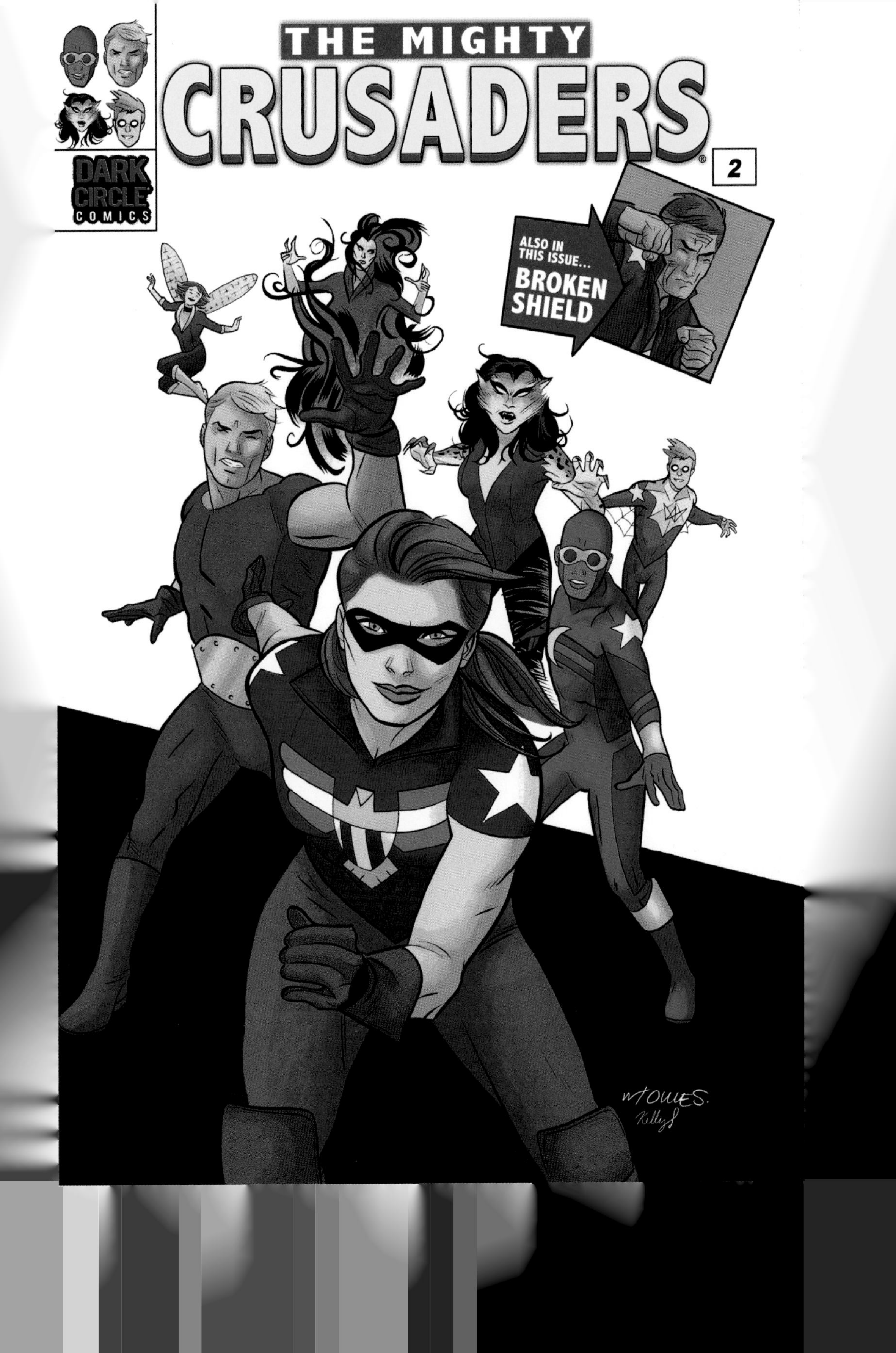
THE MIGHTY
CRUSADERS
2
DARK CIRCLE COMICS
ALSO IN THIS ISSUE...
BROKEN SHIELD

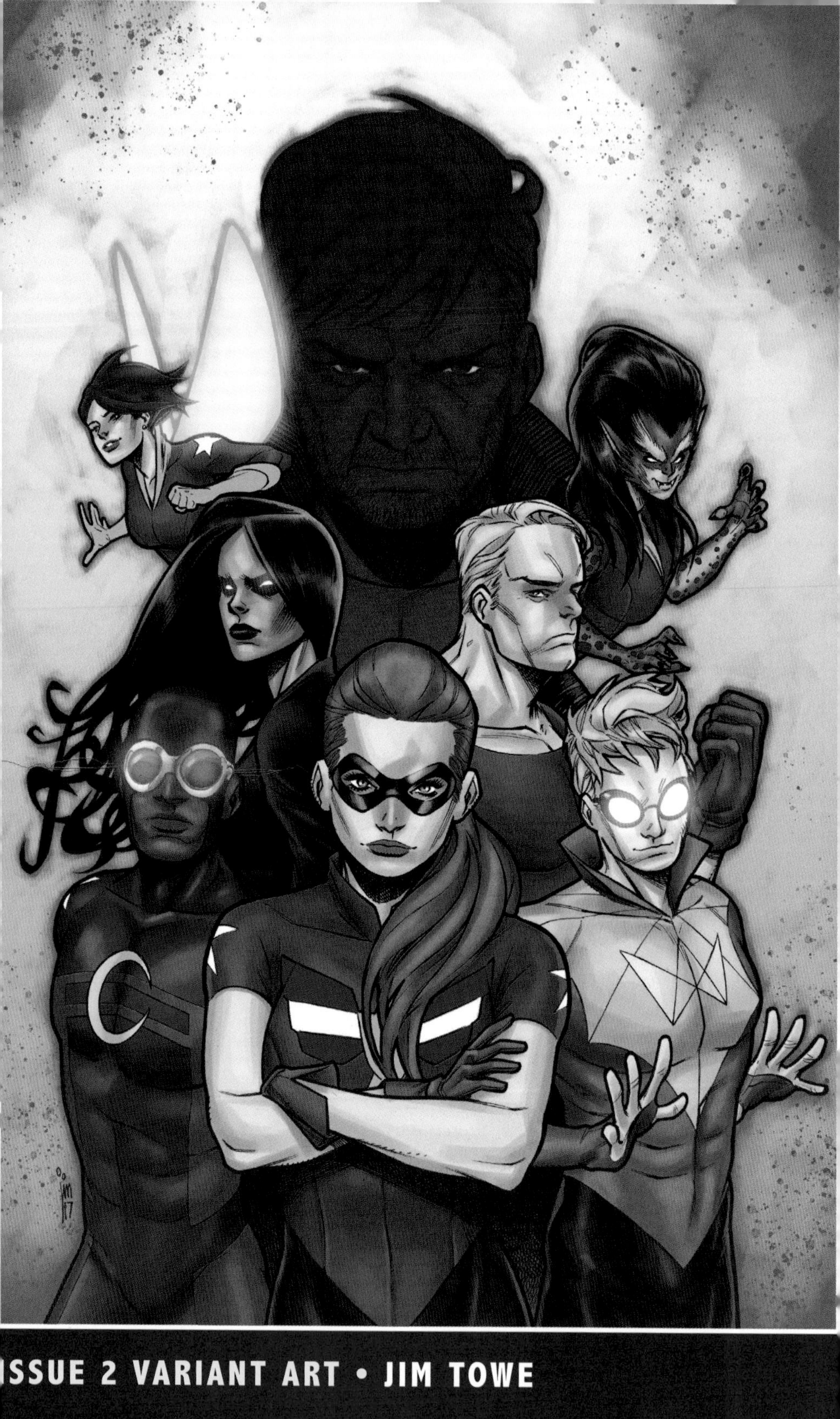

ISSUE 2 VARIANT ART • JIM TOWE

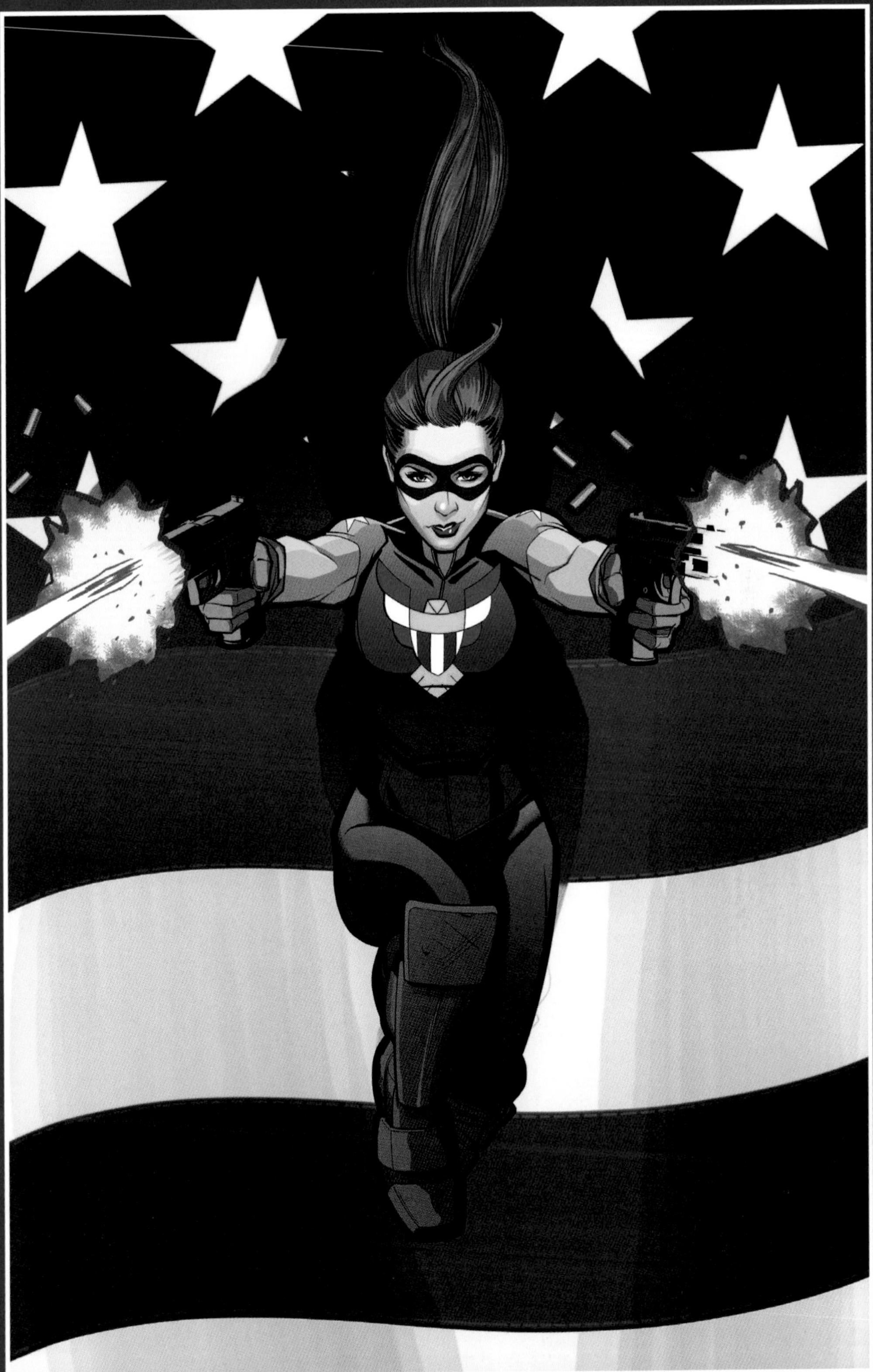

ISSUE 3 VARIANT ART • TOM FEISTER

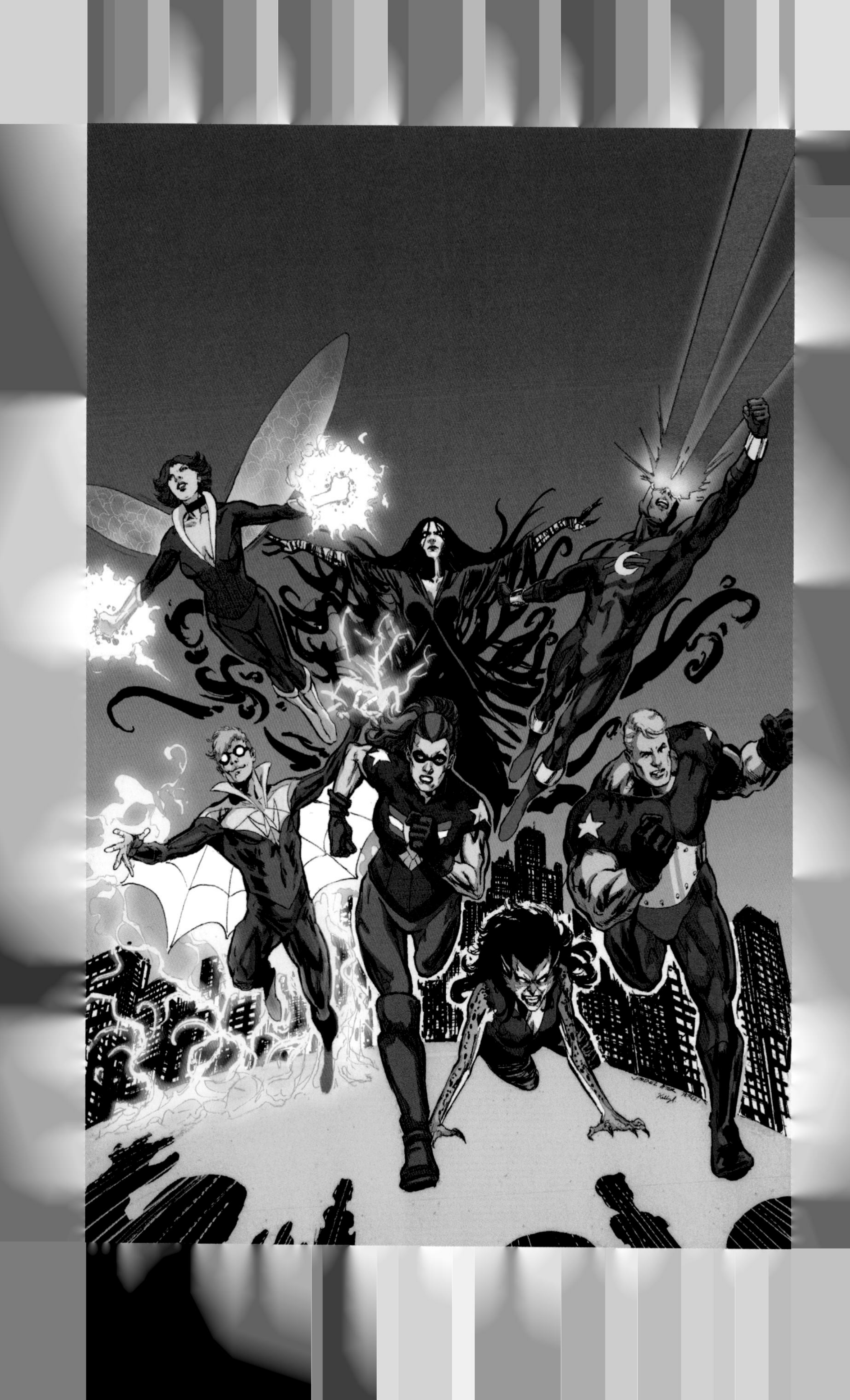

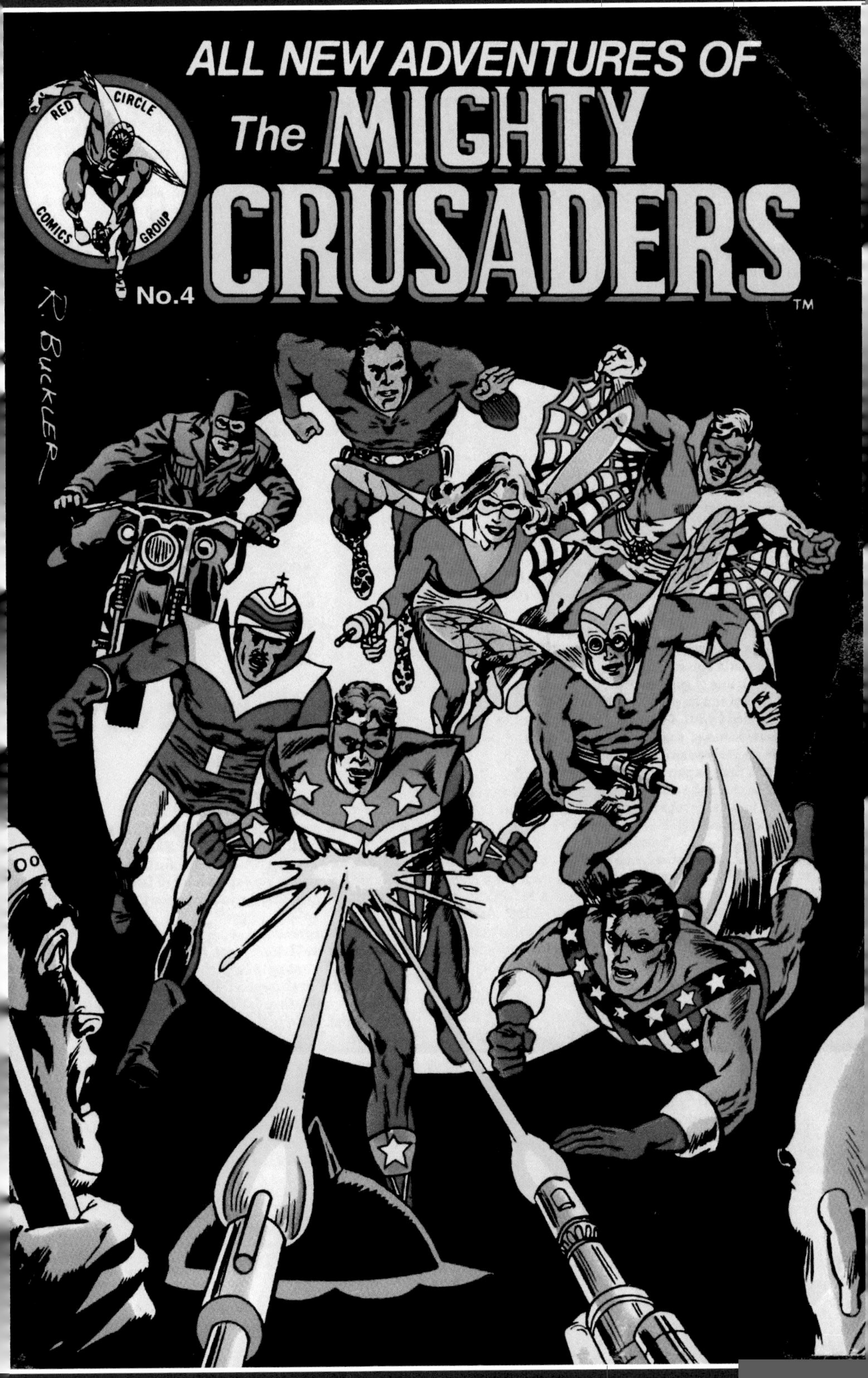
ALL NEW ADVENTURES OF
The MIGHTY CRUSADERS
TM
No.4
RED CIRCLE COMICS GROUP
R. BUCKLER

• RICH

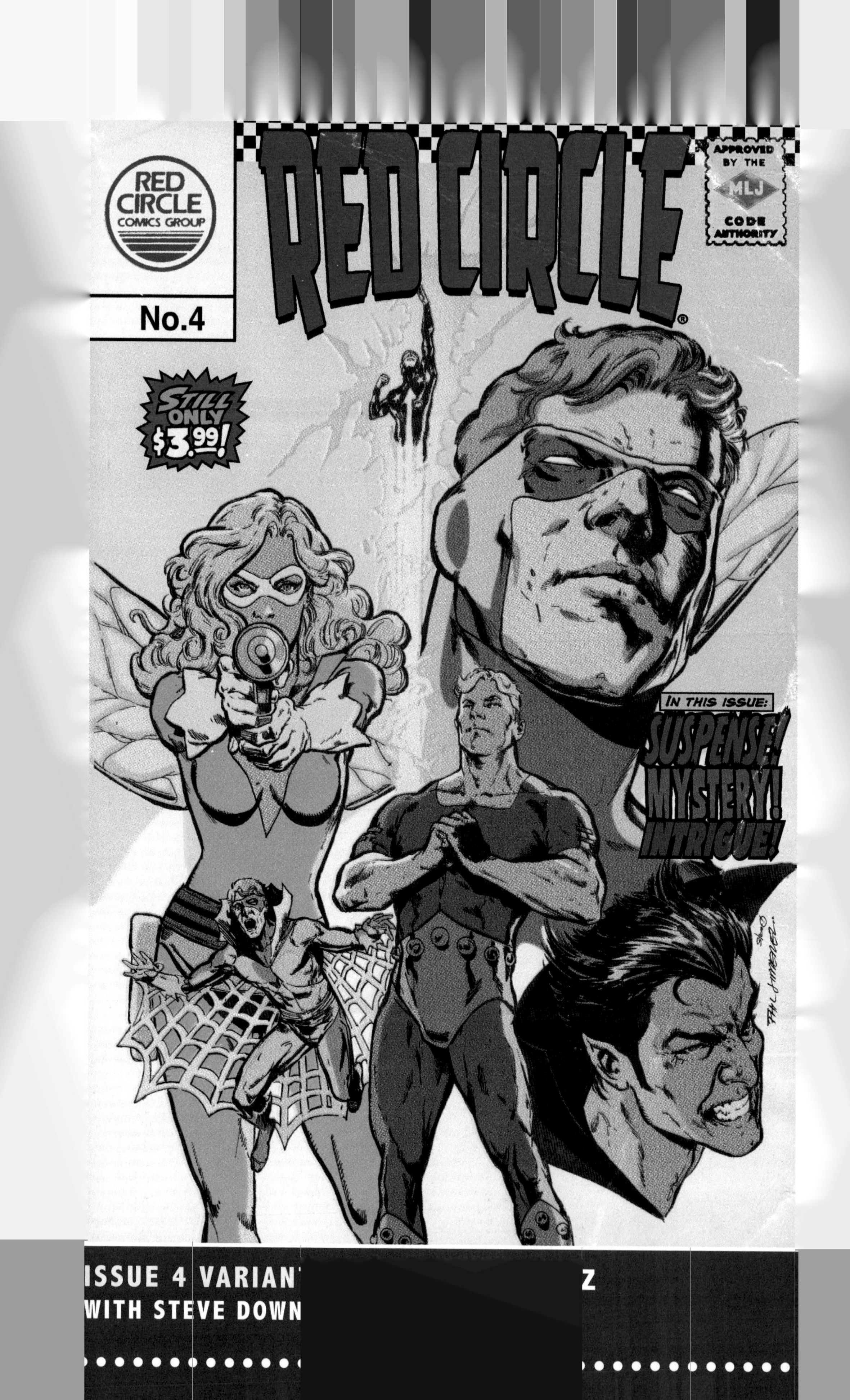
RED CIRCLE
COMICS GROUP
No.4
RED CIRCLE
APPROVED BY THE MLJ CODE AUTHORITY
STILL ONLY $3.99!
IN THIS ISSUE:
SUSPENSE! MYSTERY! INTRIGUE!

ISSUE 4 VARIANT [redacted] Z
WITH STEVE DOWN [redacted]

BONUS STORY

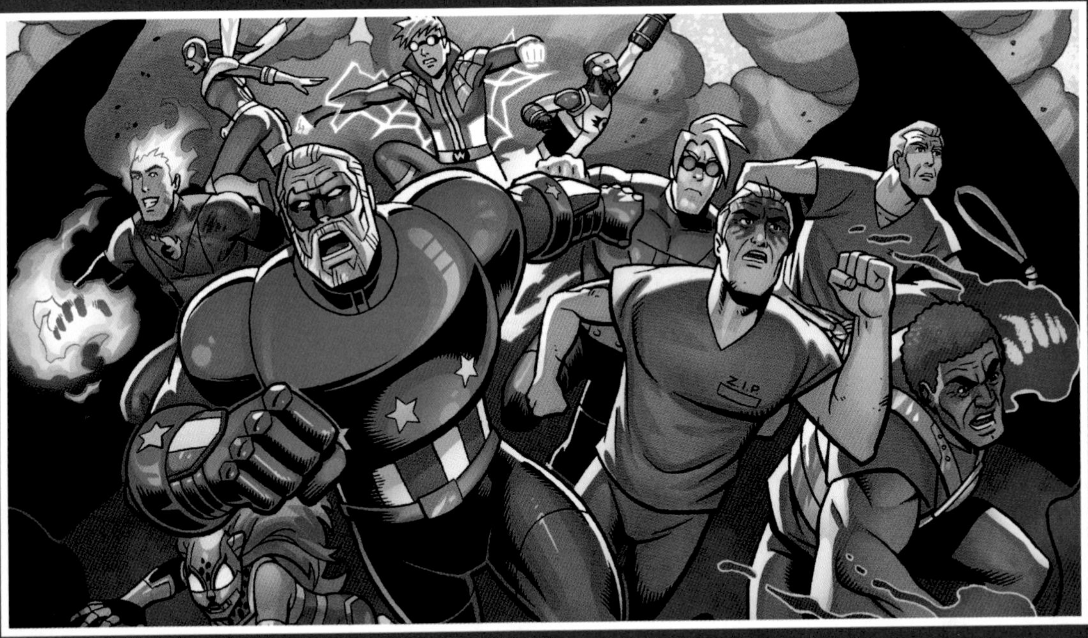

Z.I.P.

When the Brain Emperor, the most powerful villain the Mighty Crusaders had ever faced, returned from the grave and struck down his old foes, a new generation of heroes rose up to defend the world from his reign of terror. These heroes became known as the New Crusaders!

During one of the Brain Emperor's attacks on a high security prison, the New Crusaders sprang into action, but were nearly overwhelmed. As they fought to control the pandemonium (and stay alive) the Brain Emperor released a small army of super villains and made them swear loyalty to him. He escaped to Impact City with all but one...

STORY BY
IAN FLYNN

LETTERING BY
JOHN WORKMAN

EDITOR-IN-CHIEF
VICTOR GORELICK

PUBLISHER
JON GOLDWATER

PENCILS
ALITHA MARTINEZ

INKS BY
RICK BRYANT

COLORS BY
STEVE DOWNER

EDITORS
ALEX SEGURA AND
VINCENT LOVALLO

SPECIAL THANKS TO
PAUL KAMINSKI

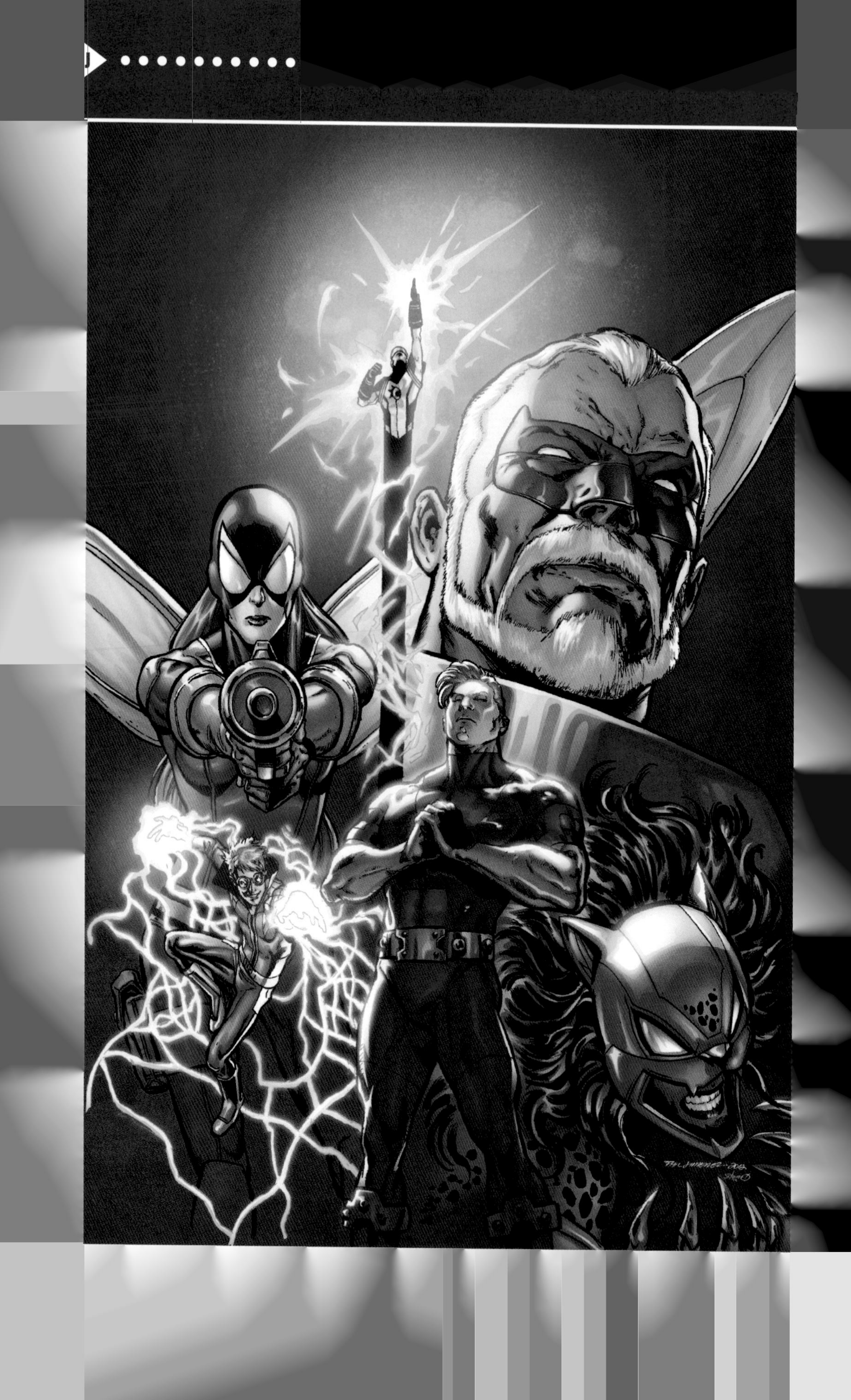

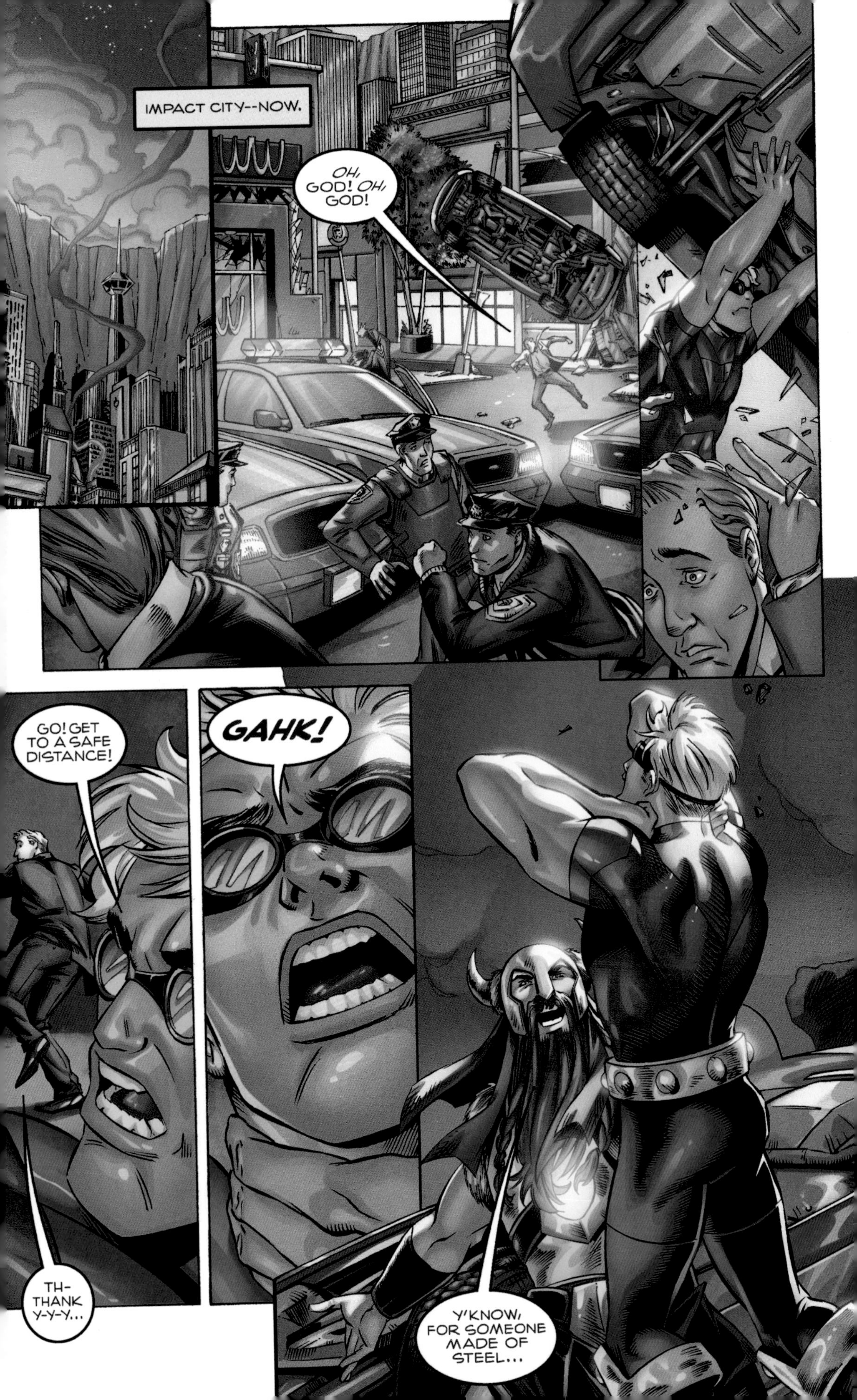
IMPACT CITY--NOW.
OH, GOD! OH, GOD!
GO! GET TO A SAFE DISTANCE!
TH- THANK Y-Y-Y...
GAHK!
Y'KNOW, FOR SOMEONE MADE OF STEEL...

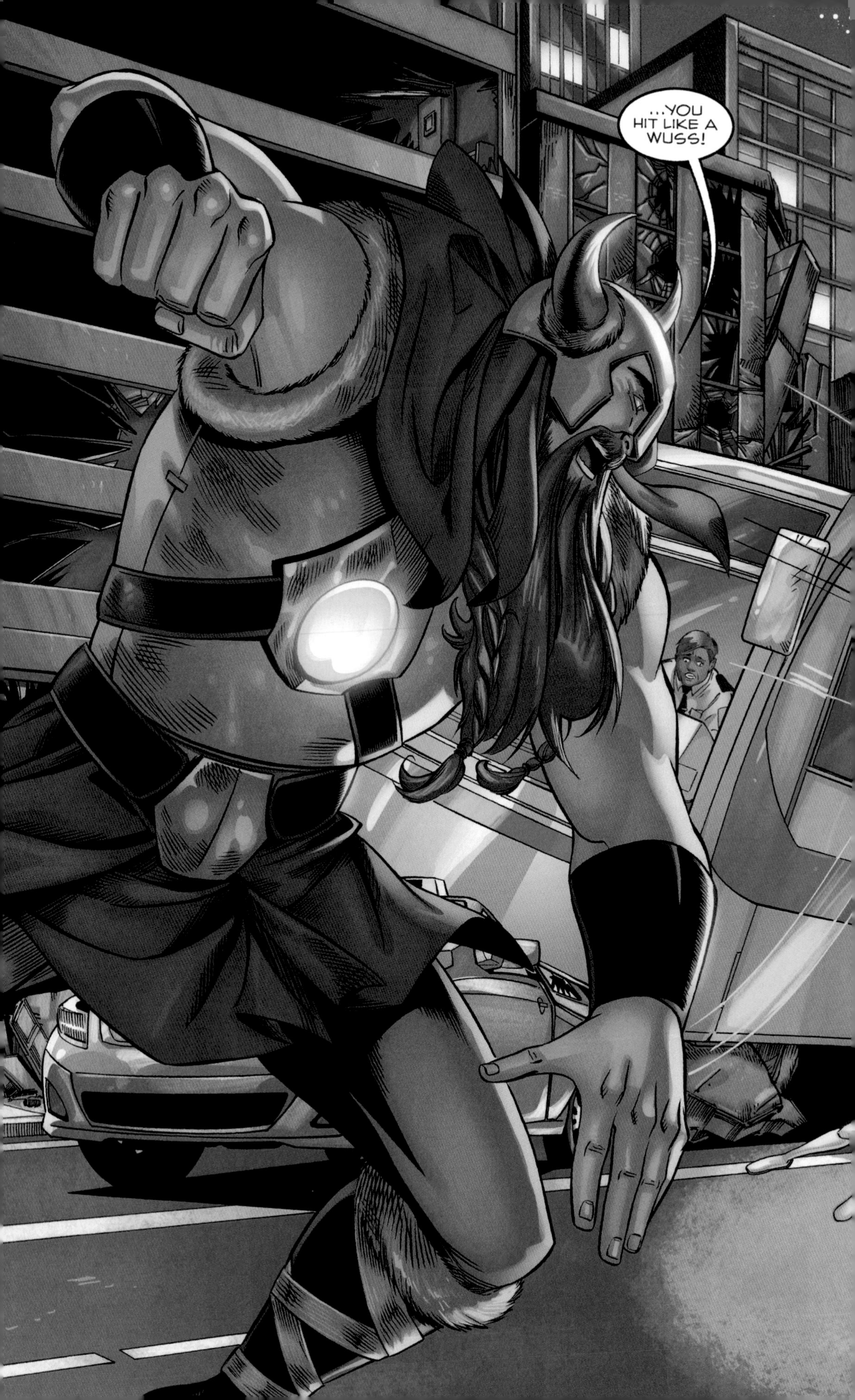
...YOU HIT LIKE A WUSS!

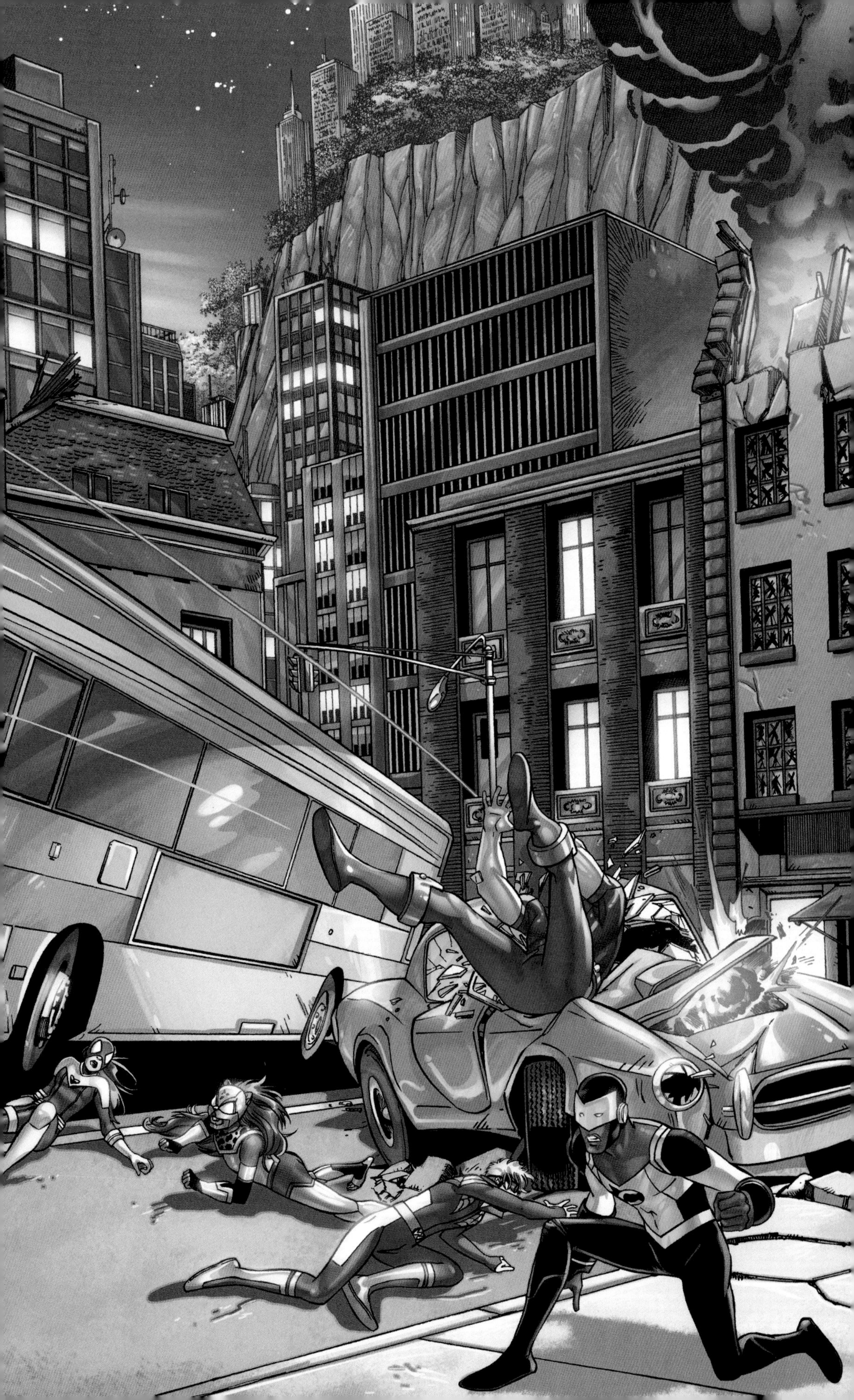

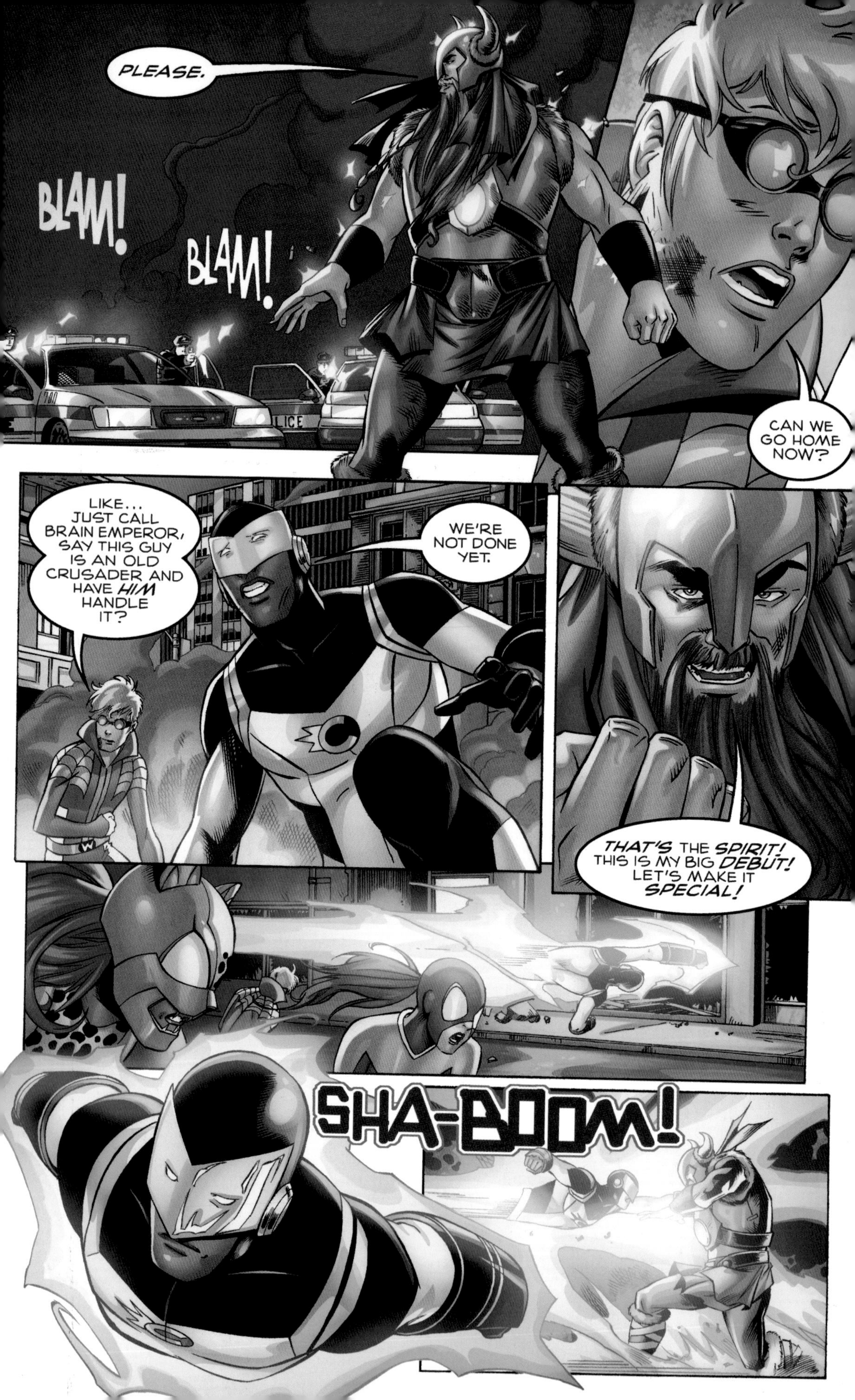
PLEASE.
BLAM!
BLAM!
CAN WE GO HOME NOW?
LIKE... JUST CALL BRAIN EMPEROR, SAY THIS GUY IS AN OLD CRUSADER AND HAVE HIM HANDLE IT?
WE'RE NOT DONE YET.
THAT'S THE SPIRIT! THIS IS MY BIG DEBUT! LET'S MAKE IT SPECIAL!
SHA-BOOM!

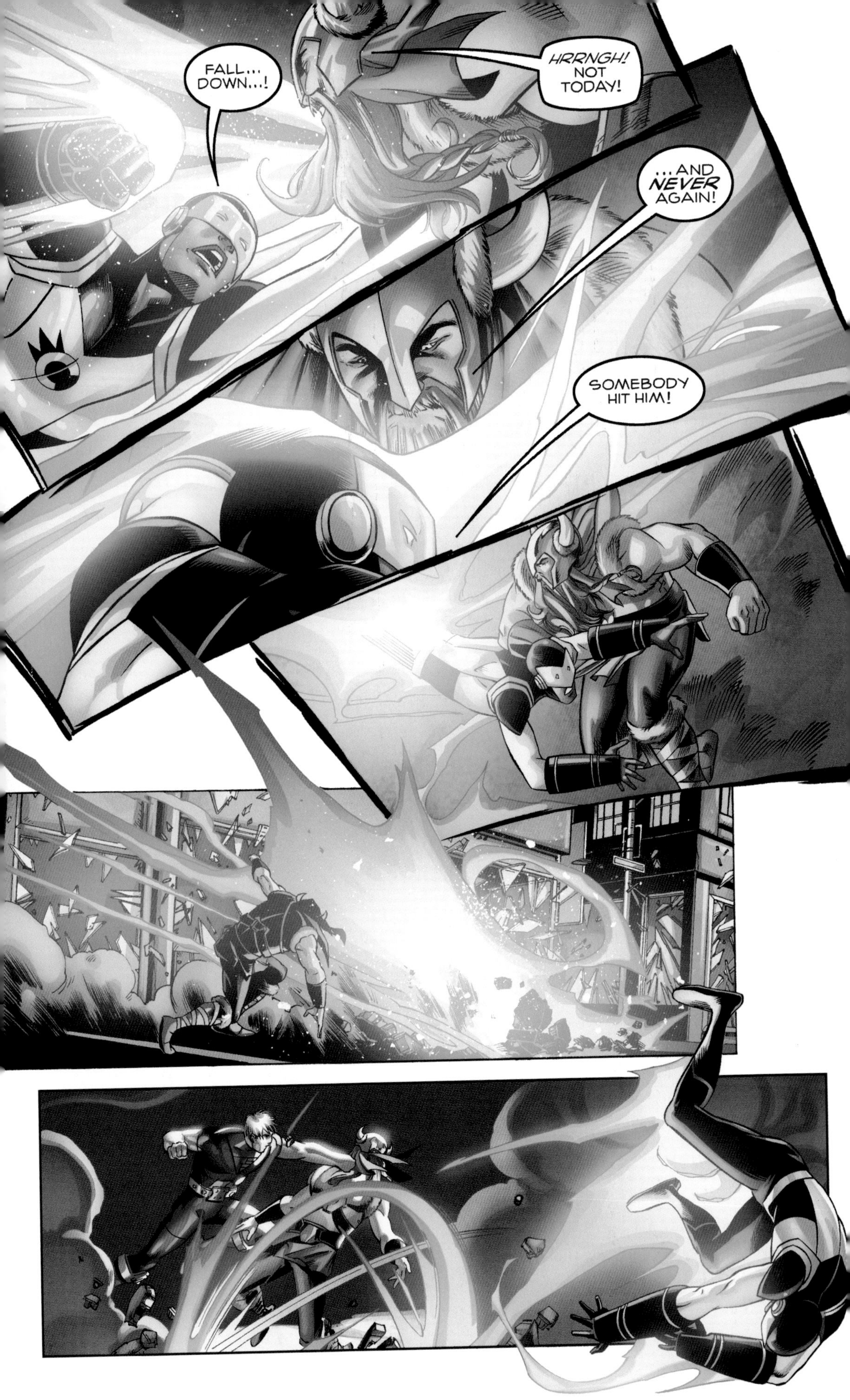
FALL... DOWN...!
HRRNGH! NOT TODAY!
...AND NEVER AGAIN!
SOMEBODY HIT HIM!

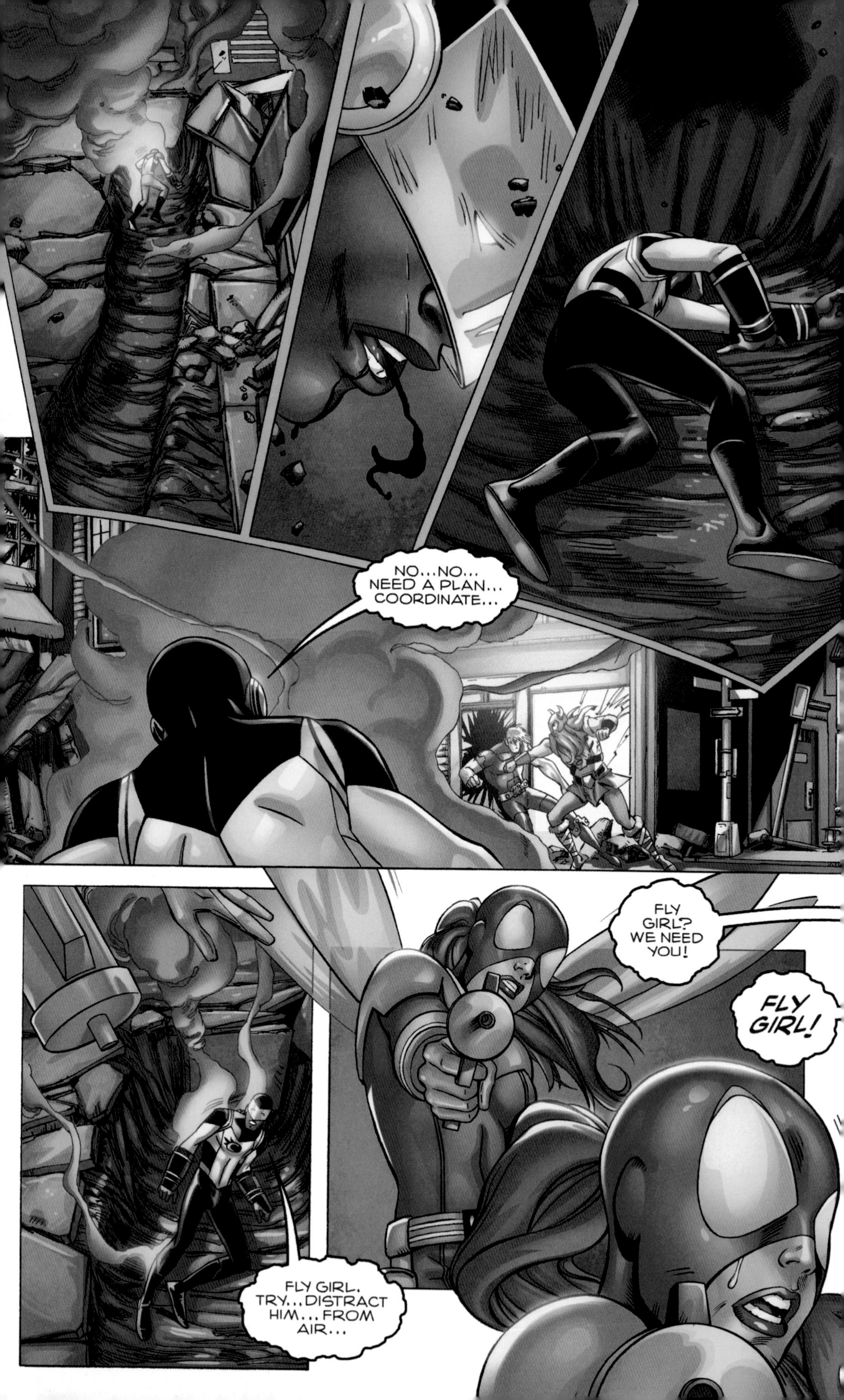
NO...NO...
NEED A PLAN...
COORDINATE...
FLY GIRL? WE NEED YOU!
FLY GIRL!
FLY GIRL. TRY...DISTRACT HIM...FROM AIR...

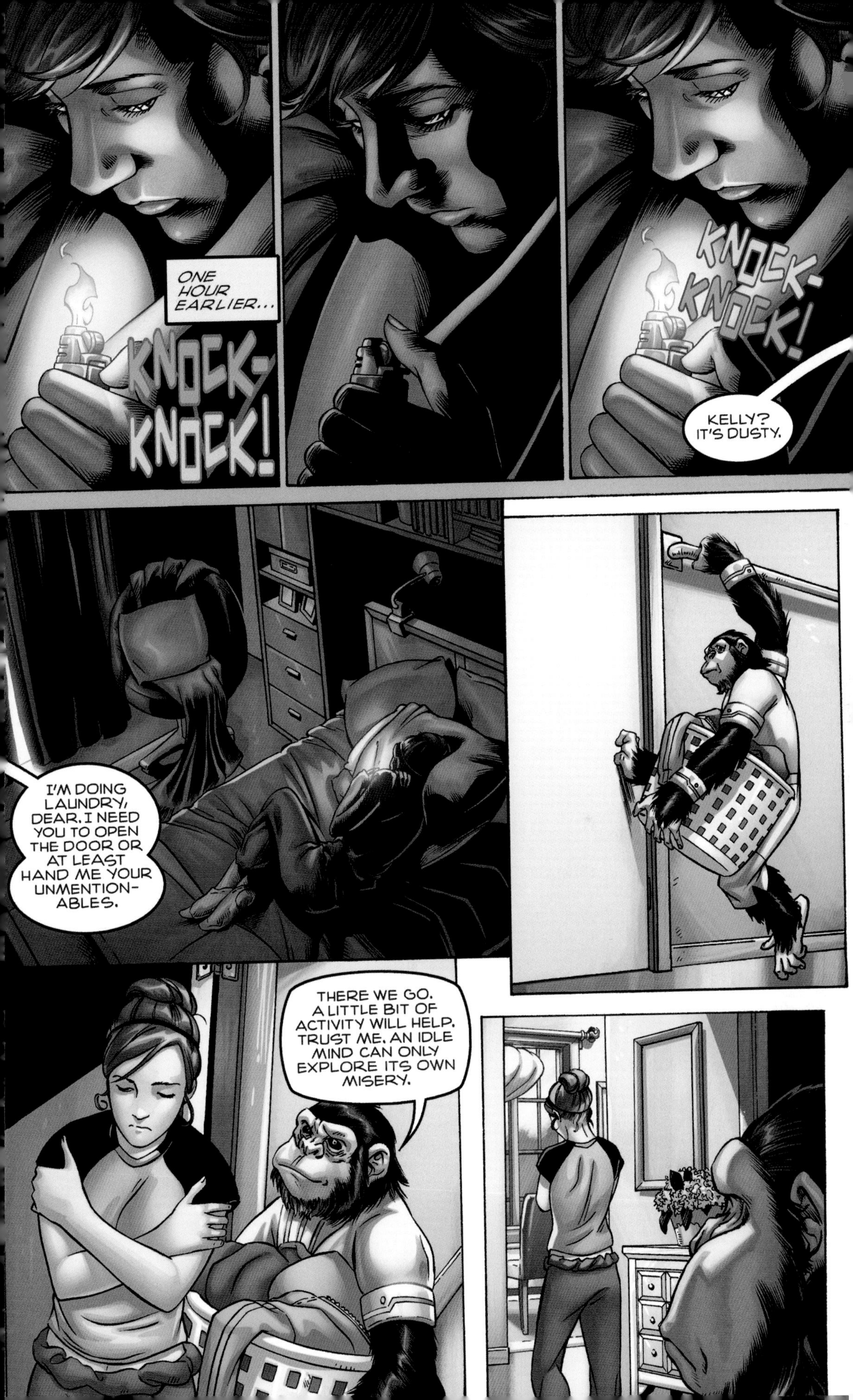
ONE HOUR EARLIER...
KNOCK-KNOCK!
KNOCK-KNOCK!
KELLY? IT'S DUSTY.
I'M DOING LAUNDRY, DEAR. I NEED YOU TO OPEN THE DOOR OR AT LEAST HAND ME YOUR UNMENTION-ABLES.
THERE WE GO. A LITTLE BIT OF ACTIVITY WILL HELP. TRUST ME. AN IDLE MIND CAN ONLY EXPLORE ITS OWN MISERY.

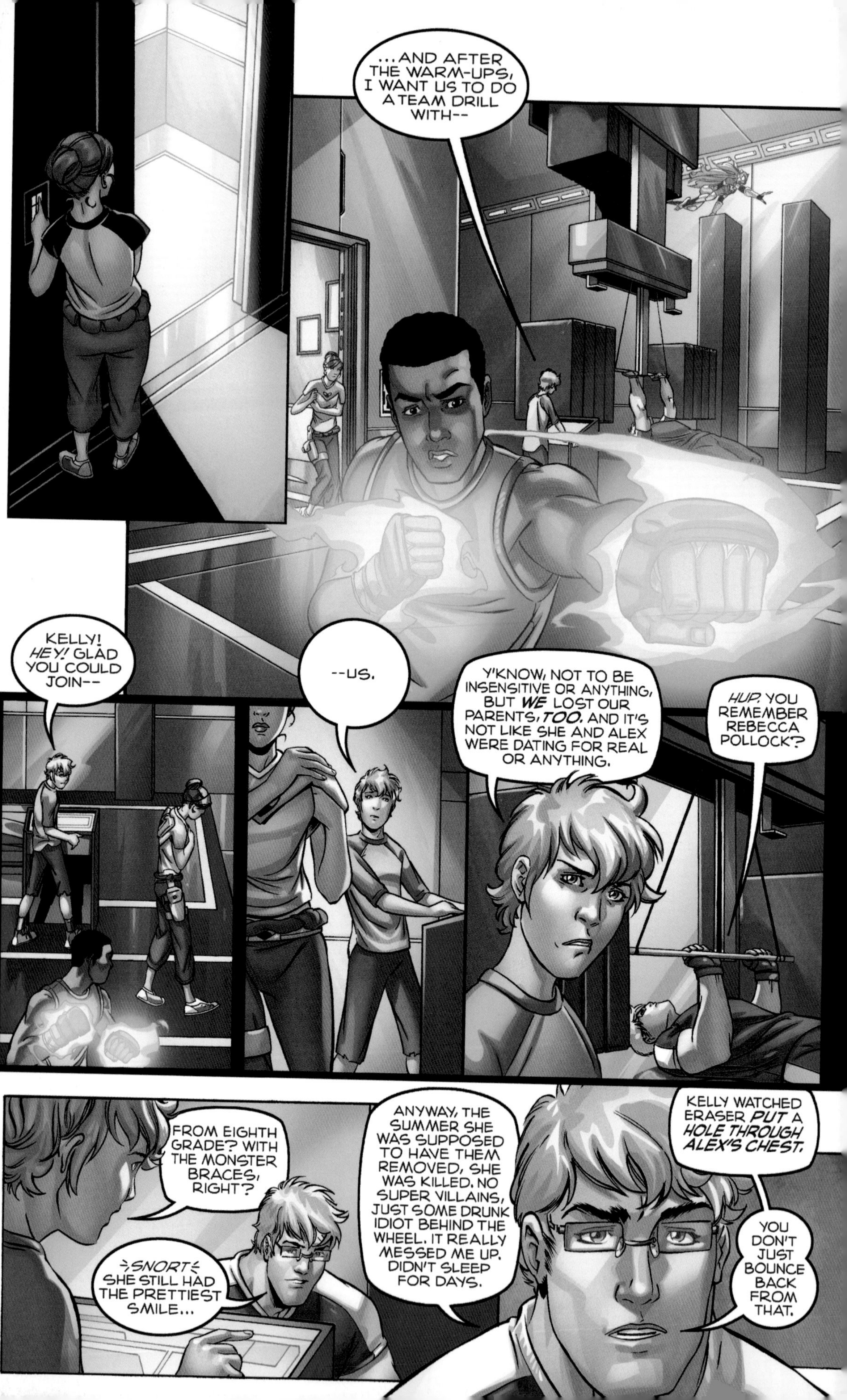
...AND AFTER THE WARM-UPS, I WANT US TO DO A TEAM DRILL WITH--
KELLY! HEY! GLAD YOU COULD JOIN--
--US.
Y'KNOW, NOT TO BE INSENSITIVE OR ANYTHING, BUT WE LOST OUR PARENTS, TOO. AND IT'S NOT LIKE SHE AND ALEX WERE DATING FOR REAL OR ANYTHING.
HUP. YOU REMEMBER REBECCA POLLOCK?
FROM EIGHTH GRADE? WITH THE MONSTER BRACES, RIGHT?
≻SNORT≺ SHE STILL HAD THE PRETTIEST SMILE...
ANYWAY, THE SUMMER SHE WAS SUPPOSED TO HAVE THEM REMOVED, SHE WAS KILLED. NO SUPER VILLAINS, JUST SOME DRUNK IDIOT BEHIND THE WHEEL. IT REALLY MESSED ME UP. DIDN'T SLEEP FOR DAYS.
KELLY WATCHED ERASER PUT A HOLE THROUGH ALEX'S CHEST.
YOU DON'T JUST BOUNCE BACK FROM THAT.

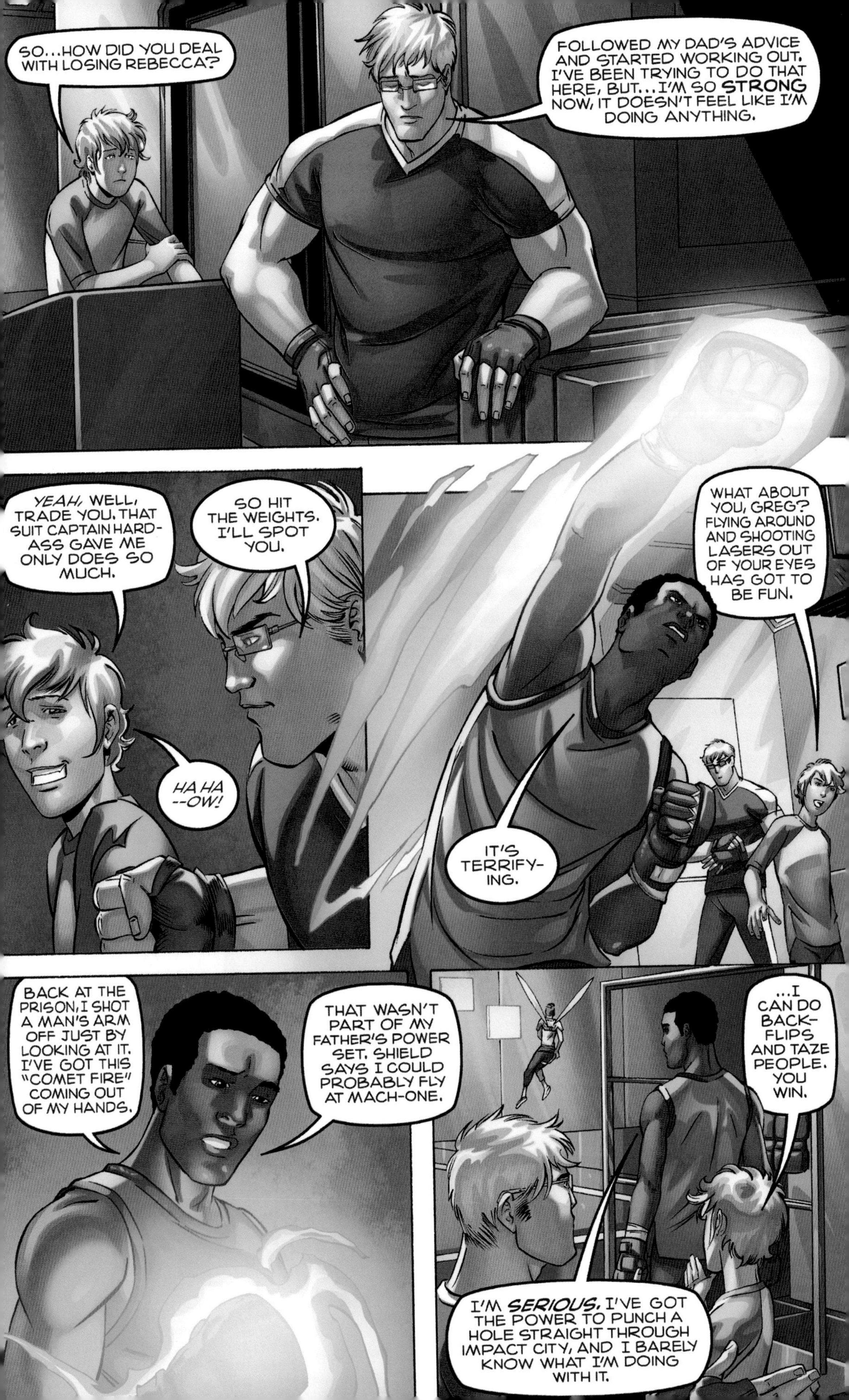
SO...HOW DID YOU DEAL WITH LOSING REBECCA?
FOLLOWED MY DAD'S ADVICE AND STARTED WORKING OUT. I'VE BEEN TRYING TO DO THAT HERE, BUT...I'M SO **STRONG** NOW, IT DOESN'T FEEL LIKE I'M DOING ANYTHING.
YEAH, WELL, TRADE YOU. THAT SUIT CAPTAIN HARD-ASS GAVE ME ONLY DOES SO MUCH.
SO HIT THE WEIGHTS. I'LL SPOT YOU.
HA HA --OW!
WHAT ABOUT YOU, GREG? FLYING AROUND AND SHOOTING LASERS OUT OF YOUR EYES HAS GOT TO BE FUN.
IT'S TERRIFY-ING.
BACK AT THE PRISON, I SHOT A MAN'S ARM OFF JUST BY LOOKING AT IT. I'VE GOT THIS "COMET FIRE" COMING OUT OF MY HANDS.
THAT WASN'T PART OF MY FATHER'S POWER SET. SHIELD SAYS I COULD PROBABLY FLY AT MACH-ONE.
...I CAN DO BACK-FLIPS AND TAZE PEOPLE. YOU WIN.
I'M ***SERIOUS.*** I'VE GOT THE POWER TO PUNCH A HOLE STRAIGHT THROUGH IMPACT CITY, AND I BARELY KNOW WHAT I'M DOING WITH IT.

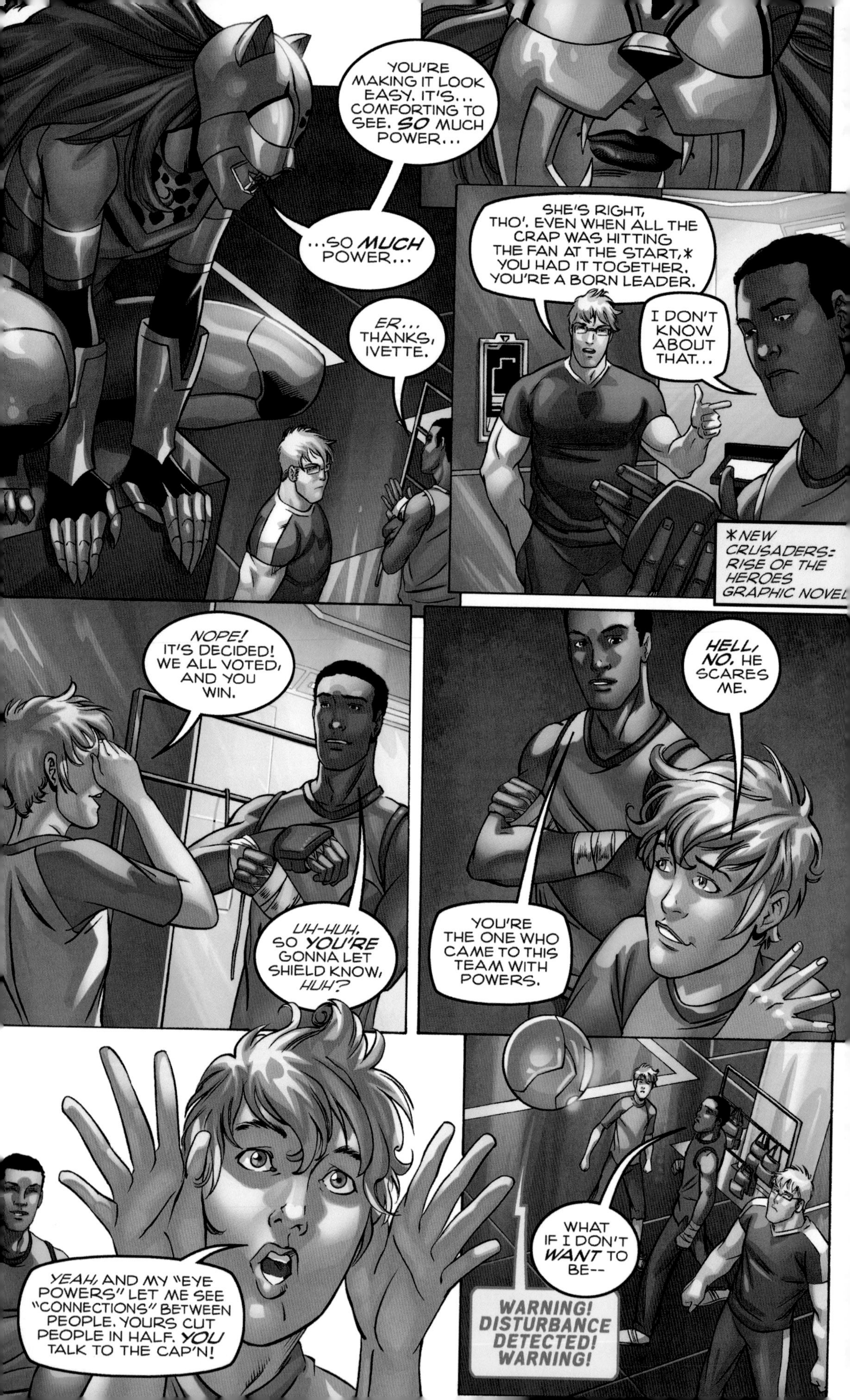
YOU'RE MAKING IT LOOK EASY. IT'S... COMFORTING TO SEE. SO MUCH POWER...
...SO MUCH POWER...
ER... THANKS, IVETTE.
SHE'S RIGHT, THO'. EVEN WHEN ALL THE CRAP WAS HITTING THE FAN AT THE START,* YOU HAD IT TOGETHER. YOU'RE A BORN LEADER.
I DON'T KNOW ABOUT THAT...
*NEW CRUSADERS: RISE OF THE HEROES GRAPHIC NOVEL
NOPE! IT'S DECIDED! WE ALL VOTED, AND YOU WIN.
UH-HUH. SO YOU'RE GONNA LET SHIELD KNOW, HUH?
HELL, NO. HE SCARES ME.
YOU'RE THE ONE WHO CAME TO THIS TEAM WITH POWERS.
YEAH, AND MY "EYE POWERS" LET ME SEE "CONNECTIONS" BETWEEN PEOPLE. YOURS CUT PEOPLE IN HALF. YOU TALK TO THE CAP'N!
WHAT IF I DON'T WANT TO BE--
WARNING! DISTURBANCE DETECTED! WARNING!

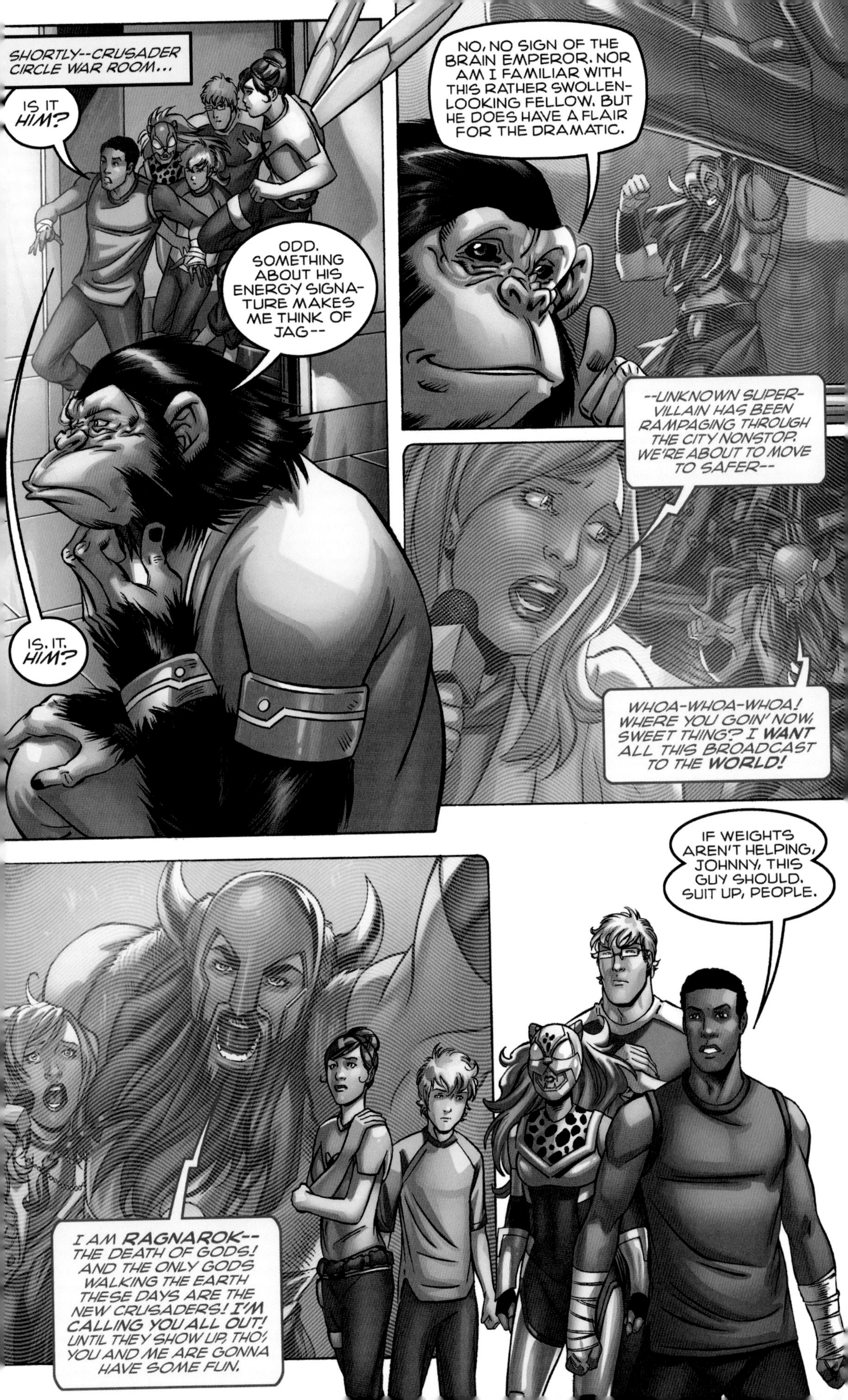
SHORTLY--CRUSADER CIRCLE WAR ROOM...
IS IT HIM?
ODD. SOMETHING ABOUT HIS ENERGY SIGNATURE MAKES ME THINK OF JAG--
IS. IT. HIM?
NO, NO SIGN OF THE BRAIN EMPEROR. NOR AM I FAMILIAR WITH THIS RATHER SWOLLEN-LOOKING FELLOW. BUT HE DOES HAVE A FLAIR FOR THE DRAMATIC.
--UNKNOWN SUPER-VILLAIN HAS BEEN RAMPAGING THROUGH THE CITY NONSTOP. WE'RE ABOUT TO MOVE TO SAFER--
WHOA-WHOA-WHOA! WHERE YOU GOIN' NOW, SWEET THING? I WANT ALL THIS BROADCAST TO THE WORLD!
I AM RAGNAROK-- THE DEATH OF GODS! AND THE ONLY GODS WALKING THE EARTH THESE DAYS ARE THE NEW CRUSADERS! I'M CALLING YOU ALL OUT! UNTIL THEY SHOW UP, THO', YOU AND ME ARE GONNA HAVE SOME FUN.
IF WEIGHTS AREN'T HELPING, JOHNNY, THIS GUY SHOULD. SUIT UP, PEOPLE.

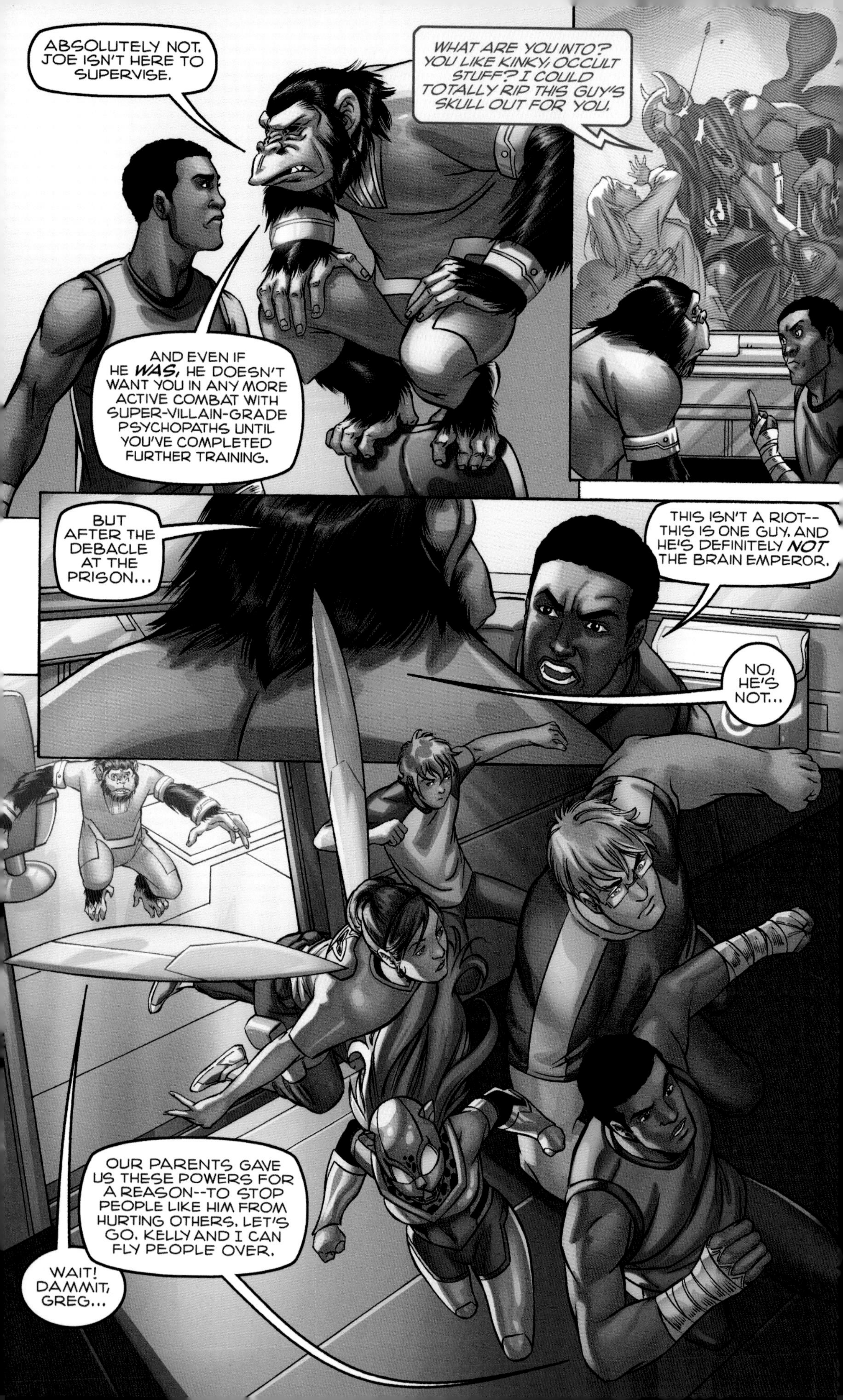
ABSOLUTELY NOT. JOE ISN'T HERE TO SUPERVISE.
WHAT ARE YOU INTO? YOU LIKE KINKY, OCCULT STUFF? I COULD TOTALLY RIP THIS GUY'S SKULL OUT FOR YOU.
AND EVEN IF HE WAS, HE DOESN'T WANT YOU IN ANY MORE ACTIVE COMBAT WITH SUPER-VILLAIN-GRADE PSYCHOPATHS UNTIL YOU'VE COMPLETED FURTHER TRAINING.
BUT AFTER THE DEBACLE AT THE PRISON...
THIS ISN'T A RIOT--THIS IS ONE GUY. AND HE'S DEFINITELY NOT THE BRAIN EMPEROR.
NO, HE'S NOT...
OUR PARENTS GAVE US THESE POWERS FOR A REASON--TO STOP PEOPLE LIKE HIM FROM HURTING OTHERS. LET'S GO. KELLY AND I CAN FLY PEOPLE OVER.
WAIT! DAMMIT, GREG...

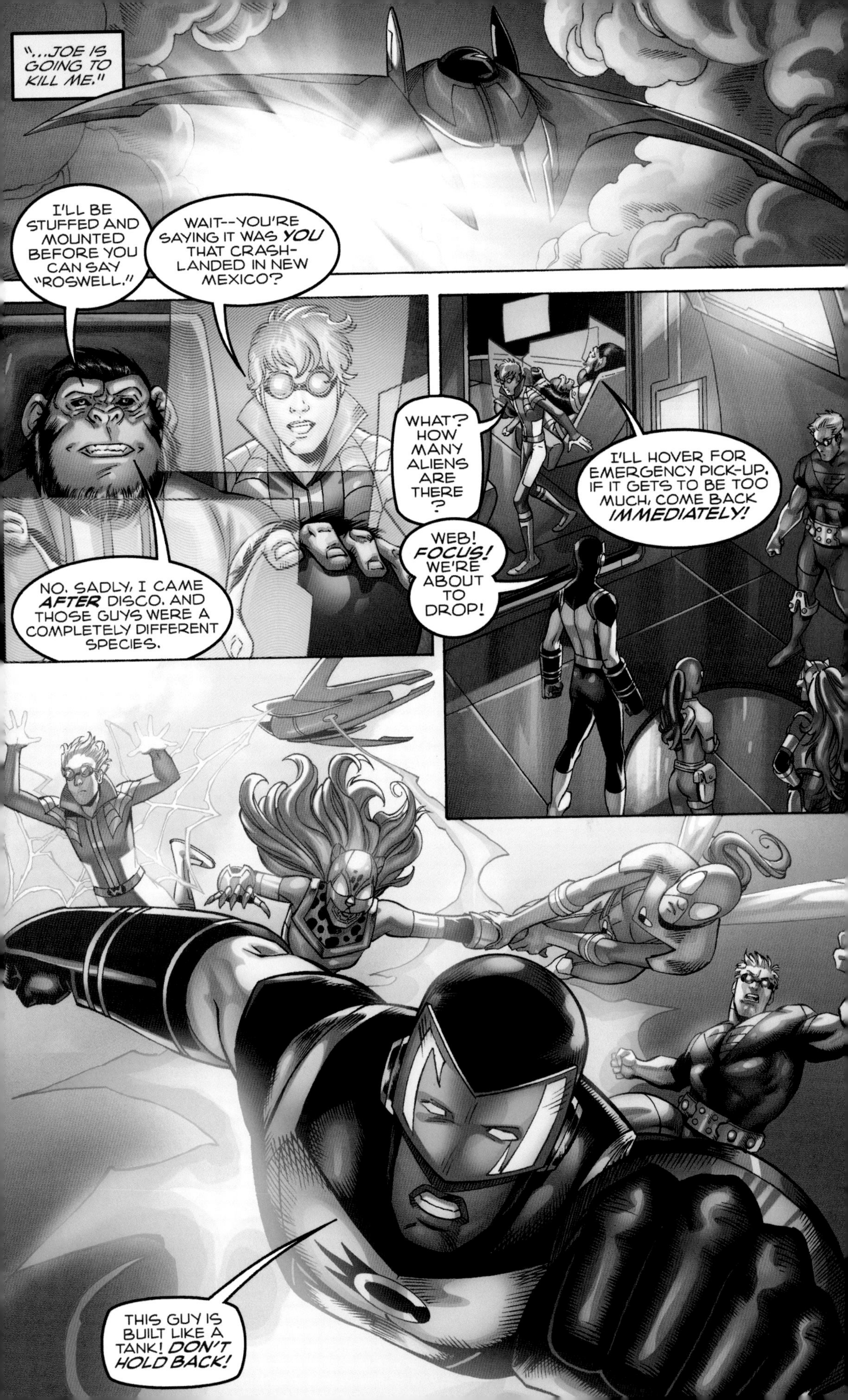
"...JOE IS GOING TO KILL ME."
I'LL BE STUFFED AND MOUNTED BEFORE YOU CAN SAY "ROSWELL."
WAIT--YOU'RE SAYING IT WAS *YOU* THAT CRASH-LANDED IN NEW MEXICO?
NO. SADLY, I CAME **AFTER** DISCO. AND THOSE GUYS WERE A COMPLETELY DIFFERENT SPECIES.
WHAT? HOW MANY ALIENS ARE THERE?
I'LL HOVER FOR EMERGENCY PICK-UP. IF IT GETS TO BE TOO MUCH, COME BACK *IMMEDIATELY!*
WEB! *FOCUS!* WE'RE ABOUT TO DROP!
THIS GUY IS BUILT LIKE A TANK! *DON'T HOLD BACK!*

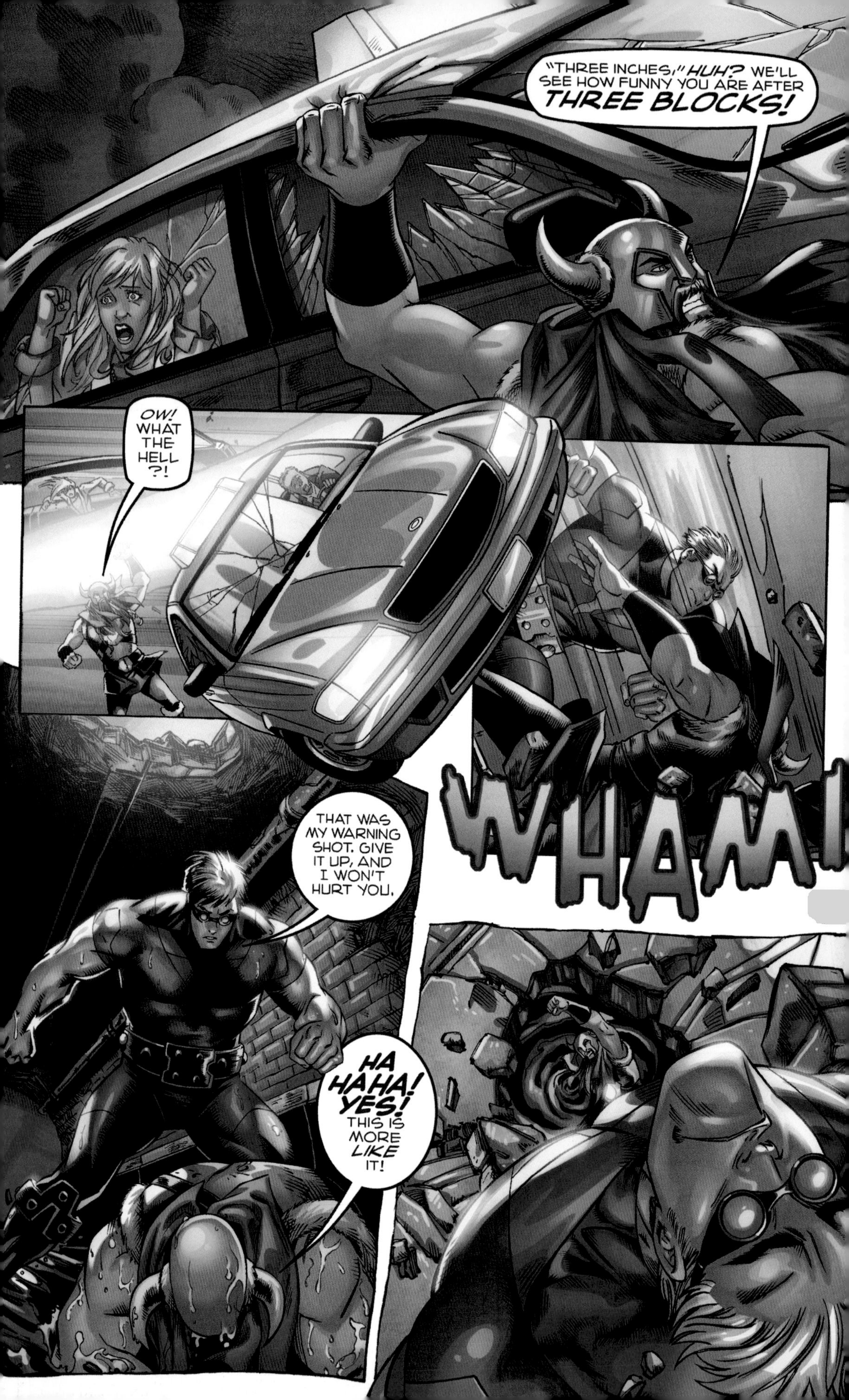
"THREE INCHES," HUH? WE'LL SEE HOW FUNNY YOU ARE AFTER THREE BLOCKS!
OW! WHAT THE HELL ?!
WHAM!
THAT WAS MY WARNING SHOT. GIVE IT UP, AND I WON'T HURT YOU.
HA HAHA! YES! THIS IS MORE LIKE IT!

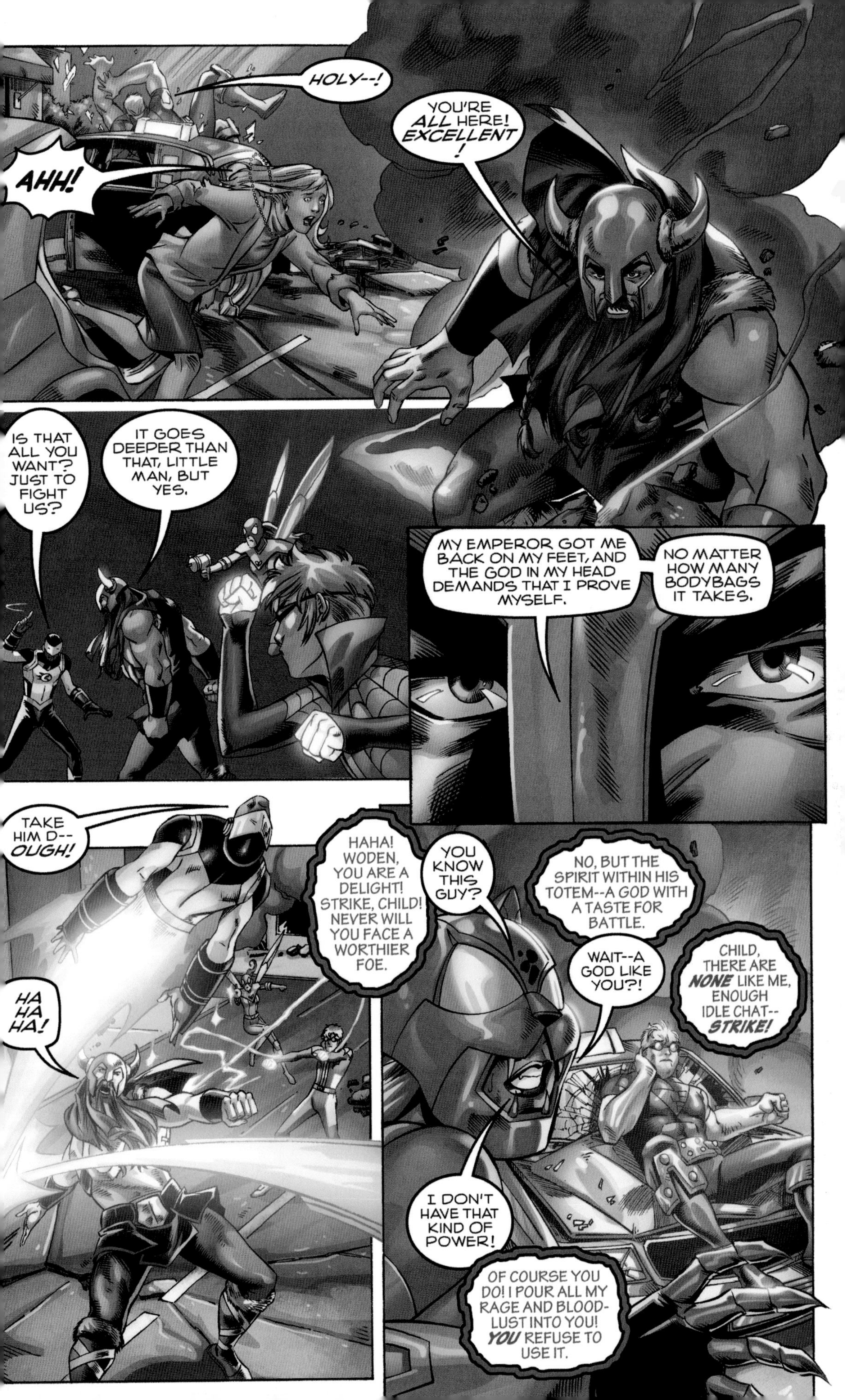
HOLY--!
AHH!
YOU'RE ALL HERE! EXCELLENT!
IS THAT ALL YOU WANT? JUST TO FIGHT US?
IT GOES DEEPER THAN THAT, LITTLE MAN, BUT YES.
MY EMPEROR GOT ME BACK ON MY FEET, AND THE GOD IN MY HEAD DEMANDS THAT I PROVE MYSELF.
NO MATTER HOW MANY BODYBAGS IT TAKES.
TAKE HIM D-- OUGH!
HA HA HA!
HAHA! WODEN, YOU ARE A DELIGHT! STRIKE, CHILD! NEVER WILL YOU FACE A WORTHIER FOE.
YOU KNOW THIS GUY?
NO, BUT THE SPIRIT WITHIN HIS TOTEM--A GOD WITH A TASTE FOR BATTLE.
WAIT--A GOD LIKE YOU?!
CHILD, THERE ARE NONE LIKE ME, ENOUGH IDLE CHAT-- STRIKE!
I DON'T HAVE THAT KIND OF POWER!
OF COURSE YOU DO! I POUR ALL MY RAGE AND BLOOD-LUST INTO YOU! YOU REFUSE TO USE IT.

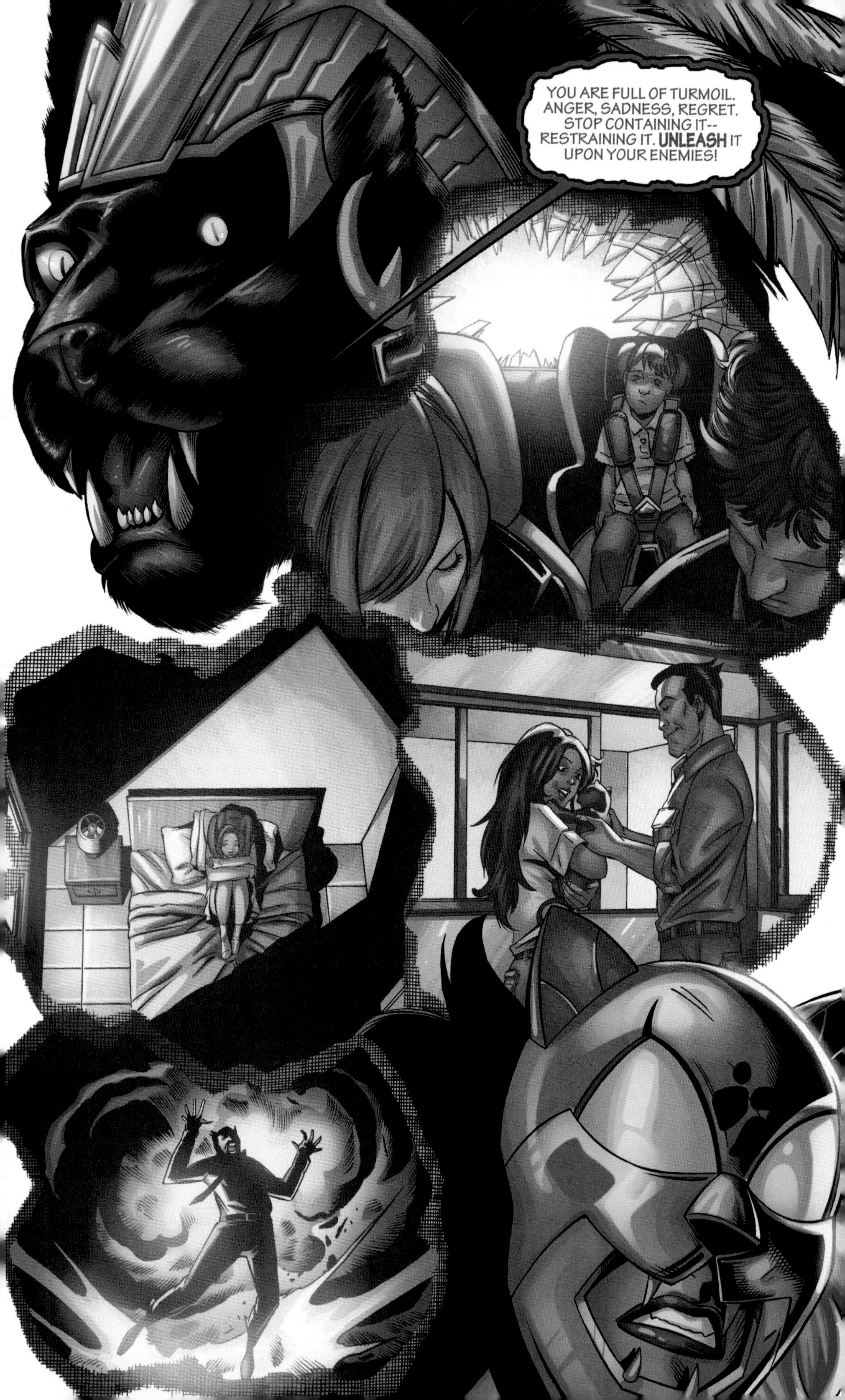
YOU ARE FULL OF TURMOIL. ANGER, SADNESS, REGRET. STOP CONTAINING IT-- RESTRAINING IT. UNLEASH IT UPON YOUR ENEMIES!

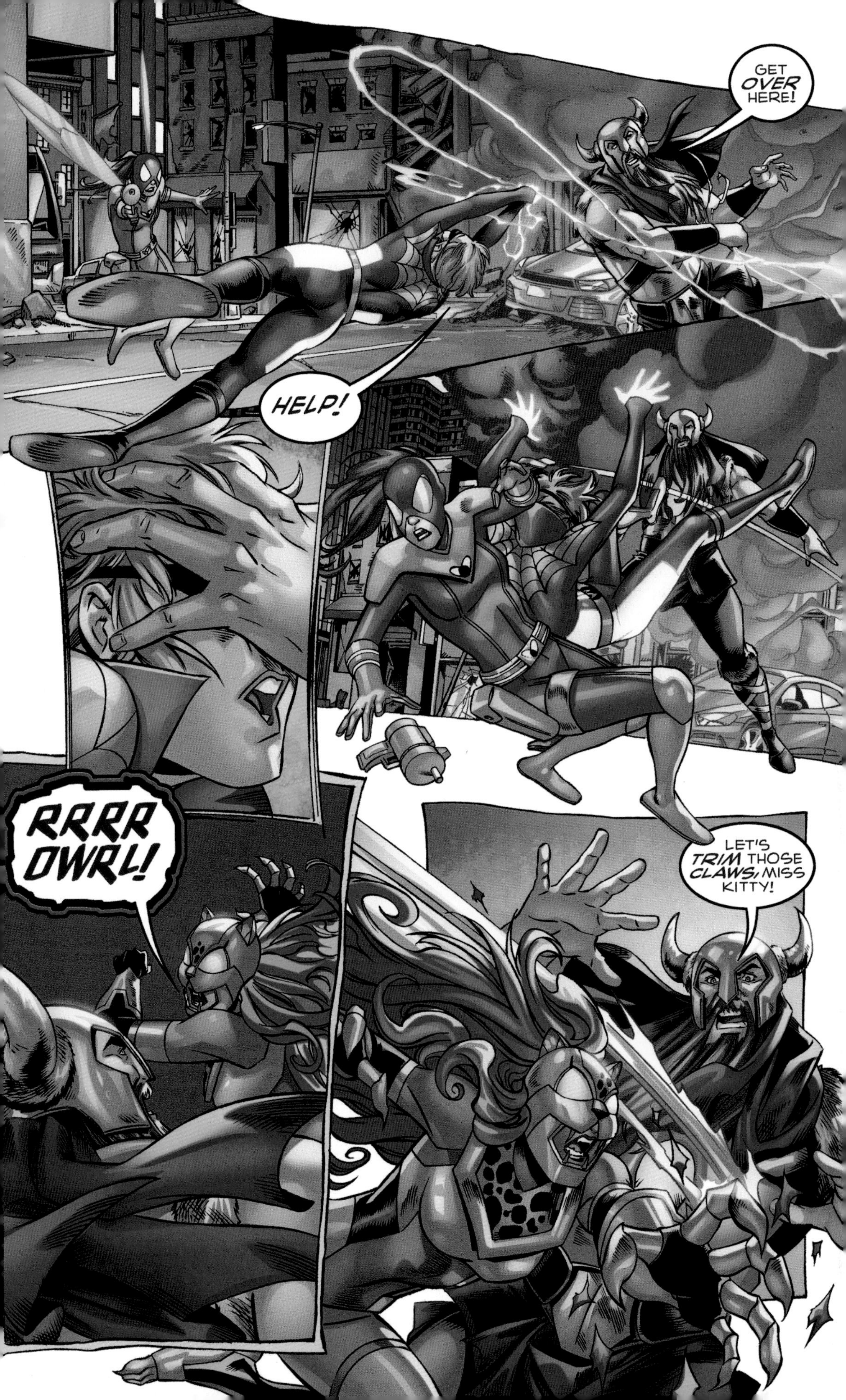
GET OVER HERE!
HELP!
RRRR OWRL!
LET'S TRIM THOSE CLAWS, MISS KITTY!

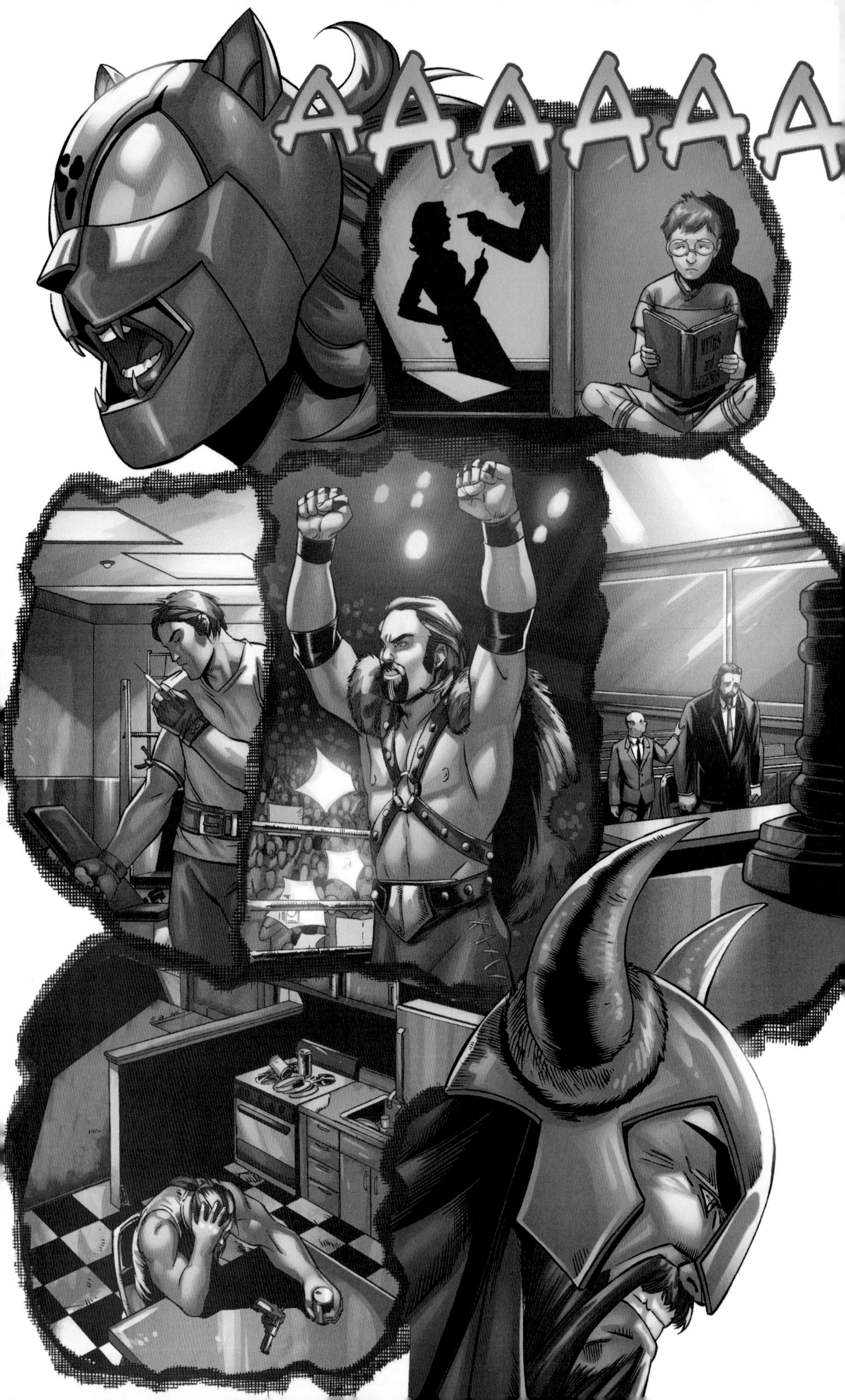
AAAAAA

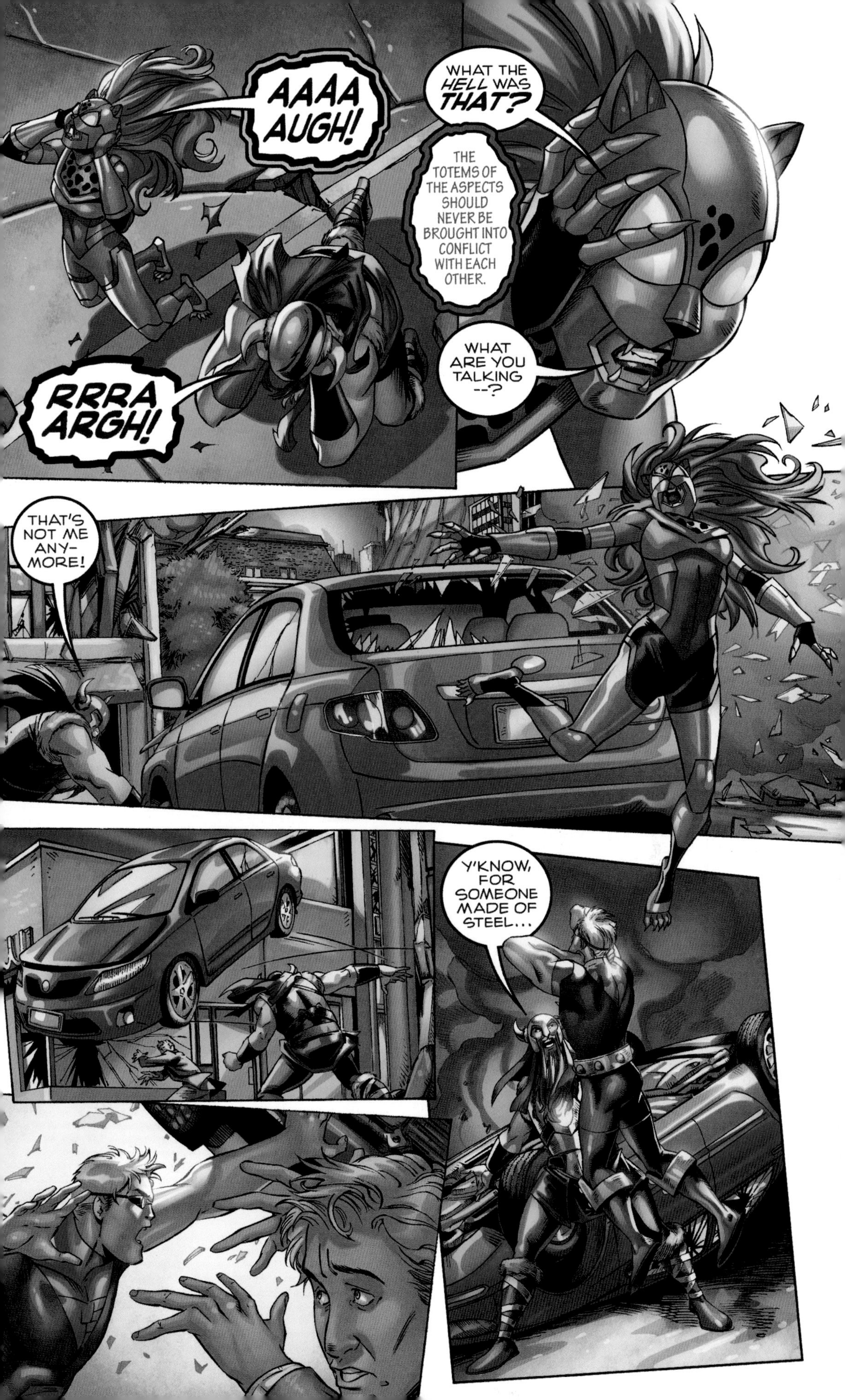
AAAA AUGH!
WHAT THE HELL WAS THAT?
THE TOTEMS OF THE ASPECTS SHOULD NEVER BE BROUGHT INTO CONFLICT WITH EACH OTHER.
RRRA ARGH!
WHAT ARE YOU TALKING --?
THAT'S NOT ME ANY-MORE!
Y'KNOW, FOR SOMEONE MADE OF STEEL...

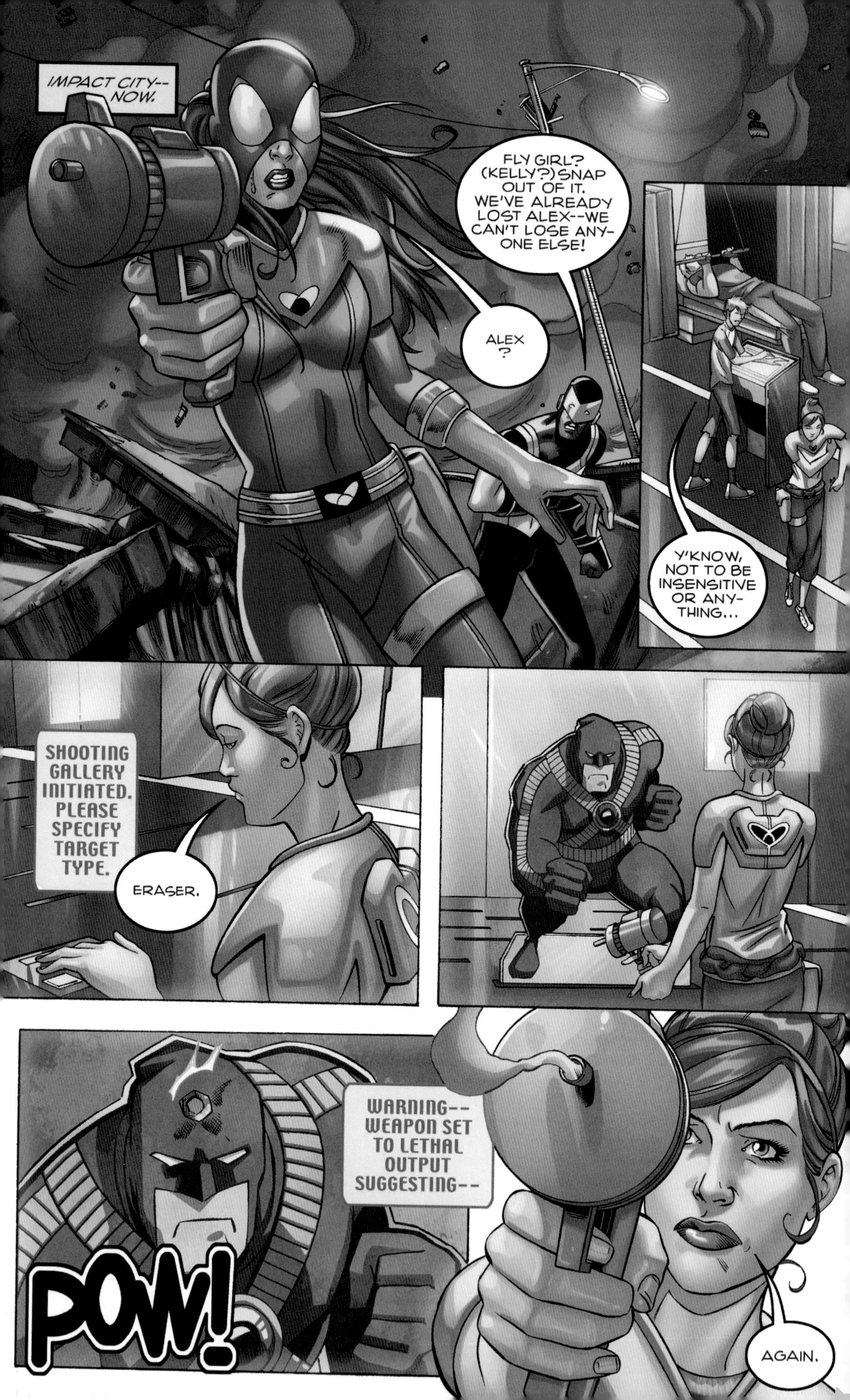
IMPACT CITY-- NOW.
FLY GIRL? (KELLY?) SNAP OUT OF IT. WE'VE ALREADY LOST ALEX--WE CAN'T LOSE ANY-ONE ELSE!
ALEX?
Y'KNOW, NOT TO BE INSENSITIVE OR ANY-THING...
SHOOTING GALLERY INITIATED. PLEASE SPECIFY TARGET TYPE.
ERASER.
WARNING-- WEAPON SET TO LETHAL OUTPUT SUGGESTING--
POW!
AGAIN.

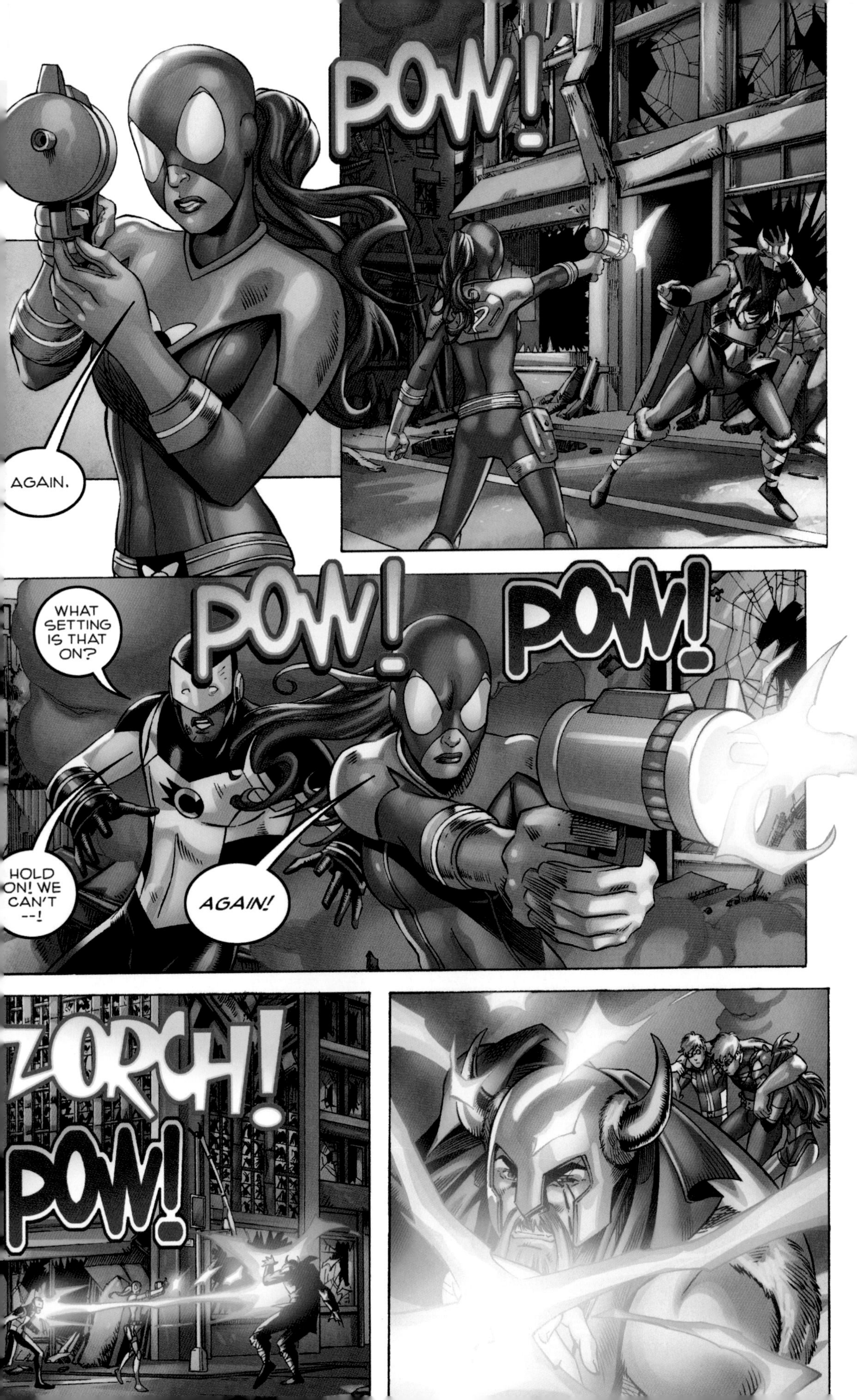
AGAIN.
POW!
WHAT SETTING IS THAT ON?
POW!
POW!
HOLD ON! WE CAN'T --!
AGAIN!
ZORCH!
POW!

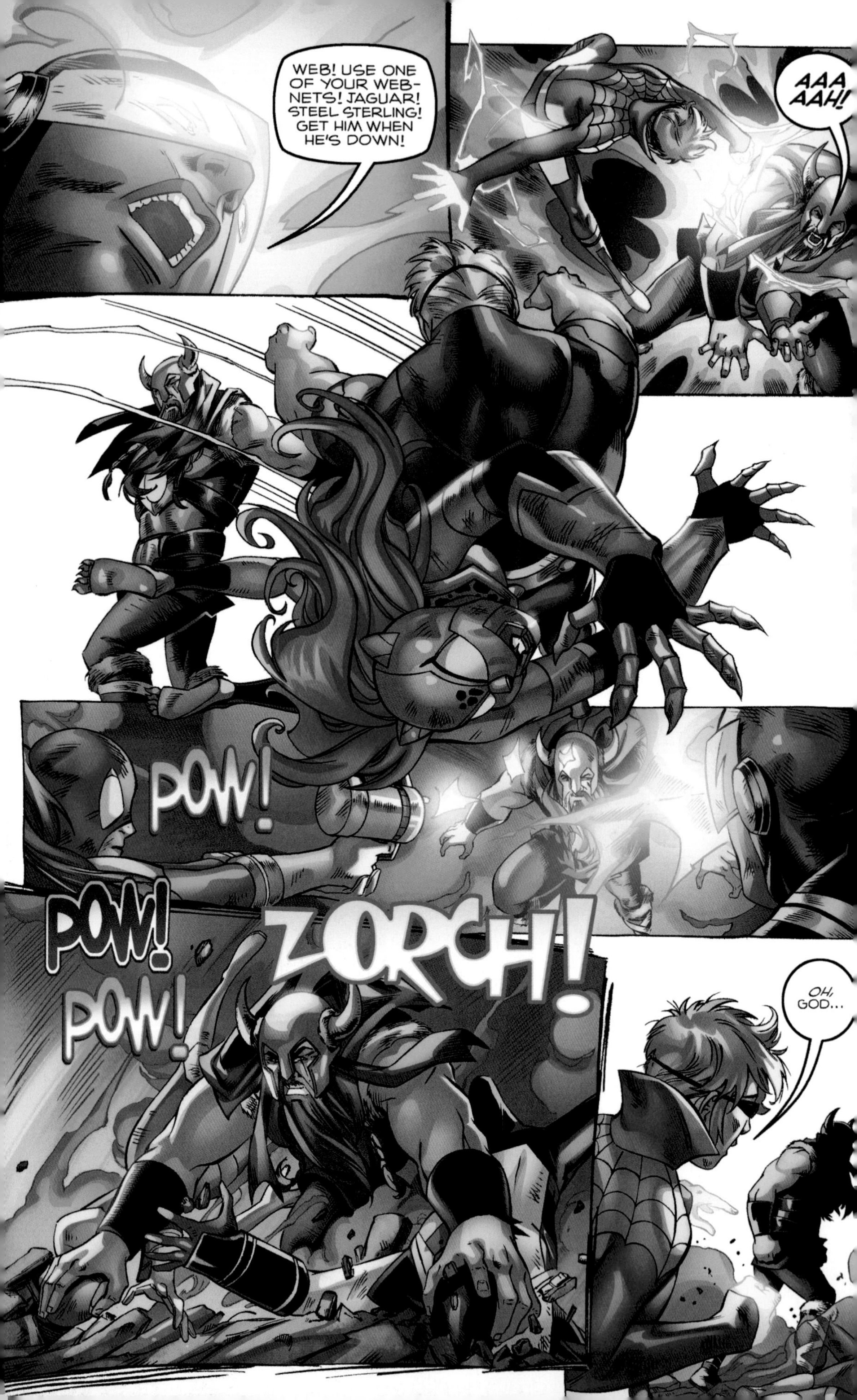

WEB! USE ONE OF YOUR WEB-NETS! JAGUAR! STEEL STERLING! GET HIM WHEN HE'S DOWN!
AAAAAH!
POW!
POW!
POW!
ZORCH!
OH, GOD...

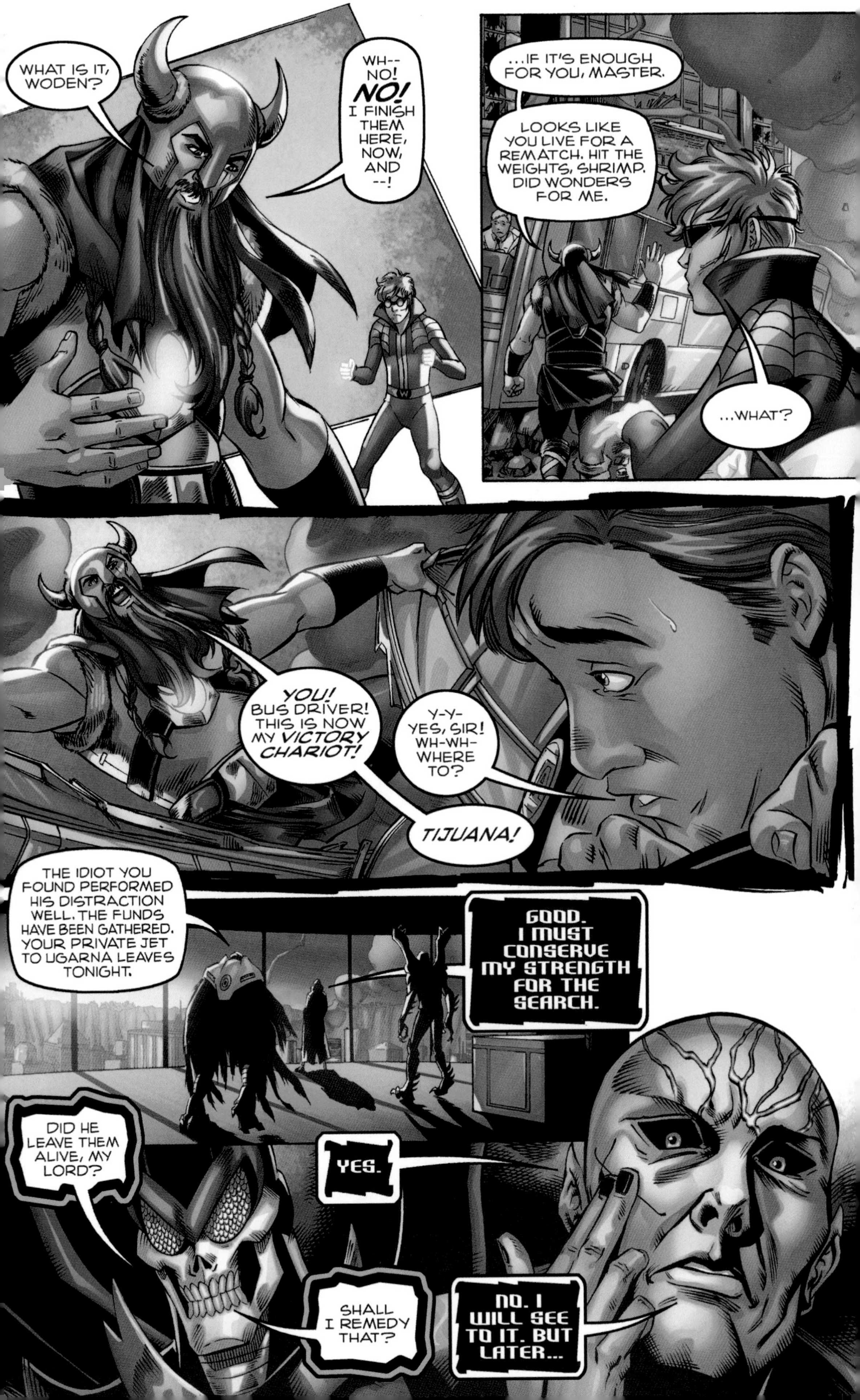
WHAT IS IT, WODEN?
WH-- NO! NO! I FINISH THEM HERE, NOW, AND --!
...IF IT'S ENOUGH FOR YOU, MASTER.
LOOKS LIKE YOU LIVE FOR A REMATCH. HIT THE WEIGHTS, SHRIMP. DID WONDERS FOR ME.
...WHAT?
YOU! BUS DRIVER! THIS IS NOW MY VICTORY CHARIOT!
Y-Y-YES, SIR! WH-WH-WHERE TO?
TIJUANA!
THE IDIOT YOU FOUND PERFORMED HIS DISTRACTION WELL. THE FUNDS HAVE BEEN GATHERED. YOUR PRIVATE JET TO UGARNA LEAVES TONIGHT.
GOOD. I MUST CONSERVE MY STRENGTH FOR THE SEARCH.
DID HE LEAVE THEM ALIVE, MY LORD?
YES.
SHALL I REMEDY THAT?
NO. I WILL SEE TO IT. BUT LATER...

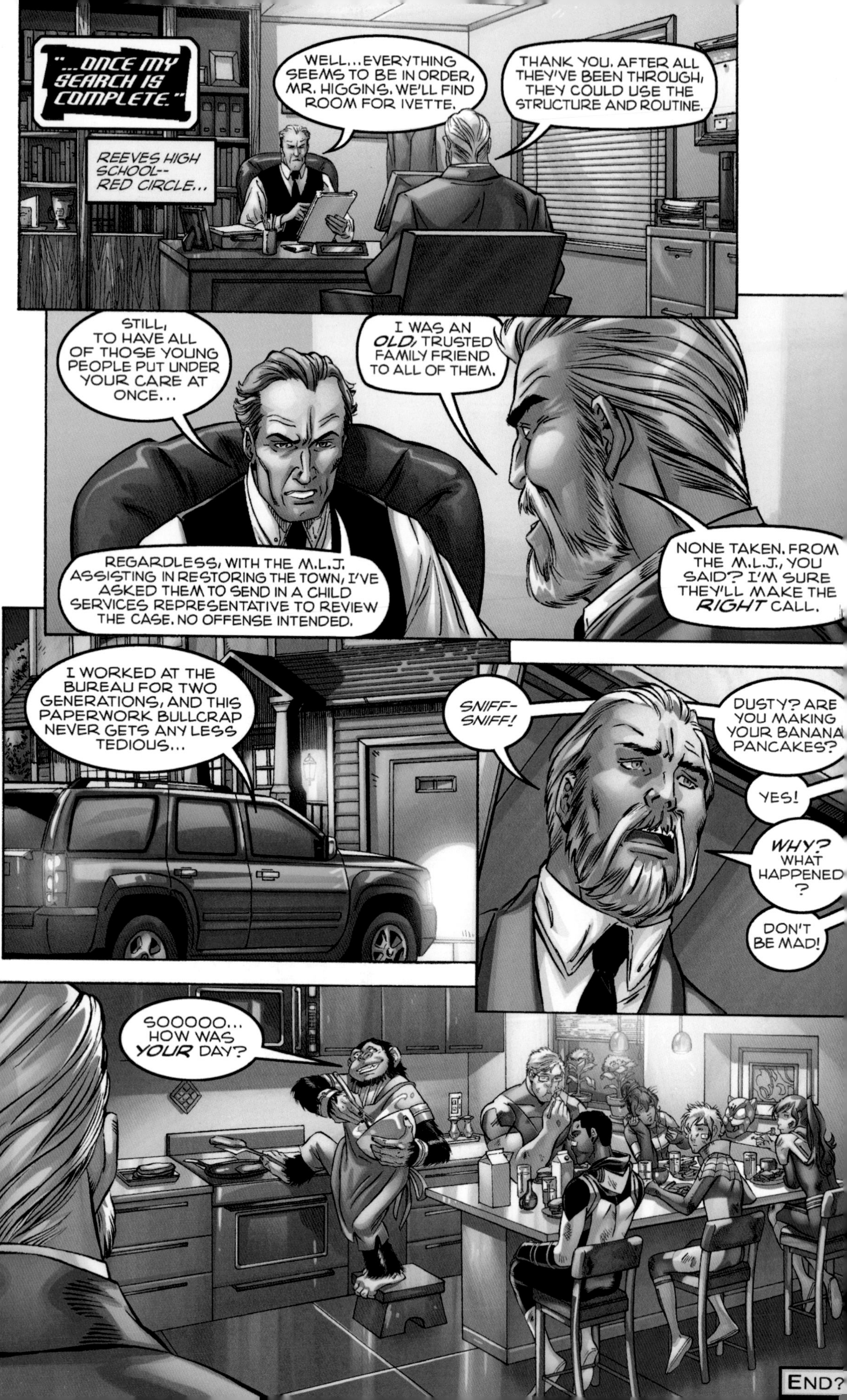
"...ONCE MY SEARCH IS COMPLETE."
REEVES HIGH SCHOOL-- RED CIRCLE...
WELL...EVERYTHING SEEMS TO BE IN ORDER, MR. HIGGINS. WE'LL FIND ROOM FOR IVETTE.
THANK YOU. AFTER ALL THEY'VE BEEN THROUGH, THEY COULD USE THE STRUCTURE AND ROUTINE.
STILL, TO HAVE ALL OF THOSE YOUNG PEOPLE PUT UNDER YOUR CARE AT ONCE...
I WAS AN OLD, TRUSTED FAMILY FRIEND TO ALL OF THEM.
REGARDLESS, WITH THE M.L.J. ASSISTING IN RESTORING THE TOWN, I'VE ASKED THEM TO SEND IN A CHILD SERVICES REPRESENTATIVE TO REVIEW THE CASE. NO OFFENSE INTENDED.
NONE TAKEN. FROM THE M.L.J., YOU SAID? I'M SURE THEY'LL MAKE THE RIGHT CALL.
I WORKED AT THE BUREAU FOR TWO GENERATIONS, AND THIS PAPERWORK BULLCRAP NEVER GETS ANY LESS TEDIOUS...
SNIFF-SNIFF!
DUSTY? ARE YOU MAKING YOUR BANANA PANCAKES?
YES!
WHY? WHAT HAPPENED?
DON'T BE MAD!
SOOOOO... HOW WAS YOUR DAY?
END?